Ethical Codes and Income Distribution

In recent years increased attention has been given to continuing disparities in income, both in the developed and in developing countries. *Ethical Codes and Income Distribution* brings an important new dimension to this important issue. Questions such as Does 'morality' affect income distribution? and What are the effects of the widespread adoption of ethical codes on the functioning of the labour market? are explored.

This book utilizes the contrasting works of John Bates Clark and Thorstein Veblen in order to illuminate the propogation of ethical codes within the two opposing frameworks, that is, the neoclassical and the institutional. John Bates Clark, in the history of economic thought, emphasized the role of market mechanisms in *spontaneously* propagating 'fair' codes of behaviour, thus giving rise to a 'just' income distribution. Thorstein Veblen underlines the importance of bargaining in the socio-political arena in determining the ethical codes adopted in a given society, in given historical contexts, arguing *external interventions* – social conflict, above all – are necessary in order to drive institutional changes in the event of the existing institutions being considered 'unjust'. Given this theoretical framework, this book also explores the effects of labour market deregulation on economic as well as on 'moral' growth.

Guglielmo Forges Davanzati is Associate Professor of History of Economic Thought at the University of Lecce, Italy.

Routledge Studies in the History of Economics

Ethical Codes and Income Distribution

A study of John Bates Clark and Thorstein Veblen

Guglielmo Forges Davanzati

Routledge
Taylor & Francis Group

LONDON AND NEW YORK

First published 2006
by Routledge
2 Park Square, Milton Park, Abingdon, Oxon OX14 4RN

Simultaneously published in the USA and Canada
by Routledge
270 Madison Ave, New York, NY 10016

Routledge is an imprint of the Taylor & Francis Group

© 2006 Guglielmo Forges Davanzati

Typeset in Times New Roman by
Newgen Imaging Systems (P) Ltd, Chennai, India
Printed and bound in Great Britain by
Biddles Ltd, King's Lynn

British Library Cataloguing in Publication Data
A catalogue record for this book is available from the British Library

Library of Congress Cataloging in Publication Data
A catalog record for this book has been requested

ISBN 0–415–36539–2

To Carla

Contents

Preface

In contemporary non-mainstream economic debate, it is a widespread idea that the functioning of a market economy needs a set of rules (i.e. institutions) which bind agents in their behaviour, allowing efficient outcomes. This idea is outside the General Equilibrium Model (GEM), where markets are pictured as working in an institutional *vacuum*, where social and historical variables play no role. However, in more recent times, a large group of economists have been working on bringing ethical issues into the economic discourse. This renewed interest can – at least partially – be explained by the growing interest shown by firms in the possible beneficial effects of adopting ethical codes. It is a *renewed* interest because as we know political economy was conceived as a branch of (moral) philosophy from ancient times to the end of the nineteenth century, when the emergence of marginalism and of the neoclassical paradigm generated a new epistemological statute of the discipline: economics as the *science* which deals with problems of allocation of scarce resources among given alternative uses.

The traditional wisdom based on the ethics *or* economics dichotomy has been replaced by the view that ethics *and* economics are compatible. Amartya K. Sen (1987a) convincingly argued that not only is the ethical discourse useful for economics, in that overcoming the narrow concept of instrumental rationality will enable effective human behaviour to be understood better, but by bringing economic variables into the equation, ethical economics can also help moral philosophers to improve their analyses. Let us consider, for instance, the main aims of economic policy: to increase employment and the rate of growth, with price stability. Why should the maximum rate of growth be an end in itself? The most obvious answer is that the higher the growth rate, the higher the per capita income. However, even if this link holds, one needs an explanation as to *why* the increase in income is an end in itself, and this explanation cannot avoid ethical considerations.

Note that, while philosophers usually approach the issue by asking what individuals *should* do, economists are interested in the *effects* of the adoption of moral norms on the dynamics of market economies, that is, their functional value above all. This book follows this line of research, with a special focus on the labour market and income distribution. The works of John Bates Clark and Thorstein Veblen will be discussed as representative efforts to analyse the genesis and the propagation of ethical codes within opposing theoretical frameworks. Their contributions can be conceived as highly significant in two contrasting paradigms, that is, the neoclassical and the institutional; also significant is their direct approach to the ethical dimension of income distribution. This is not to say that *only* John Bates Clark and Thorstein Veblen have dealt with this topic in the history of economic thought (Wicksteed, Edgeworth, Pigou, among the others, provided relevant contributions), but that (a) since Clark was the major neoclassical scholar in the United States in the years between the end of the nineteenth century and the beginning of the twentieth century and Veblen had a similar position within the rising institutional paradigm; and (b) since Clark and Veblen debated, in that period, the questions treated here, the comparison of their contributions can also help to understand better the cultural climate of the period in the United States. As Stabile (1997) convincingly points out: 'Veblens's criticisms of Clark's works suggest that both have taken different intellectual paths in analyzing similar issues'. However, contributions from other economists of the past as well as those drawn from the contemporary debate will also be examined. In this sense, this book is not only devoted to exploring questions proper to the history of economic thought: present contributions will be used in order to understand past contributions, and vice versa, in the conviction that the history of economics does not evolve from 'error to the truth' but competing lines of thought are always present in past as well as in contemporary debates.

Sparing use has been made of mathematical tools. Casual sequences will be employed in order to show the *logical* links between the variables considered. For the sake of the arguments presented here, the emphasis on cause-and-effect alone is sufficient and the use of formal models is not strictly necessary. Moreover, since this book – by its very nature – is directed to economists as well as to philosophers, the language used is designed to be understandable for both. Finally, the focus will be on the links between ethics and income distribution with sole reference to 'developed countries': the treatment of ethical issues within 'developing' economies would need a space (and competence) which is not available here.

Acknowledgements

I wish to thank Lilia Costabile for her useful suggestions in my search for contemporary contributions within the institutional theoretical framework, Sergio Cremaschi for his criticisms on Chapter 1, Luca Fiorito for his useful comments on my treatment of Veblen's thought, Antonio Luigi Paolilli for his precious help in improving my treatment of altruism (Appendix I), Mario Signore for his useful suggestions on my dealing with Catholic ethics, Stefano Zamagni for his useful opinions on the links between ethics and economics relating to Chapter 1; Francesco Biondo for his suggestions on Chapter 1; Andrea Pacella for his effort in improving the treatment of uncertainty and for helping me write Appendix II; Lucia Assunta De Siena for helping me in bibliographical research. Luigino Bruni helped me in approaching Pareto's theory of the labour market (Chapter 2); Riccardo Realfonzo provided relevant suggestions in the treatment of Keynesian thought (Chapter 4). Augusto Graziani and Stefano Perri read a preliminary draft of Chapter 2 and provided extremely useful clarifications on the marginal productivity theory. Joan McMullin put in considerable effort into improving my English.

The usual disclaimers apply.

Guglielmo Forges Davanzati
Lecce, June 2005

Outline of the book

The book is organized as follows. Chapter 1 deals with the genesis and the spread of moral codes, within two contrasting views: the so-called 'inside-the-market' approach, which emphasizes the role of market mechanisms in promoting the spontaneous growth of both national income and the 'degree of morality'; and the so-called 'outside-the-market' approach, where the origin and the nature of moral norms is the outcome of bargaining in the socio-political arena, among agents with different degrees of bargaining power. The distinction can be read in the light of the distinction between the neoclassical and the institutional paradigm, which will be the focus of the final chapter. This discussion is opened by a rereading of the different philosophical views on the nature of moral norms. The aim of Section 1.1 is to provide a synthetic description – with no presumption of originality – of the main philosophical approaches to morality, which may be useful for economists, although it does not present new arguments for philosophers. Appendix I deals with a particular topic in ethical economics, that is, altruism and its effects on exchanges and on economic development. Appendix II reproposes Sidney and Beatrice Webbs' analysis of the functioning of the labour market, based on the idea that the relationships between firms and workers are deeply affected by ethical codes. Chapters 2 and 3 are devoted to the study of John Bates Clark and Thorstein Veblen's thought, with particular reference to their views on the role of morality in affecting income distribution. Chapter 4 proposes a comparison between the contemporary neoclassical and institutional theoretical framework in terms of the different conceptions of the nature and the functions of social and moral norms in the operation of market mechanisms and of the different analyses of the rules governing income distribution.

Although the chapters could be read as independent contributions (particularly Chapters 2 and 3), it is hoped that with the background of the introduction the entire work will form something more of a complete whole.

1 The genesis and the spread of ethical codes

The inside-the-market versus the outside-the-market approach

In charity there is no excess.

(Sir Francis Bacon, *Of Goodness, and Goodness of Nature*, 1625)

The world has achieved brilliance without conscience. Ours is a world of nuclear giants and ethical infants.

(General Omar Bradley)

A man's ethical behavior should be based effectually on sympathy, education, and social ties; no religious basis is necessary. Man would indeed be in a poor way if he had to be restrained by fear of punishment and hope of reward after death.

(Albert Einstein)

1.1 Introduction

The basic assumption underlying this book is that moral norms significantly affect agents' behaviour and, therefore, the functioning of a market economy. The 'single-spot interaction paradox' provides an example supporting this assumption.[1] Suppose that individual A, finding herself in a city where she knows she will never return, acquires a good x and that, in the shop considered, payment is due *ex post* (i.e. after the purchase). A is anonymous, that is, completely unknown to the seller, and has to choose whether to pay or not. Non-payment should produce a level of utility higher than the opposite solution, under the condition that – being anonymous – the probability of receiving a *formal* sanction is approximately nil. Accordingly, a purely rational agent should choose not to pay, but evidence shows that people tend to behave differently. This paradox can be solved only by inserting some moral rules (e.g. 'the duty to pay') into the paradigm of economic behaviour.[2]

In line with this example, three questions are in order. First, what is the *nature* of a moral norm? Second, what are the possible *causes* that can generate the emergence of a norm? Third, what are the *effects* that the widespread adoption of a norm is likely to produce?

This chapter is devoted to providing answers to these questions, and the focus will be on questions relating both to income distribution and, more generally, to justice.

The first question is a purely philosophical question and, for the purpose of this book, it does not need a definite answer. The main theoretical positions in the contemporary debate can be summarized as follows.[3]

The French School

Its major exponent – Sartre (1936) – believes that *a moral act is simply an act of freedom*. In this sense, art, in that it is a creative act, constitutes the highest expression of creativity and therefore of morality. Freedom is essentially liberation, and it is the *only* basis of values. Moreover, in Sartrean thought, political commitment is the natural corollary (or specification) of moral commitment: this is because since freedom is liberation, it belongs both to the individual sphere and above all to the sphere of social organization. From this point of view, freedom as liberation stands for the freeing of the proletariat from its subjection to capital (hence its proximity to the positions of the French communists in the first half of the 1900s). The ethic of freedom therefore translates into the 'ethic of commitment' (see Faracovi, in Viano 1990, pp. 23 ff.).

Utilitarianism

Its first and main exponents – in particular, Bentham, at the beginning of the 1800s, and Sidgwick, at the end of the 1800s – embrace the (Benthamite) argument that

> Nature has placed mankind under the governance of two sovereign masters, pain and pleasure. It is for them alone to point out what we ought to do as well as to determine what we shall do. On the one hand, the standard of right and wrong, on the other the chain of causes and effects, are fastened to their throne.
>
> (Bentham 1970 [1789])

It follows that *the morality of an act is determined by the consequences that the act itself produces in terms of social welfare*. In other words, an action can be considered morally acceptable if, even unintentionally, it produces an increase in the utility of the community.[4]

While contemporary utilitarianism accepts the basic approach just mentioned, it is divided by convention into two main stances: act utilitarianism (Smart) and rule utilitarianism (Harsanyi). Smart, the main exponent of the first position, re-propounds a radical form of utilitarianism, taking up the 'progressive' Benthamite view that what is needed in the question of ethics is to set ethics (and individuals) free from all ties with traditions, customs and habits (see Bentham 1970 [1789]). This viewpoint ends up denying any difference between pleasures and denying that an intrinsically bad pleasure can exist (see Viano in Viano 1990, pp. 54 ff.). Harsanyi's rule utilitarianism places greater emphasis on the effective dimension of social actions, stating that the ethical rule amounts to maximizing utility under uncertainty (see Selten 2001).[5] As Carlo Augusto Viano argues (in Viano, 1990, p. 55, my translation), 'Harsanyi believes that effective behaviour must rely on a system of social roles considered equally probable, with each of which the humanitarian spectator could identify.' Consequently, unlike that of Smart, his theory ultimately proves to be a *hypothetical* theory of social action (based, that is, on a model of society) not a *descriptive* theory.[6]

Neo-contractualism

Its main exponent, John Rawls – author of the widely discussed work *A Theory of Justice* (1971) – takes up the hypothetical model of modern contractualism (Locke, Rousseau, Kant), postulating a state of nature (*original position*) in which individuals – covered by a *veil of ignorance* – make a hypothetical rational choice about the distribution of resources in the final position; in other words they decide the norms of the society in which they will live. Rawls shows that, given the hypothesis of aversion to risk, and adopting the maximin principle,[7] the optimal choice is such that a fair distribution of income is achieved in the final position. The rationale of this conclusion lies in the statement that since the chooser fears being classified as 'poor', he tends to minimize the gap between the resources of the potentially 'rich' and the potentially 'poor' in the final position.[8] For the purposes of our discourse, what counts most is the neo-contractualist idea that *justice equals fairness* and, even more, that *a moral action is one that guarantees the maintenance of a 'well-ordered society'*. The latter is defined by Rawls as a society in which each person accepts, and knows that the others accept, the same principles of justice, and in which the social institutions respect, and are known to respect, these principles.

The liberal ethic: Nozick

Author of a work which, like that of Rawls, has had a great effect on the philosophical, political and economic debate about moral norms – *State, Anarchy and Utopia* (1974) – Robert Nozick does not consider Rawls' attempt to find a scientific basis for the 'common sense of morality' starting from a hypothetical state of nature to be productive. This is due to the fact that there exists nothing that can be unambiguously called 'social justice', unless one presupposes the existence of something that is entitled to establish the criteria for the sharing out of the resources produced. Moreover, even if this thing exists, the most it can do is to establish *how* to distribute, but not *how much* to distribute, since production must obviously take place first. Discarding Rawls' thesis obviously means starting from a different hypothesis. According to Nozick, it is perfectly reasonable to start from the assumption that in every socio-historical context and independently from the distribution of income, individual rights are granted, and these cannot be purely negative: reference is made in particular to the rights of non-aggression and non-interference. It follows that all the existing distributions resulting from processes in which no individual right has been violated must be considered fair (the so-called theory of entitlement). It also follows that *a moral action is one that respects the rights of others to non-aggression and to non-interference* and, on the political plane, that the state – being non-omniscient and not having been officially appointed to establish distribution criteria – must confine its operation to the defence of legitimately acquired rights, with particular reference to private property (the so-called minimum state).[9,10] One may argue that the normative prescriptions of Nozick's approach can lead to his thought being classified under the label of libertarian, more than liberal.[11]

Christian morality

Although there are a variety of theoretical and theological positions,[12] the basic value here can be said to be constituted by *the dignity of man* (see Banner 1999). It is therefore understood that *an action is to be considered moral as long as it promotes, or at least does not injure, the dignity of an individual, whatever may be his political affiliation, religion and social status*. The economic policy rules – or rather, the order of priorities to assign to the final goals of political action – deriving from this approach are basically the following.

i   *Full employment*. The full employment of the workforce is seen as the foundation of a fair economy, because the work of man possesses a special dignity and is the key to the achievement of justice in society.

ii   *A fair wage and dignity in conditions of employment*. In Christian economic theory, it is believed – and this is a widespread conviction – that the wage cannot be determined solely by market forces.

While respecting the freedom of private enterprise and the rules of the market, and *precisely because work is not goods*, it cannot and must not be subjected to the criteria governing price-setting for goods. In particular, it is believed that the wage must not only take labour productivity into account (as the market would establish it) but also, and above all, some at least of the workers' subsistence needs, which are socially and historically determined. Similarly, it is believed that the employer's freedom to organize production within his/her own firm cannot and must not be unlimited. This is due to the different bargaining power held by employers compared with their employees. The resulting guidelines aim to ensure – also within the production process, which is more than a mere technical event – that the dignity of the worker is respected and promoted, in that it is the dignity of man.

On the economic plane, the different views of the market within this approach are worth noting. Blank (in Blank and McGurn 2004, pp. 22–26) argues that five theological imperatives contrast the support for market economies. First, from the point of view of Christian ethics, the idea that individuals are solely self-interested is unacceptable: 'concern for others' is the cornerstone of Christian morality and egoism is its opposite. Hence, insofar as the operation of market economies rests on self-interested behaviours (and economic models – accepting this assumption – show that self-interested behaviours lead to the best outcomes), the political support for them is not admissible in the light of the principle of 'concern for others'. Second, for Christians the model of behaviour is based on 'self-giving love', which is outside both the actual functioning of market economies and the economic models. Third, while economics takes for granted that *more is better*, Christian ethics conceives 'abundance' not as abundance of material goods but as 'abundance of the Spirit' (ibid., p. 24). Fourth, while economics sees that more *choice* is better, Christians cannot support some choices, such as the production/ consumption of pornography, prostitution or abortion. Finally, Christian teachings emphasize the 'concern for the poor' and this clashes with economics on two levels: first, this principle establishes that certain choices (those that assist the poor) have a greater value than other choices; second, it leads to not supporting the idea – and/or the fact – that workers are paid according to their (marginal) productivity. In Blank's view, these considerations do not lead to a moral rejection of the market: 'The key question' – she clarifies (ibid., p. 13) – 'is not "Should there be a market?" but "What are the limits to markets as an organizing structure for economic life?"' Her response advocates public intervention moulded on Christian principles and devoted to promoting 'the common good' and 'human development', by inducing individuals to behave according to 'prosocial' values and by limiting the access to goods and services (and by regulating contracts) which conflict with human dignity: 'When market values (efficiency, productivity, incentives)' – she writes (ibid., p. 52) – 'become core secular values, the church needs to serve as a counterweight.'

The position of William McGurn is very different from that of Blank. His approach to the issue is twofold, involving the empirical level and the theoretical grounds. In what follows, the main arguments will be presented. McGurn starts by assuming that 'economic freedom is a good' (ibid., p. 62) and that work is the instrument by which the dignity of man is preserved. Hence, without external intervention, the joint operation of capital and labour generates constant increases in social wealth, which, although unintentionally, guarantees an increase of well-being for all individuals who take part in market mechanisms. Accordingly, 'the worker also contributes to the wealth of [his/her] neighbor' (ibid., p. 62). Since the market is assumed to be the mechanism which generates the maximum level of production, and since production is also distributed in favour of the poor, it produces the twofold positive effect of increasing revenues and, strictly linked with this, of promoting freedom. Moreover, the increase in revenues and the greater degree of individual freedom acts, in turn, as a disincentive to dishonest behaviour: in this sense, the market is moral.[13]

Marxist ethics

Although Marx did not write directly on problems of moral philosophy, 'the relationship between Marxism and ethics is often alluded to' but rarely explored (Kamenka 1972, p. 1). Kamenka emphasizes Marx's distinction between man's universal essence – *Wesen* – and his existence as a particular (factual, empirical) being. Alienation, in the capitalist system, both in the form of worker's alienation from the product of his/her work and in the form of the degradation of his/her personal life to the sole dimension of producer, becomes 'alienation from his own universal being' (Kamenka 1972, pp. 75–76). Moreover, insofar as money is the very essence of alienation, morality is outside the realm of the capitalist system: people honour money and hence its possessor *even if dishonest*. Man's universal essence results in a 'rational State', where *freedom* is not only apparent but *true* and no privileges and differences exist.[14] In the 'truly human' society – that is, Communism – human activity 'is not subordinated to ends outside the activity' (Kamenka 1972, p. 110); it is inherently creative and no hierarchical relationship is admitted. Within the Marxist theoretical framework, and with particular regard to the space for 'justice' in labour relationships, Engels' contribution is worth noting. In his article on the 'just wage', published in 'The Labour Standard', 7 May 1881, Friedrich Engels defines the just wage in a purely descriptive sense: a wage is just if it allows workers to survive and reproduce, according to the standard of living prevailing in the society where they live. This means only that a just wage is to be considered *just* only within the logic of the capitalist system, which is, in turn, both 'irrational' and 'unjust' in itself. The real notion of *justice* – according to Engels – should be based on the idea that since the whole social product is made by human labour, workers should receive a real wage equal to the product of their labour.[15] Engels adds that the very notion of a just wage – although not really referring to an ethical view – is a powerful *practical* instrument that stimulates workers' (and unions') claim to it: a claim which should take second place to the demand for the transition to an economy based on the socialization of the means of production.

Contemporary Kantian ethics

Immanuel Kant maintained that the moral law is an *objective* law, independent of human desires, so that morality is pursued for no other purpose than for morality itself (see, among others, Friedrick 1949). A rule is morally acceptable only if it can be universalized: 'Act on a maxim which can also hold good as a universal law. Every maxim which is not capable of being so is contrary to morality' (Kant 1909 [1785], p. 282).[16] Kant's categorical imperatives, based on *general laws*, give rise to a duty-centred morality. At the cost of oversimplification; Kant's view can be summarized in the idea that the moral law requires one *always to act in such a way that one treats others as ends and never merely as means*.[17,18] The 'universality principle' respects the difference between moral rules and behavioural rules. A modern representative of the Kantian view is Amitai Etzioni (1986), who maintains that agents act according to two independent kinds of utility, that is, moral utility and pleasure utility. Moral utility stands independent of pleasure utility and of the optimization of such utility, according to a multiple-self approach. The two functions, for Etzioni and other scholars of the multiple-self approach, are not only in conflict but also inconsistent in the sense that they cannot be reconciled by a common algorithm or reduced to a higher-level utility function. Therefore, *a moral act is one that respects the objective canons of morality*.

The socialization approach

Mead (1934) maintains that agents organize their codes of behaviour in order to gain the approval of their significant peer group.[19] According to this line of thought, called 'symbolic interactionism', agents' sense of self is moulded by the society where they live, and *moral behaviour is the result of the ability to see themselves from the viewpoint of others* ('empathic preferences'). This argument appears *prima facie* close to that of Adam Smith. As we know, one of the basic principles stated in *The Theory of Moral Sentiments* (*TMS*) is that *sympathy* is to be regarded as the basis of social behaviour, being, in the broader sense of the concept, 'our fellow-feeling with any passion whatever' (Smith 1976b [1759], p. 10). By extending this principle at the *macro* level, the following result holds: 'All members of human society' – he writes (Smith 1976b, p. 85) – 'stand in need of each other's assistance, and are likewise exposed to mutual injuries. Where the necessary assistance is reciprocally afforded from love, from gratitude, from friendship, and esteem, the society flourishes and is happy.' And: 'Man [...] has a *natural love for society*, and desires that the union of mankind should be preserved for its own sake, and though he himself was to derive no benefit from it' (ibid., p. 88, italics added). The 'natural love for society' acts as an ethical constraint, and it is reflected in the *habitus* of the 'prudent man' (see Pesciarelli 1991; see also part 1.3 later in this chapter).[20]

However, as Khalil (1990) notes, Mead's theory does not need an independent source of conscience, such as the Smithian 'impartial spectator', but it seems unable to provide an answer to the question: where do the group's expectations arise from? In other words, the proposition 'a group expects an agent to behave in a particular way' presupposes that the members of this group must have already formed their expectations as to such 'fair' behaviour. But, in this theoretical framework, the mechanisms which lead to the origin of expectations remain unexplained.[21,22]

Frankfurt School

First and second generation. This school proposes a critical theory of present society based on a revolutionary perspective of a free and unalienated future society. This critical, negative view of reality is capable of unmasking the deep, secret contradictions of society, using a utopian model that becomes a revolutionary spur for radical change. In this sense, the Frankfurt School follows from Hegel, Marx and Freud as a dialectical criticism of the present society. The school is divided into two generations. Two of the most important exponents of the *first generation* are Theodor Wiesengrund Adorno and Max Horkheimer. The main peculiarity of Adorno's whole theoretical contribution is his opposition to the habits of thought typical of the capitalist system and his polemical view of positive dialectics. With Horkheimer in *Dialektik der Aufklärung* (1947), he criticizes the technological society and the 'cultural industry', a tool in the manipulation of individual consciences, created to preserve the 'system' and to subject the population. Individuals – it is argued – are not the subject but the object of the cultural industry. They are not free individuals because they are indoctrinated by the ideology of the mass media. In their free time, too, individuals are indoctrinated by the cultural industry, although they believe they are 'happy' and free. The era of liberty is a time without repression, different from Kantian moral time, with its components: law, obligation, respect and duty. The era of liberty, connected to the Freudian principle of pleasure, is (or should be) a time without moral law.

One of the most important exponents of the *second generation* is Jürgen Habermas. In contrast with Adorno, he tries – in a theoretical context where communication strategies play a crucial role – to reformulate Kantian theory about the question of basic norms. Habermas (1991) tries to defend the concept of *right* rather than the concept of *good*. By contrast with classical ethics, connected to matters of a *good life*, Kantian ethics is connected to matters of 'right' acts. First of all, Habermas deals with Hegel's objections to Kantian ethics: to formalism, to abstract universalism, to the impotence of pure duty, to the 'terrorism' of pure intention. And in this way Habermas is able to provide a solution to the problem of applying Kantian moral principles, through *Diskursethik*, that is, the participation in social dialogue. Philosophy denies nobody moral responsibility. He maintains – following Horkheimer – that a materialistic theory of society is necessary if the utopian character of Kant's representation of a perfect constitution is to be overcome.

According to his interpretation, Kantian ethics is not concerned with the applicability of norms, but no norm possesses the rules for its own application. A kind of prudence or reflective judgement is needed in order to apply rules to actual cases, because in this way moral theory is not connected to well-founded reason. Habermas's purpose is to reformulate Kantian theory thanks to *Diskursethik* and defend it against the sceptical attitude to values. *Diskursethik* is represented in one essential formula: 'A well-founded norm should have the assent of all concerned, on condition they participate in practical discourse.' According to Habermas, practical discourse is not a procedure designed to produce justified norms, but to examine the validity of existing norms that have become problematical and are examined as hypotheses. This moral principle gives rise to an explanation of the validity of norms relating to human interaction. Justified norms regulate matters of life in common in the interests of the common good and they are *equally good norms* for all concerned. For this reason, moral obligations refer to 'people regardless of their arguments'; no attention must be paid to self-centred convictions that individuals might add to plausible general arguments. On the other hand, the moral principle owes its universal content to the fact that arguments are paramount regardless of their origin, and therefore 'regardless of people'. No one can start a discussion if she/he does not presuppose a dialogue based on the principle of free public access, even-sided participation, the truthfulness of all concerned and lack of compulsion when people adopt a position. Those concerned convince each other, thanks solely to the force of the best argument. It is important to distinguish this situation from the institutional arrangements that force some people to get involved in given arguments on given occasions. These institutions impose restraints on rationality, but presuppositions of communication do not have the value of rules. These presuppositions have an enabling role in the practice that serves as argumentation for all those involved in practical discourse.

Responsibility ethics

Hans Jonas (1979) suggests responsibilty ethics as a way to raise consciousness of the unforeseeable long-term effects resulting from technological advances.

In this theoretical context, the notion of a 'heuristic of fear' is extremely relevant: it must persuade us – in a state of uncertainty – to expect the worst. By contrast with the dimension of *hic et nunc* in Kantian ethics, responsibility ethics is interested in the future dimension. The individual subject of a moral act becomes a collective and universal subject, related to new perspectives with a global dimension. In his *Das Prinzip Verantwortung*, the emphasis is put on the concern for future generations, as the cornerstone of a new dimension of the ethical discourse where responsibility is *above all* responsibility towards those who cannot influence present economic choices. Accordingly, technical progress should take the long-term interests of the whole society (the society of today as well as that of tomorrow) into account, and political strategies are to be conceived as designed to improve – or, at least, not to damage – future generations.

Intuitionism, subjectivism, emotivism

George Edward Moore is considered the author who best described the intuitionist view. The basic idea is that agents accept moral norms on the basis of what they consider, solely by intuition, good or bad, independently of the consequences that their behaviour produces. As a result, just as a colour cannot be defined, nor can good itself: a colour – like a moral precept – can only be perceived. And even if people tend to rationalize their beliefs in moral disputes, this is not proof that moral beliefs are based on rational arguments (see Edwards 1965). 'Good' includes the appreciation of beauty and the pleasure derived from friendship (Moore 1903, p. 17). Furthermore, moral beliefs may arise from subjective feelings or in reaction to contrasting views and hence no moral judgement is objective or true. Similarly, it is also argued that moral judgements are the result of emotions (Ayer 1936), particularly of repugnance to certain acts. At least in their naive forms, these views fall into moral nihilism, although it is reasonable to maintain that *some* fundamental ethical propositions are based on personal feelings (Edwards 1965).

Naturalism

Mackie (1984) asserts that moral theory *must* be based on rights and that rights are *natural* and hence *objective*. Within an Aristotelian framework, it is maintained that rights derive from human nature, which is conceived here as showing constant features over time and space. Piderit (1993) adds that reason serves the purpose of discovering which actions are natural (and hence moral), so the whole process of 'civilization' is conceived as a constant attempt to select what is good, thanks to the progressive improvement in man's capability to find the good by means of reason.[23] Although the ideas that (i) morality must be based on rights and (ii) all rights are natural and hence independent of historical and institutional settings may appear questionable, it seems obvious that 'any acceptable doctrine must conform to nature in the sense of not requiring impossible actions or behavior enforceable only at excessive cost' (Yeager 2001, p. 215).[24]

The human development and the 'capability' approaches

The human development approach – derived from (and linked to) the capability approach of Amartya Kumar Sen and Martha Nussbaum[25] – emphasizes the standard of living and quality of life. Standard of living is defined as 'personal well-being related to one's own life' (Sen 1987a, p. 29), and the conditions for well-being depend on the individual's set of 'functionings' and 'capabilities'. Functionings are the characters of the lifestyle and can be ranked from basic matters (such as being well nourished, decently dressed, being in good health) to more complex ones (such as taking part in the life of the community). In this context, the 'real opportunities', – that is, the set of available capabilities of a person in order to function – are the basic preconditions to achieve a standard of living which makes it possible to realize individual potentialities, that is, to reach more complex 'functioning'. Real opportunities, in turn, crucially depend on *freedom* (hence the possibility of enabling a person to improve his/her living standard), but – differently from the liberal tradition – freedom is here *substantive* freedom.

Sen also explores the issue of *inequality*: since individuals differ in the variety of their conditions, the concept of inequality should itself be regarded as relating to *specific* cases. Moreover, inequality is a multidimensional variable, so that it is difficult to interpret it in one single way. He maintains that the ambitious egalitarian project can be realized solely by opposing a *pre-existing inequality*. In this view the measurement of inequality depends on some basic variables (happiness, income, wealth, and so on), and comparison between individuals and groups should be made on these bases. And then if individuals were identical, equality in one sphere (i.e. in opportunities and in income) should be coherent with equality in other spheres (i.e. the capability of functioning). However, in actual fact there is an absolute 'human inequality' and equality in one sphere coexists with inequalities in other spheres: equal incomes coexist with different capabilities (a healthy man and a sick man with equal incomes may adopt different behaviour).

By rejecting the welfarist approach, Sen maintains that a 'good life' is such that the 'basic capabilities' are available in order to develop 'internal' (personal aptitudes) as well as 'external' (absence of circumstantial impediments) capabilities. Basic capabilities enable personal aptitudes to be activated in a context where no significant external constraints exist. Sen questions the relation between welfare and utility, which is at the foundation of mainstream economics. The Human Development Index (HDI), developed by the United Nations (UN) starting from 1990, was designed to take the place of traditional economic indexes (gross domestic product (GDP), above all). The HDI has the goal of translating the concept of welfare based on availability of goods into a concept based on the possibility of a dignified life. And the *Human Development Reports*, published annually since 1990, represent an extensive and sustained effort to translate the ideas of the capabilities approach into operational policy prescriptions. This approach believes it is necessary to review the distribution of real capabilities of individual choice that may lead to criticism of policies based merely on the idea that market mechanisms can generate both efficiency and 'equality'. In fact,

Sen maintains that the equality level of a society must guarantee an advantageous quality of life or general well-being (without the constraints of instrumental and economic parameters). His approach is ultimately based on the idea of 'development as freedom', and in this view he returns to the Greek tradition of Aristotelian *eudaimonia*. The Greek *eudaimonia* is not English happiness, but corresponds to *fulfilment* and it can be explained with the metaphor of a *flourishing life*, a life flourishing in its potentialities. However, Sen's *eudaimonia* appears to be in contrast both to the ideal of welfare economics and to the Aristotelian monistic formulation of *eudaimonia*. Following this line of thought, the Aristotelian mistake lies in formulating a universal list of well-grounded functioning, neglecting the individual. According to Sen, since individual goals are different, there must be a plurality of capabilities (see particularly Sen 1987a,b).

The philosophical debate summarized here ultimately rests on the idea that the concept of morality – however it is defined – can be established on a purely theoretical *a priori* ground, that is, without reference to the possible *economic* causes that may generate a moral norm and without reference to the *economic* effects that a moral norm can produce. In contrast, in what follows, the relationships between the functioning of market mechanisms and the origin and propagation of moral norms will be explored, in line with two distinct approaches to the role of economic variables in generating such norms. For the sake of the arguments developed in the next sections, it is sufficient to refer to a 'neutral' definition of moral norm, that is, a definition which – based on the maximum degree of generality – can be used without necessarily referring to a specific moral view. Attitudes towards cooperation, benevolent motivations, trust, altruism, honesty, concern for the environment and future generations can be seen as ethical codes within the debate on the *economic* effects of morality. In this context, morality – in purely economic terms – *can* be conceived as the individual propensity to constrain or to moderate the search for private gains (i.e. an inner constraint on self-interest),[26] and it *can* derive from both 'intrinsic' and 'instrumental' motivation (i.e. being moral as an end itself or being moral if it is convenient, in the short run or in the long run). Moreover, the notion of 'fairness' – and of 'justice' – can rest on two distinct grounds, both acceptable for the following arguments. First, leaving aside the role of formal rules, A's behaviour can be defined 'unfair' (or 'unjust') towards B if it violates some aspects of B's *perception* of fairness (i.e. a *subjective* dimension of justice). Second, fairness can be linked to impartial normative principles, based on an *objective* dimension of justice (see Barry 1995).[27,28]

1.2 The origin of moral norms

In the contemporary debate, as well as in the history of economic ideas, it is possible to trace two contrasting approaches, here called the *inside-the-market* and the *outside-the-market approaches*, towards the role of market mechanisms in generating and propagating moral norms.

The inside-the-market approach

It is argued here that the market is an effective instrument for generating moral codes, as well as for ensuring that they are respected, and, hence, that external intervention is not necessary for this purpose.

Although his work has been the object of numerous interpretations, and although the questions approached here were not the main focus of his thought, F. von Hayek provides the basic theoretical framework of the ideas being discussed. In dealing with the issue of solidarity, he distinguishes between solidarity within small groups – that is, in pre-capitalistic economies – and solidarity in the 'great society' (i.e. contemporary capitalism), where impersonal interactions prevail. In this context, morality in intentions (i.e. acting on the principles of solidarity) implies immorality in results. Solidarity – Hayek suggests – expresses itself mainly for the benefit of known persons, and the 'great society' is characterized by the possibility of increasing production for the benefit of the greatest number of individuals. There would therefore be *immorality in results* if resources were used in order to help a few known individuals, since it is possible – via the increase in production and *unintentionally* – to improve the living standard of a far greater number of persons (Hayek 1979). Accordingly, market economies are instruments for solidarity (Antiseri 2000, p. 48).[29]

In contemporary literature, the contributions of Taylor (1987), Schotter (1986), Axelrod (1984) and Sudgen (1986) are worth noting. They show that moral norms – conceived here as a leaning towards cooperation – emerge via interaction among agents in the marketplace, in contexts where the rules of the game are of a 'tit for tat' type, giving rise to a *spontaneous order* (see Costabile 1998). The reasoning runs as follows. Suppose that two agents, *A* and *B*, interact and that they are both able to punish each other if one of them defects (i.e. does not cooperate). In particular, *A* and/or *B* can stop the game when the other behaves in an opportunistic way (*endogenous sanction*), so that each individual is subject to a *conditional cooperation* on the part of the other. Even if, in the first game, individuals defect (such as in the Prisoner's Dilemma), it can be shown that cooperation emerges spontaneously *when the game has an infinite time horizon*, or when its length is unknown to the players.[30] The rationale for this is that – if the game finishes at time *x* – it would be profitable for both the players not to be cooperating in the interaction at time *x*. As a result, moral behaviour (i.e. cooperative behaviour) is privately convenient and it is adopted spontaneously.[31]

It should be noted that this theory is unable to provide a *general* framework in order to explain the origin of moral codes. In fact, according to this approach, cooperation (i.e. moral behaviour) is profitable only insofar as agents know they will meet and, by contrast, it is not convenient in contexts where agents expect to meet occasionally.[32] More precisely, the larger the number of individuals, the more the single agent will tend to underestimate the effects of his/her behaviour on the macro plane, mainly owing to the fact that his/her identity (and hence reputation) will matter less and less. In other words, this is a theory capable of explaining the origin of norms within groups which systematically interact. Moreover, as Baland and Plateau (1996, ch. 6) note, the crucial question – in explaining the origin of moral norms by using game theory – is what gives rise to the initial belief.

Vanberg (1987) argues that the adoption of moral rules is rational and, as a result, external interventions – in the form of formal enforcement – are inadequate. Respecting rules is more convenient than making case-by-case decisions for three main reasons: (i) saving on decision-making costs; (ii) reduction of the risk of erroneous choices, resulting from scarce or incorrect information; (iii) increase in the focus on long-term interests. The morality of the rules is strictly linked to *reputation* and it is *social capital*. Social capital, in turn, is closely linked to *trust* (see Granovetter 1985). Once rules have been internalized, 'moral routine' is in operation and calculation is not required. Granovetter (1985) also argues that social networks deeply affect individual choices (the so-called theory of 'embed-dedness') and that decisional processes are to be viewed as 'path dependent', in the sense that past events are *not* irrelevant for present decisions. In more general terms, path dependency is a phenomenon where technological change in a society depends quantitatively and/or qualitatively on its own past. A well-known example of technological path dependence is the QWERTY keyboard: it is used today only because this convention was established in the past (David 1985). A technique which is casually chosen at time t is likely to have an advantage over possible rival techniques at time $t + 1$, until 'lock-in' effects come into operation, determining the impossibility of changing the technological paradigm. This mechanism gives rise to 'non ergodic' processes (see Davidson 1994). However, as van Dun (1994) points out, 'good' reputation deriving from individual moral-ity can occur only where a *critical mass* of 'moral agents' exists. In other words, only if most people are honest will being dishonest produce a loss of reputation, while in the opposite case, dishonesty is the optimal strategy. More generally, one can state that *the individual propensity to respect norms increases as the social propensity to respect norms increases* (see Shavell 1987). Furthermore, where immoral behaviours prevail, a vicious circle is likely to occur. Consider the norm 'no littering in the street': if this norm is not respected in town x, then individual A, in that town for the first time, will be tempted not to respect the rule, both because A's ethical constraint is weakened by the absence of a social sanction and because his/her possible contribution to the cleanliness of the street would be irrelevant. A's behaviour, though unintentionally, reinforces the common belief that 'no littering in the street' is not a binding constraint (Conte and Castelfranchi 1996).[33]

A possible extension of the inside-the-market approach – which is particularly relevant for the purposes of this chapter – is related to firm–consumer interac-tion (see Section 1.3 that follows): if consumers express a demand for 'social responsibility' on the part of firms, it would be profitable for firms to react by satisfying this demand, in order not to lose reputational capital and hence their market share.

The outside-the-market approach

In the field of economics proper, the inside-the-market approach emphasizes the role of consumers in orienting corporate strategies, and – in a context where consumers are 'ethically oriented' – firms are induced, via market mechanisms, to adopt ethical codes. The point of departure of this alternative view is the rejection of the principle of consumer sovereignty. It can be pointed out, in fact, that this principle is acceptable on the plane of reasonableness at the microeconomic level, but it is logically inapplicable at the macroeconomic level. This is because *the consumer may want goods not yet produced or not yet put on sale, but she/he cannot demand them*.[34] But if the consumer is not 'sovereign', it follows that the adoption of ethical codes on the part of firms cannot be the result of a 'demand for social responsibility' expressed by consumers. From this point of view, therefore, the genesis of a moral norm depends on variables that are different from market variables, and not based on a purely rational choice.

Buchanan (1994, pp. 63 ff., italics added) suggests that the acceptance of moral norms derives from the '*cognitive limits* of our capacities, especially in situations that are unfamiliar for us'. In these cases, he argues, it may be 'rational to adopt relatively rigid rules or constraints, some of which may be moral in nature'. Buchanan also maintains that 'ethics are not contractual' (ibid., p. 73) and that ethical constraints are likely to emerge via social interaction and, particularly, by means of investments in mutual persuasion which aim at modifying the preferences of others so as to produce the desired changes in others' behaviour. Rereading Hobbes, Yeager (2001, pp. 130–131) assumes that 'a just person acts from a settled disposition that maximizes his prospect for security', although this does not imply that 'being a virtuous person is [...] a necessary and sufficient condition for personal success'. This line of thought is based on the idea – mainly due to the philosopher Moritz Schlick in the 1930s within the 'Vienna Circle' – that acting with the aim of social cooperation is likely to be successful in the long run and in *probabilistic terms*. Huck and Kübler (2000) emphasize the role of social pressure in promoting cooperation. They show that – in a context where n agents have to finance public goods – if $n - x$ agents contribute, then social pressure (and the consequent feeling of guilt at the expense of the potential free-rider) will induce x to contribute as well. They also stress the importance of uncertainty in triggering this effect, since – in a world of complete and perfect information – it is easier to avoid the payment by cooperating for the purpose of not contributing. Furthermore, it is also argued that external interventions – insofar as they increase the degree of uncertainty about the source of contribution – determine a further incentive for social cooperation, giving rise to a 'crowding in' effect. The role of uncertainty[35] in spreading social and moral norms has recently been explored by Hogg and Mullin (1999) and Bordia *et al.* (2004), who stress that 'uncertainty reduction is the primary motivation for group identification' and – in view of this purpose – it requires common rules of behaviour. Following this argument, uncertainty would lead to cooperation. However, according to Greer (2000, p. 7), in a context of (Keynesian) fundamental uncertainty 'individuals often simply do not know what the future will bring and therefore allow their decisions to be affected by apprehension and even undue conservatism about the future'.[36] This idea can be expanded by emphasizing that a 'prudent' attitude resulting from uncertainty is likely to enforce self-interested behaviours, which, in turn, may produce conflict. In other words, as the degree of uncertainty increases,[37] one can argue that the *perceived* scarcity of resources[38] increases and it therefore becomes more difficult to share resources, giving rise to behaviour designed to preserve the available resources. Moreover, if the number of individuals who can acquire the available resources increases, self-interested behaviours are likely to change into conflictual attitudes. Consider, for instance, individual A who earns an income Y at time t and that – owing to an increase in the immigration rate (let us call the immigrants B) which, in turn, may produce an exogenous increase of uncertainty (owing, for instance, to the fear of dismissal) – A perceives a reduction of Y at time $t + 1$. This event is likely to change A's attitude towards immigrants in the sense that (i) she/he will not give to charity in the situations she/he previously did, because of the perception of a higher degree of scarcity of resources (which gives rise to pure self-interested behaviour) and (ii) she/he will oppose the immigrants (for instance, by means of his/her political choice), insofar as she/he sees them as competitors (for a further development of this argument, see Yaari (1996) and Chapter 4 in this book).

In a different theoretical framework, an argument explaining the adoption of moral norms – which does not rely on the operation of market mechanisms – has recently been proposed by Bowles and Gintis (2002). The basic idea is that agents tend to internalize norms because they experience *prosocial emotions*, such as shame, guilt, pride, regret, joy. Accordingly, norms are respected not on a rational basis, that is, the explicit cognitive optimizing process, but via the operation of 'gut reactions'. More precisely, Bowles and Gintis maintain that, even if agents *can* perform cognitive operations, they usually *do not* when faced with problems of respecting codes of behaviour involving emotions.[39] Herbert A. Simon ([1990] in Zamagni 1995, pp. 344–347) suggests that the individual acceptance of moral norms may depend on agents' 'docility'. Docility is the tendency to be 'adept at social learning' and, in a context where society can instil norms of behaviour oriented to cooperation, altruism and the respect of others – which, in turn, depends on the number of 'docile' individuals – moral norms are likely to be widely respected. Dennis C. Mueller ([1986] in Zamagni 1995, pp. 181 ff.) argues that cooperative behaviours can derive from a social sanction in the specific form of *taboos* and that they are ultimately the result of *learning*.

These arguments will now be examined further, in the light of the study of possible ways in which norms are propagated.

1.3 Propagation effects

The question we intend to answer here is the following: once a moral norm has been generated, through what mechanisms can it spread and be accepted by a particular group?

The answer refers to the different theoretical approaches mentioned earlier.

Propagation through the market

According to the authors who identify with the inside-the-market approach, the moral norm can spread through the spontaneous operation of market mechanisms. Two approaches will be taken into consideration.

i   *On the microeconomic level*, it is argued (see Sacconi 1997, pp. 66 ff.; Fudenberg and Levine 1989) that moral behaviour can be seen as an investment in order to gain reputation. Sacconi shows that – in a game with a 'constant player' and 'multi-periodal players' – if the constant player adopts an ethical code (i.e. non-misuse of his/her power), and if she/he is endowed with foresight, she/he gains the maximum payoff in the repeated game by *always* playing in a cooperative (i.e. moral) way. The rationale of this argument is to be traced in the idea that beliefs tend to change over time, so that a 'patient' ethical player can induce a change in the way other agents interact with him/her. A possible application of this theoretical framework is in a context where 'ethical' or 'socially responsible' firms (fixing high wages and low prices) *A* are likely to generate a *crowding out* effect over their competitors *B*. This is because – if the labour force and goods are sufficiently substitutable – *A* can gain a greater market share at the expense of *B*, forcing *B* to 'convert', that is, to become an ethical agent. Similarly, Kahneman, Knetsch and Thaler (1986) suggest that fairness can affect pricing policy, and provide evidence on this issue: once a widespread conception of a 'just price' has been formed on the part of consumers, suppliers are reluctant to charge a price that consumers may judge to be unfair.

ii *On the macroeconomic plane*, it is pointed out that *reputation* can significantly affect agents' behaviour (see Kreps and Wilson 1982), with particular regard to corporate strategies. Let us assume – for instance – that fair treatment in the conditions of employment is considered a moral norm, and that consumers prefer – *ceteris paribus* – to acquire goods produced under these conditions (i.e. demand for corporate social responsibility, see Almender 1984). Where the firm recognizes that unfair treatment of its employees causes a drop in demand for its products, it is *in the interests of the firm* to adopt strategies of *fairness* towards its employees (see Schlict 2002). Thus, the emergence of a demand for social responsibility is linked to economic growth.

Let α be an indicator of the degree of fairness in social relations, so a low value of α indicates, for example, the existence (publicly known) of child labour in a firm. Let D_f and S_f respectively be the demand and the supply of 'the firm's social responsibility', expressed respectively by consumers and by firms. Let Y/N be income per-capita. Sequence 1.1 illustrates the effect of propagation, in the theoretical framework discussed here.

The increase in per-capita income generated by economic growth,[40] brings about an upward shift in consumers' needs in Maslow's hierarchy (in other

Sequence 1.1 Economic growth as moral growth

$$\uparrow Y/N \rightarrow \uparrow D_f \rightarrow \uparrow S_f \rightarrow \uparrow \alpha(\ldots)$$

words, once the basic physiological needs and security needs are satisfied, individuals also express the need for solidarity).[41] This involves consumers demanding greater social responsibility from the firm, and – so as not to lose its reputation and therefore its market share – a parallel improvement in what the firm offers, with the result that the degree of *fairness* in social relations tends to grow progressively.

A variant of this approach – the so called *group selection theory* – is based on the idea that some individuals or groups have a 'moral gene', which, in the course of social evolution, becomes dominant via natural selection. In other words, it is argued that 'pro-social' traits, insofar as they favour coop-eration, favour greater reproductive success than groups formed by purely selfish – that is, non-'moral' – individuals (Frank 1988; Wilson 1983). Accordingly, moral norms propagate spontaneously.

In this vision, therefore, economic growth is accompanied by (or determines) 'moral growth'; or, in other words, economic growth (meaning the increase in income per-capita over time) determines economic development.

Propagation through social negotiation

In this approach, which is the one proposed here, the market is not thought to be capable of either generating (see earlier) or propagating moral norms. The reasoning underlying this thesis is the rejection of the argument that econo-mic growth is the spontaneous result of the operation of market mechanisms. But, even if this argument is accepted, the existence of fluctuations in national income (which may not depend on external intervention) leads to the conclusion that ethical codes are respected solely in periods of growth, while recession would lead to the adoption of unfair rules: in fact, ethical codes rely solely on market mechanisms and no process of internalization is theoretically admitted in this context.

A similar argument can be traced in Adam Smith's thought, with particular reference to his picture of the working of the labour market. In *The Wealth of the Nations* (*WN*), he proposes at least two different theories of wages: the subsistence wage theory, based on the idea that 'masters' – owing to their superior bargaining power and to their tendency to collude – fix wages at their minimum level, and a theory of the 'decent wage', according to which – once a standard of fairness has been fixed in labour relationship – no firm finds it convenient to modify it. This thesis leads to consideration of the links between the path of labour demand and labour supply and the respect of ethical codes. One can interpret Smith's thought on this topic by arguing that 'sympathy' – the basic principle stated in $(TMS)^{42}$ – conceived as the search by individual A for moral approval on the part of all other members of the same social group, where the closer the others are, the more intense is the search for approval (Smith 1976b, p. 10), is also what drives entrepreneurs' choices in industrial relations. Once a 'decent wage' has been settled, entrepreneurs would not find it convenient to fix their employees' wage at a lower level, since this wage policy would imply the break of social links related to sympathy and, ultimately, ostracism. This ethical constraint is reflected in the *habitus* of the 'prudent man'. As emphasized by Pesciarelli (1991), in Smith's view, prudent men, as entrepreneurs, widespread in society,

> direct self-oriented initiatives towards social ends. In other words, in the exercise of his economic activity, the prudent man submits his own action to a certain degree of *self-control* in order not to harm others and in order to receive their approbation. The prudent man *unconsciously* promotes the interests of society because he *consciously* sets limits on the pursuit of his interests.
>
> (Pesciarelli 1991, p. 216)[43]

Owing to the existence of these ethical constraints, the need for social cohesion becomes dominant, and, ultimately, it *forces* employers to respect the code of behaviour of paying 'decent' wages. Moreover, a high wage policy is also convenient insofar as high wages determine an increase in labour productivity: 'The wages of labour are the encouragement of industry, which, like every other human quality, improves in proportion to the encouragement it receives' (Smith 1976 [1776], p. 99). From this analysis, a more general theoretical conclusion may be drawn, that is: *it is because of the existence and spread of ethical constraints that social efficiency can be achieved.*[44] Given his idea of social efficiency (i.e. the wealth of the maximum number of people),[45] there are two states of the world to consider.

STATE 1 – *Relative scarcity* → *incentive to compete* → *efficiency*
STATE 2 – *Relative plenty* → *incentive to collude* → *inefficiency*

As 'scarcity' and 'plenty'[46] are the clearest features or indexes of the business cycle, for Smith it follows that *norms of behaviour change during the cycle.* In a growing economy, the 'pre-market' (or exogenous) ethical constraint – collusion among 'masters' – is relaxed and 'converted' into the *temporary* absence of ethical constraints. By contrast, in a stationary (or declining) economy, the 'pre-market' ethical constraint holds, and no factors can modify it.

The inside-the-market approach rests on the idea that agents are 'ethical' only if it is profitable; however, the assumption that different types of agents (i.e. 'socially responsible' and 'pure maximizing' firms) exist and that some of them are 'intrinsically' ethical can be inserted into this schema. In so doing, a harmful effect is likely to occur. Assume that, in a given economy at a given time, consumers are 'ethically oriented' and two types of firms exist: type-*A* firms (socially responsible, in the sense that they would behave 'morally' even if consumers did not express a demand for 'morality') and type-*B* firms (maximizing profits). If being 'ethical' is profitable, type-*B* firms would find it convenient to temporarily 'convert' into socially responsible firms, even (temporarily) adopting higher standards of 'morality' than their competitors. As a result, a crowding out effect will occur at the expense of type-*A* firms and, in the long run, consumers will find only the products of type-*B* firms. Since no competition on the part of type-*A* firms will exist, type-*B* firms will revert to behaving as pure profit-maximizers.[47] A similar mechanism is likely to occur within a different path. Relaxing the assumption of homogeneous agents, suppose that the economy is formed by, say, 'unscrupulous' (type-*B*) and 'benevolent' (type-*A*) entrepreneurs (*UE* and *BE*), where the former are non-ethically oriented agents and the behaviour of the *BE*s is based on 'fair' treatment of their employees: they basically differ in their wage policies (low wages in the first case and high wages in the second case). The higher costs of production of the *BE*s will lead them to sell at higher prices with respect to their competitors and, under the assumption that goods/services produced by *BE*s are substitutes (although not perfect substitutes) of those produced by *UE*s, in a deregulated market for goods, unscrupulous entrepreneurs will prevail and benevolent entrepreneurs will be forced to adopt 'immoral' codes of behaviour.[48]

In view of these considerations the first link of sequence 1.1 is not necessarily proven and consequently neither are the logical links implied there. Moreover, the assumed scale of wants is also questionable, since it is based on the idea that individuals have the *same* order of needs independently of the social, historical and institutional environment in which they live, that is, a scale of wants which presumes that human psychology is basically 'universal' (involving *all* men) and 'constant' (no changes over time and space are considered). By contrast, anthropologists find that solidarity is often a *prerequisite* for exchanges, particularly in 'developing' countries, and that the search for *individual* subsistence is basically absent in pre-capitalistic society, where cohesion within groups is necessary in order to produce goods needed for the *subsistence of the group* (see Schneider 1974). Reisman (2002, p. 157) questions Maslow's approach on the theoretical plane, pointing out that

> Rank-ordering can differ: risk-lovers such as war correspondents put self-actualization before safety and security since a long life without excitement seems to them like no life at all. Rank-ordering can be in conflict: loners like visionary hermits are unwilling to put integration before creative freedom lest too little self-ownership deprive them of the initiator's self-respect.

Two possible alternative approaches to the inside-the-market view are suggested here.

a *Ethical codes in a microeconomic approach.* The basic idea of this approach consists of pointing out that the propagation of moral norms derives from *intolerance effects*, that is, from the reaction of weak agents who are repeatedly subjected to 'incorrect' behaviour by the strong agents with whom they have social relations. It is likely that the intensity and/or rapidity of the reaction is proportionate to (i) the amount of damage suffered and (ii) the propensity to risk on the part of weak agents, since they may suffer from reprisals by the strong agents, *if* reaction has a *rational* ground.[49] Following the reaction, the degree of *fairness* will then be established given the bargaining powers of 'weak' and 'strong' agents. This view *can* also presuppose that reaction is driven by emotions (such as anger or indignation, in this case), so that 'Anger may cause cessation of calculation of benefits and costs' (Schmid 2004, p. 36), and the propensity to risk does not play a relevant role. Jack Knight (1992, pp. 129 ff.) has proposed a similar approach to the issue (however, based on the bargaining game under the assumption of rationality) in search for a 'micro-level explanation of the decentralized emergence of social institutions'. In his view, resource asymmetries, credibility, risk aversion and time preferences are the key variables in foreseeing the outcome of bargaining among agents who have different powers.

Moreover, one can argue that the perception of fairness is likely to depend on the communication strategies adopted by firms: advertising, for instance, can induce workers to perceive as a just wage a level of wage which allows them to enjoy a standard of living similar to that experienced by the 'representative' agent (resulting from communication strategies), *within their social group*.[50] Advertising, in turn, and under the assumption of non-satiation on the part of workers as consumers, determines an increasing difference between the actual real wage and the *desired* real wage and their consequent possible reaction, in the form of conflict. 'Envy' can also be taken into account in explaining conflict, giving rise to a solution where a condition of 'fairness' should be such as to generate an 'envy-free' allocation of resources: no agent would find it profitable to obtain resources from others, given the cost of this action (see Varian 1974).

b *The spread of ethical codes on the macroeconomic plane.* Within the institutional theoretical framework (see North 1990 and Chapter 4 in this book), it is stressed that formal, informal and moral norms basically derive from the interaction among agents in the social and political arena, and that the market is only one possible locus where the economic process takes place. Douglass C. North (1990, p. 48, italics added) points out that

> Broadly speaking, political rules in place lead to economic rules, though the causality runs both ways. That is, property rights and hence individual contracts are specified and enforced by political decision-making, *but the structure of economic interests will also influence the political structure.*

An extension of this argument results in the following schema, based on the so-called theory of revolution (Silver 1974; Tullock 1971) and under the basic assumption that agents do not enjoy the same bargaining power. Bargaining involves *at least* three macro-agents: firms, workers (or unions) and the government. Let us assume that all agents are self-interested and that their aims are, respectively, to maximize profits, to maximize utility (deriving from wages and labour conditions) and to maximize consent,[51] and that firms call for labour market deregulation (producing a decrease of the unitary wage) and workers oppose this policy.[52] Let us also assume that the initial condition is unemployment equilibrium. The rules governing firm–worker relationships (with particular regard to wages) are the object of negotiations, in a context where firms – both the individual firm and firms as a whole – aim at setting wages at the lowest level (w^0) and workers aim at obtaining a higher wage ($w*$), consistent with the no-bankrupt condition.[53] The degree of 'fairness' in working conditions and the level of 'desired' wages is assumed to depend on what workers *perceive* as 'just', which – in turn – may depend on social, institutional and historical variables. Government faces a double constraint: imposing $w*$ (or, more generally, following a 'pro-worker' policy) would guarantee consent from workers but would induce firms to threaten disinvestment and/or delocalization of production (what Bowles and Gintis (1976) define as a 'capital strike').[54] This, in turn, may produce a reduction in national income and income per-capita and hence a reduction in the probability of obtaining high levels of consent to the advantage of the government. Therefore, the 'morality' underlying firm–worker relationships (at least in the sense of 'fair' labour conditions and wages) will ultimately depend on (i) firms' capability credibly to threaten government, which, in turn, is the outcome of the institutional setting governing capital mobility and labour relations in other countries. The higher the corporate bargaining power with respect to government, the worse the prevailing treatment of workers will be; (ii) degree of worker solidarity, which affects their bargaining power and allows problems of free-riding behaviour to be overcome by their joining the union (Tullock 1971);[55] (iii) government propensity to a deficit spending policy in order to avoid the perverse effects of corporate disinvestment. This basic schema referring to the outside-the-market approach may lead to the results described in sequence 1.2.

Sequence 1.2 Social conflict and the spread of ethical codes

$$\uparrow m \rightarrow \uparrow (FBP - GBP) \rightarrow \downarrow w \text{ and } \alpha \rightarrow \text{social conflict} \rightarrow \uparrow w \text{ and } \uparrow a \text{ (if } dm = 0; dG > 0)$$

The increase in corporate bargaining power with respect to that of the government (FBP, GBP) owing to the increase in capital mobility (m) determines (according to the assumptions above) a reduction in wages (w) and in the degree of fairness in labour relationships (α). Given worker (or union) bargaining power, this is likely to lead to an increase in social conflict,[56] which, in turn, may produce an increase in wages and the degree of fairness in labour relationships,[57] if (i) m does not increase and/or (ii) if policies of deficit spending (G) are put in place (or state-controlled firms are created in order to increase employment and incomes). If condition (i) does not hold, policies of deficit spending – when possible – are profitable for a self-interested government (also independently of its ideological background) for the sake of obtaining workers' consent. If both condition (i) and condition (ii) do not hold, social conflict produces a further delocalization of firms, hence a decrease in wages and employment and consequently the workers' opposition to the government via voting.[58]

This argument falls within the Keynesian approach. One can argue that social conflict, insofar as it determines an increase in wages, produces a growth in effective demand and, as a result, in employment and the rate of growth (starting – as assumed here – from an unemployment equilibrium):[59] therefore, the higher the wage demanded (and received) by workers (which, in turn, reflects their *perception of fairness*), the lower the resulting unemployment rate. Accordingly, while conflict is not profitable for the *individual* firm – since it produces a decrease of output (if workers' claims are not satisfied) – it is *socially* profitable (if workers' claims are satisfied) because of the increase in effective demand. An inflationary pull can occur in the event the market wage in a context of full employment is lower than the wage demanded, and received. Note that, as in the inside-the-market approach, economic growth is moral growth, but the basic difference lies in the fact that in the outside-the-market approach economic growth is driven by *external interventions* (unions and/or the state). Moreover, in both cases – where propagation effects are considered – agents behave 'ethically' basically because it is privately convenient and in both cases it is necessary for *one* agent (or group of agents) to call for ethical behaviour on the part of the others: the basic difference lies in the fact that in the inside-the-market approach *consumers* are those who 'demand', and orient the firm's production, under the principle of 'consumer sovereignty'; while in the outside-the-market approach *workers* are those who 'demand' and their claims are *not necessarily satisfied*. The 'demand' for ethical behaviour, in turn, depends – in the first case – on 'natural' needs and – in the second case – on needs which are socially and historically determined.

This simplified schema aims at showing that the spread of ethical codes (conceived here as 'fair' treatment of workers) (i) is not driven by market mechanisms, (ii) is independent of the search for reputation, (iii) is not necessarily connected with economic growth and (iv) basically refers to dynamics within the production process, the labour market, the socio-political arena, while not necessarily involving changes in the goods market. More generally, following Douglass C. North (1990, p. 48), it is maintained here that rules are not linked to efficiency: they are 'at least in good part, devised in the interests of private well-being rather than social well-being'.[60] Jack Knight (1992, p. 19) proposed a similar view, by emphasizing that 'social institutions are conceived as a product of the efforts of some to constrain the actions of others with whom they interact'. This does not imply that in a condition of 'institutional stability' a Pareto-optimal solution is reached: institutional stability – that is, a situation where 'no one wants to deviate from the institutional rules' (Knight 1992, p. 37) – can be consistent with the existence of individuals or groups who do not maximize their objective function, because the process of institutional change is too costly. The cost of institutional change, in turn, is strictly linked to the degree of uncertainty that 'unsatisfied' individuals and groups face, and the benefits of stability are, by contrast, linked to the reduction of uncertainty that institutional stability produces. Moreover, the schema proposed here is based on the view that labour markets as well as labour relationships are ultimately a 'political product', since the political arena affects economic variables just as economic variables affect political choices, basically in line with Soskice's (1990) concept of 'coordinated market economies'.

Note that social conflict is excluded in the inside-the-market approach on the grounds that it presupposes discontent on the part of some agents or group of agents; but since, within this approach, the genesis and the spread of ethical codes is consensual and results from bargaining among 'equal' agents, the existence of discontent is not admissible.[61]

The contrasting views discussed here are based on two opposing visions of the functioning of market economies. In the first case, it is argued that *cooperation* among agents in the marketplace allows not only an efficient allocation of resources, but also the spontaneous spread of ethical codes. In the second case, emphasis is put on *conflictual* relationships among agents with different and largely contrasting aims. Moreover, while in the first case the widespread adoption of ethical codes is *unintentional*, not planned and not necessarily foreseen, in the second case ethical codes are likely to emerge *via deliberate* actions by firms, workers and the government.

The schemes presented here are conceived as the theoretical frameworks for interpreting the reflection of John Bates Clark and Thorstein Veblen on the role of market versus institutions in setting rules of behaviour reflecting ethical codes.

Appendix I

*Altruism, exchange and economic development**

Within the theoretical framework of ethical economics, the issues of the nature of altruism and its economic and social effects are the subject of an interesting debate (see Sacco and Zamagni 2002, among others; Sen 1979, 1984; Zamagni 1995). Two main questions are in order: first, what is the *nature* of altruism? And, second, what are the possible *effects* of the spread of altruistic behaviours on the number of transactions and, more generally, on economic development? In what follows, these themes will be explored.

The nature of altruism

Following Khalil (2003), three different approaches to the question have been proposed: the 'egoistic' approach, the 'egocentric' and the 'alterocentric' approaches.

The egoistic conception of altruism[62] is based on the idea that altruistic behaviours may be convenient insofar as they produce future benefits, and future benefits can occur in the case of repeated games, particularly under 'tit for tat' rules (see Axelrod 1984; Bergstrom and Stark 1993; Taylor 1987). Carlo Augusto Viano (1990, pp. 43 ff., referring to Sidgwick 1907) maintains that the attempt to make altruistic behaviours consistent with the basic neoclassical paradigm (based on the Pareto criterion and on utilitarianism) is likely to be unsuccessful.

---

* This appendix is partially derived from G. Forges Davanzati and A. L. Paolilli, 'Altruismo, scambi e sviluppo economico', in L. Tundo Ferente (ed.) 2004. *La responsabilità del pensare. Scritti in onore di Mario Signore*. Napoli: Liguori, pp. 289–307.

A Pareto optimal change benefits at least one agent while harming no other and a Pareto optimum is a condition where no change is possible. In Viano's interpretation, this statement presupposes that agents differ because of their different *natural* capacities and, therefore, this anthropological view seems to exclude the possibility of taking altruistic behaviours into consideration, at least in a 'significant' way. In contrast, Collard (1975) finds the analytical conditions for Pareto optimality with interdependent utility, by inserting a 'coefficient of effective sympathy'[63] into the utility function. This result is generated in a context of what the author names 'positive utilitarianism' – referring to Sidgwick and Edgeworth – which arises when it is admitted that individuals attach weights to the utilities of others. Moreover, as Yeager (2001, p. 239) points out, 'The Pareto criterion itself involves value judgements, however hidden, including the judgement that all persons' tastes and preferences are to count equally according to their intensity.'

The 'egocentric' perspective (Becker 1976; Dawkins 1976; Hochman and Rodgers 1969) argues that the altruistic agent *A* includes *B*'s utility in his/her utility function. *Emotional proximity*, in turn, determines actual altruistic behaviour, giving rise to different degrees of altruism according to parental or friendship relationships. Note that – in this case – the reason *why* individuals behave in an altruistic way is not identified; it is the *way* altruistic individuals reach their aims.

According to the 'alterocentric' view, a moral gene ultimately favours pro-social behaviours, *independently of calculation*. Sober (1991) finds that the stronger the social cohesion, the higher the probability that a social group will be successful in natural (as well as social) selection. Accordingly, social evolution has supposedly selected the norms which promote cohesion, altruism included (Frank 1988).

The nature of altruism with respect to its effects on social interaction (particularly in the form of gifts) is also the subject of extensive debate. Marcel Mauss (1950) maintains that gifts are social devices in order to establish alliances, since a gift generates a persistent relation of dependence among agents. The potlach, widespread in the indigenous population of North America, represents – according to this view – the most significant example of the gift as an instrument to subject the other to one's rule: unfriendly relations produce dependence via gift exchanges. Moreover, it is argued that the gift is also a strategy in order to acquire – or not to lose – prestige. By contrast, Sahlins (1965) emphasizes that 'pure' relations of friendship, where a gift is involved, cannot involve the economic dimension, by their very nature. Hence, the command to 'reciprocate' occurs only in the event where the 'degree' of friendship is low: in the case of pure friendship, the gift by *A* to *B* does not imply the expectation, on the part of *A*, to receive something from *B*.[64] What is (or what should be) the *content* of exchanges between altruistic agents? 'A real altruist' – it is suggested – 'would urge you to stop eating chocolates, because although you may like the taste of chocolate, it is not in your best interest to eat them' (Lutz and Lux 1988, p. 109). Zamagni (1995, p. xvi, italics added) suggests classifying altruistic individuals 'when they feel and act as if the *welfare* of others were an end in itself'. The welfare of others – one can maintain – is likely to depend on the inter-temporal discount rate of the altruist, in the sense that, by expanding Lutz and Lux's argument, altruistic agents (like all agents) can be 'myopic' – thus giving chocolates – or 'long sighted' – thus *not* giving chocolates, provided that eating chocolates produces damages in the long run.

Origin and effects of altruistic behaviour

The main theoretical problem which arises in approaching the issue of the origin of altruistic behaviour is connected to the so-called Darwinian paradox of the survival of altruists (Becker 1976). This paradox derives from two assumptions: first, natural selection favours stronger individuals; second, altruists are more vulnerable than self-interested agents. It should follow that social (and natural) evolution determines the progressive disappearance of altruistic agents, which is counterfactual. However, the questionable assumption on which this paradox is based is that altruistic agents are more vulnerable than self-interested individuals. Following Sober's argument (1991), one can reach the opposite conclusion: provided cohesion within social groups (and hence the existence of pro-social attitudes including altruism) promotes efficiency, then self-interested agents are likely to be more vulnerable. Moreover, it is both the intensity of competition among self-interested and altruistic agents (where, almost by definition, an altruistic agent does not compete with other altruists) and the 'critical mass' of one of the two groups which ultimately affect the supremacy of these contrasting codes of behaviour.

Two questions are now in order:

a *What theoretical conditions must be considered in order to conceive exchanges among altruistic agents?* The question is significant because of the possibility (although highly hypothetical) that an economy where solely altruistic agents operate is an economy without exchanges. Let us assume that

i   all agents are *pure* altruists, in the sense that they maximize the utility of others without considering their own interest. For the sake of simplicity, consider two individuals A and B, with these utility functions: Max $U_A = f(U_B)$ and Max $U_B = f(U_A)$, with $f' > 0$ in both cases.

ii neither A nor B wants the other to lose resources and the choice has to be made in a given unit of time (for instance, A wants to go to see a football match while B wants to go to the theatre, and both the events are on at the same time).[65]

In view of these assumptions, neither A nor B acts and the number of exchanges is zero, because neither wants the other to reduce his/her utility.[66] This result – which can be described as *the paradox of bilateral pure altruism* – although not significant empirically, shows that the functioning of a market economy necessarily requires either that agents should be only partially altruistic (i.e. should consider their own interests too) or that, when interacting with pure altruists, they should be selfish or, finally, that a significant number of self-interested individuals should exist. However, by relaxing the assumption of pure altruism, one can argue that, by comparing an economy in which solely selfish agents operate with an economy of altruistic individuals, there is a higher number of exchanges in the latter. This is because solidarity also implies providing resources in the absence of monetary gains. Moreover, by assuming that 'it is impossible to be happy if surrounded by unhappy individuals',[67] it may be *rational* to be altruistic, within a given (and reasonably small) group.[68] This view can be linked to the Smithian concept of 'the pleasures of harmony': in Amos Witzum's interpretation (in Porta *et al.* 2001, p. 147) this means that

> Initially, the *need* to survive makes people aware of the importance of wealth. As they are equally motivated to maximize the pleasures of harmony they must choose now between *acting* in a way that will command the respect of the public [...] or accumulating wealth and gaining the public's respect through the deception of nature and the pleasure of 'utility'.

  b *Can altruistic behaviour promote economic development?* There are at least four reasons that may establish a positive relation between altruism and economic development.[69] First, altruism is likely to positively affect the propensity to work. If *A* wants to help *B*, one would expect *A* to produce a higher quantity of goods/services than if she/he were only self-interested (think, for instance, of non-profit organizations).[70] Second, altruism – as a pro-social attitude – is associated with the respect of social norms and hence its spread is likely to increase social capital, which, in turn, acts as an input for economic development (see Sacco and Zamagni 2002). As Chillemi (in Sacco and Zamagni 2002, p. 493; see also Chapter 4) notes, within the firm, the existence of cooperative attitudes among workers can generate an increase in productivity because of the lack of free-riding behaviour. Third, in a Keynesian theoretical framework, if altruism implies an increase of the lowest income, this produces a growth in effective demand, employment and economic growth.[71] Four, altruism can directly or indirectly affect social capital. The rationale for this argument is made clear – among other possible cases – if we consider a situation where, in a labour market where jobs can be obtained via corruption, 'ethical voters' do exist (see Hudson and Jones [1994], in Zamagni 1995, pp. 196–205). Ethical voters are altruists in the sense that they vote by considering above all the effects of their choice on the welfare of the whole community, thus rejecting the possibility of obtaining private advantages through corruption and taking only their ideological convictions into account. Corruption, in turn, determines inefficient social outcomes, mainly because – if jobs are given on the basis of illegal transactions – job allocation does not reflect individual abilities. Accordingly, the more ethical the voters, the lower the probability of 'dishonest' politicians being voted in and, as a result, the greater the number of 'honest' politicians.

  The main theoretical argument opposing the idea that altruism can promote economic growth and hence should be encouraged lies in the view that 'charity' disincentivizes work, a view frequently put forward in the history of economic thought.[72] The underlying assumption relies on a vision of human behaviour where (i) labour always implies disutility; (ii) man is solely self-interested. However, on the macro plane, this view (and its consequent policy prescriptions) appears questionable. As Richard Titmuss has convincingly shown, gift relationships are effective devices for ensuring social cohesion (see Fontaine 2004)[73] and, more generally, the fact that individuals are unable to earn at least a subsistence wage is likely to produce social conflict. The costs of repressing conflict may be higher than the costs of the possible decrease in production owing to the (assumed) disincentive effect associated with gifts. As a result, and also accepting assumptions (i) and (ii), a society where 'charity' is in operation (on both the individual and political planes) may produce a higher level of social efficiency than a society based only on self-interested behaviour.

A further theoretical argument supporting the inefficiency of altruism is based on its supposed 'informational inefficiency': it is argued that exchange relations via the market presuppose a higher level of information than gift exchanges. In other words, an altruistic agent – unlike a purely selfish agent involved in market transactions – may not know the *precise amount* of resources that the beneficiary needs. Serge-Christophe Kolm ([1983] in Zamagni 1995, pp. 244 ff.) strongly criticizes this view on the grounds that '[altruists] can also do some other things which egoists cannot do'. For instance, 'Altruists can reveal their preferences for "public goods", [and] internalize in their calculation the "externalities" which they create.'

Appendix II

*Sidney and Beatrice Webb: the ethical foundation of the labour market**

This section will address the Webbs' analysis of the labour market, mainly found in *Industrial Democracy*, and within the theoretical economic framework of the Fabians. The basic idea is that public intervention – and hence the increase in wages – solves a lack of coordination problem which arises when 'ethically oriented' firms compete with 'non-ethical' firms, in a context where a 'crowding out' effect beneficial to 'non-ethical' firms is in operation. By assuming that wage increases determine increases in labour productivity and/or in working hours (owing to human capital accumulation and reduction of social conflict) – and since 'non-ethical' firms do not find it profitable to increase wages as this only produces positive externalities on the part of their competitors – regulation promotes the adoption of a code of behaviour which leads entrepreneurs to follow a high wage policy, which, in turn, determines increases in demand and in aggregate output. The result is reinforced by the emergence of asymmetric information problems between entrepreneurs and traders. Thus, their analysis may also be read in the light of contemporary debate on labour market deregulation and the reflections on the institutional foundations of the labour market (see Saint-Paul 2000).

Sidney and Beatrice Potter Webb were the undisputed leaders of the Fabian Society,[74] an upper-middle-class intellectual group that emerged in 1884. They became known after the publication of *Facts for Socialists* (1884) by Sidney Webb. The Fabian Society, including George Bernard Shaw, William Beveridge,

---

* This section partly reflects par. 2 of my paper (with Andrea Pacella) on the Webbs' theory of the labour market published in the *History of Economic Ideas*, 12, no. 3, 2004.

Sydney Olivier, Graham Wallas, Ramsay MacDonald, G. D. H. Cole and H. G. Wells, rejected the Marxist revolutionary solution 'against the evils of late – nineteenth century capitalism' (Minion 2000, p. 237) because of its inherent incapacity to maximize welfare and the allocation of resources (Trentmann 1997, p. 95). In addition, it was more directly involved in 'the reconstruction of society in accordance with the highest moral possibilities' (Pease 1963, p. 31), in the sense that each individual right should be balanced with social responsibilities (see Marton 2003; Prideaux 2001) and with politics and practical advances in favour of the working class, such as good wages, short hours, fair conditions and regular work (in the contemporary debate, the issue is brought up again by Checchi and Lucifora 2002, among others).[75] Their political project focused on a *gradual* transition to socialism. In particular, as Wright stresses, Fabians 'emphasized the organizational attributes of socialism in arranging efficient production and egalitarian distribution' (Wright 1987, p. 81). Bevir (1989) and Trentmann (1997) maintain that – within the Fabian Society – economic and political ideas went beyond both liberalism and Marxism.[76] With specific reference to Sidney and Beatrice Webb's economic and political ideas, Cole (1972, p. 489) maintains that 'their social philosophy [...] rested upon [...] the principle of utilitarianism, "the greatest happiness of the greatest number"', so that their view of the economic process, as well as of economic policy, is seen to be in line with the Benthamite tradition. Crowley (1978, p. 1) considers Sidney Webb a 'utilitarian socialist planner', who basically followed J. S. Mill's ideas on socialism. By contrast, Bevir (2002, p. 223, italics added) points out that

> Although [Sidney] Webb seems [...] to accept a utilitarian position, we need to be careful in our analysis. Utilitarianism can be a slippery doctrine [...] Webb, like many of his contemporaries, played on the ambiguous nature of utilitarianism, sometimes appealing to it as a principle, but always with a notion of happiness that made him scarcely a utilitarian at all. For Webb, *individuals have a duty to act for the social good rather than their own happiness.*

Schumpeter (1954, book II, ch. IV) interprets the Webbs' approach to economics as a result of the reception, in England, of the methodology of the German Historical School.

These latter interpretations appear more convincing,[77] although the interpretations of the Webbs' thought are complicated by their enormous bibliography. Following Schumpeter's view, the Webbs' economic methodology can be summarized as follows: first, agents are not always and everywhere self-interested. Second, human behaviour is not independent of the historical and institutional conditions where it takes place. Third, even if the rational choice paradigm is adopted, this does not imply that *all* agents behave according to this paradigm, and generalizations are admitted once empirical evidence has been traced (see Harrison 2000; S. and B. Webb 1919b, 'Preface'; S. and B. Webb 1932, p. 219–221; Webb 1905).[78] Accordingly, empirical evidence plays a crucial role in the Webbs' approach to economics (see S. and B. Webb 1932, p. 219, p. 221) and – by rejecting the neoclassical picture of a purely self-interested *homo oeconomicus* – they oppose the mathematical *architecture* of the dominant economic theory.

It is on this basis that the analysis of the working of the labour market is carried out and the reflections on institutional changes (i.e. the passage to socialism) are made.

The analysis of the labour market in the capitalist system

The starting point is the criticism of the classical picture of the labour market, with particular regard to the wages fund theory and to the Malthusian principle.

1 The wages fund theory. In its crudest shape, this theory – proposed by J. R. McCulloch and re-proposed by John Stuart Mill in his influential book of 1848 (*Principles of Political Economy*) – states that the amount of capital devoted to paying workers is a given, in a given moment, and, hence, that the volume of employment results from the capital/unitary wage ratio in a competitive labour market.[79] In his review of Thornton's *On Labour*, published in the *Fortnightly Review* in May 1869, Mill himself rejected the wages fund theory (his so-called recantation). However, according to the Webbs (1919b, p. 604), this theory 'still lingers in the public mind'.[80]

They maintain that the wages fund theory is not a theory, but a truism: if the capital devoted to paying workers is predetermined, it is quite obvious that the unitary wage is given by the capital/number of workers ratio, or that the volume of employment results from the capital/unitary wage ratio. The Webbs also reject the assumption underlying the wages fund theory that wages are paid in advance, that is, before the production process has been finished: so-called advance economics (see Schumpeter 1954). The rationale for this position is to be found in the empirical evidence that wages are not paid from the capital previously accumulated, but from corporate earnings deriving from the sale of products. In their own words:

> Whatever may be the task on which the workmen are engaged, they are, as a matter of fact, fed, *week by week, by products* just brought to the market, exactly in the same way as the employer and his household are fed. They are paid their wages, week by week, out of the current *cash balances* of their employers, these cash balances being daily replenished by sales of the current product.
>
> (S. and B. Webb, 1919b, p. 619, italics added)

It is worth noting that the same criticisms were also put forward, in that period, by most of marginalist/neoclassical economists (see, in particular, Jevons 1871; Walker 1876).[81] One can argue that the basic difference between these two streams of criticism lies in the different view of the role of the working class in the production process. 'Advance economics' suggests that workers are instruments of production: early neoclassical authors, by contrast, tried to picture the economic process as beneficial to workers as consumers, in order to show that socialist claims lacked a scientific basis.[82] On the contrary, the Webbs' criticism is justified on the grounds of the outcome of the wages fund theory in terms of economic policy, that is, the possibility of increasing wages only at the expense of a reduction in employment.[83]

2 The Malthusian principle. As we know, according to this principle, population tends to grow faster than wage goods. The Webbs strongly reject this view, on two points. On the methodological plane, they find the idea that it is possible to find *universal* economic 'laws' questionable. On the empirical level, they show that – in the context they look at – 'no connection can be traced between [the fall in the general death rate of the United Kingdom] and any rise of wage' (S. and B. Webb 1919b, p. 635). The decline in the death rate is to be explained in view of an institutional change (i.e. the improvement of sanitation conditions), which is, in turn, the outcome of the increase in worker bargaining power (ibid., pp. 642 ff.).

While the Webbs' argument clearly and explicitly reflects their political position, that is, the rejection of the practical consequences of the Malthusian principle (the ineffectiveness of union action), it is not so clear why the neoclassical economists of the period (excluding Pareto and Wicksell) continued to consider the principle 'true', although they left it out when elaborating their (static) models. Schumpeter (1954) interprets this choice as the acceptance of what he calls 'a bogey'. A different interpretation – suggested here – relies on the neoclassical political and economic framework: the Malthusian principle may be useful in demonstrating that workers' claims are not only pointless, but also counterproductive, a conclusion in line with the neoclassical picture of the labour market.[84]

The Webbs picture the labour market as ruled by formal and informal norms, paying particular attention to (a) the nature and the ends of entrepreneurs and (b) the possible effects of high wages in promoting economic growth. Let us look at these theses.

a *The nature and ends of entrepreneurs.* Unlike the neoclassical conception of the entrepreneur as a pure profit-maximizing agent, the Webbs' approach takes two types of entrepreneurs into consideration. The first type is defined 'unscrupulous employer' (S. and B. Webb 1919b, p. 552, hereafter UE): his/her aim is to maximize profits *via* reduction in wages and/or increase in working hours and/or reduction in comfort in the workplace. The second type is defined the 'good' or 'benevolent' employer (hereafter BE), described as follows (ibid., p. 662):

> the typical capitalist manufacturer of the present generation, with his increasing education and refinement, his growing political interests and public spirit, will, so long as his customary income is not interfered with, take a positive pleasure in augmenting the wages and promoting the comfort of his workpeople.[85]

Incidentally, they maintain that the BE can be a rational (and self-interested) agent (ibid., p. 661), although this is not his/her main characteristic:

> A capitalist employer who looks forward, not to one but to many years' production, and who regards his business as a valuable property to be handed

down from one generation to another, will, *if only for his own sake*, bear in mind the probable effect of any reduction upon the permanent efficiency of the establishment.

(Italics added)[86]

The following remarks are now in order.

(i) Unlike the neoclassical picture, which excludes ethical considerations from the economic discourse, the Webbs argue that the aim of profit can be reached in two distinct ways, resulting from two distinct ethical codes: by worsening the conditions of workers or by improving them. They attach a negative value judgement to the first strategy and a positive judgement to the second. It is worth noting that these judgements do not apply to the aim (profits), but to the means selected to achieve it. The rationale can be found in Sydney Olivier's (1891 [1889]) reflections on ethics. He maintains that individual behaviour should be considered moral insofar as it preserves the existence of a society and contributes to avoiding (or minimizing) social conflicts.[87] Hence, the Webbs' UE is a self-interested immoral agent because – by worsening worker conditions – she/he generates high profits on the one hand, but possible negative externalities on the other hand, as a result of deterioration of the quality of the workforce, increase in social conflict and reduction in demand. By cutting wages, UEs can reduce prices and, hence, take market share away from BEs, who, in turn, in order to avoid bankruptcy (or keep profits at the normal level), are forced to cut wages. In other words, competition between the BE and UE determines a 'crowding out' effect beneficial to the UE. They also suggested that the easiest strategy is that of worsening workers' conditions: 'it is so hard to spend laborious nights and days in the improving process. It is so easy to find workmen eager for a job at 10 per cent below the standard rate' (S. Webb 1906, p. 6). In this respect, competition modifies the codes of behaviour on the part of benevolent employers, in the sense that – while they are 'ethically oriented' *ex ante* – they are forced to behave in an unscrupulous way. This leads, in turn, to what Sidney Webb calls 'demoralization' (S. Webb 1906, p. 4).

(ii) The Webbs also consider the case of asymmetric information between the entrepreneur and the wholesale trader. In this context:

> He [the manufacturer] [...] is told that the price of his product is too high to attract consumers [...] and that there are just come an offer from a rival manufacturer to supply the same article at a lower price. The manufacturer may doubt these statements, but he has no means of disproving them.
>
> (S. and B. Webb 1919b, p. 664)

In other words, the asymmetric information problem arises because entrepreneurs – unlike traders – do not have complete information on the amount of the demand for their products/services. Traders aim at obtaining the maximum difference between the price of goods sold and the price set by the entrepreneurs. As a result, the BE is forced to reduce prices and therefore wages, so that – also for this reason – *via* competition UEs tend to prevail.

The resulting overall reduction in wages determines two main consequences: (a) emigration of the more productive workers and deterioration of the quality of the workforce; (b) social conflict, which forces government to increase taxes in order to finance repression.[88] This may imply a migration of firms if taxes are imposed on profits.[89] Since these effects reduce both working hours and productivity, as well as demand, it remains to be seen why firms find it convenient to cut wages. The rationale for this strategy is that while cutting wages is advantageous on the *micro* plane (insofar as it allows the individual firm to increase its expected profits), it is counterproductive on the *macro* plane. In fact, the increase in the quality of the workforce, the reduction in social conflict and the increase in demand – resulting from high wages – should be conceived as positive externalities for competitors and, hence, they are not taken into account in determining the individual firm's wages policy.[90] In what follows the policy implications of this model will be discussed.

b *Union action and the high wages theory.* The Webbs strongly emphasize that employers and workers have very different bargaining power. Although this assumption may appear quite reasonable, it was not so in the theoretical debate of the time. The prevailing view supported the idea that 'whilst the wage-earners must starve if the employers stand out, the employers may be driven into bankruptcy if the workmen revolt' (S. and B. Webb 1919b, p. 656, footnote no. 1).[91] By contrast, they argue that:

> [capitalists] go on eating and drinking, working and enjoying themselves, whether the bargaining with the individual workman has been made or not. Very different is the case with the wage-earner. If he refuses the foreman's terms even for a day, he irrevocably loses his whole day's subsistence.
>
> (Ibid., p. 656)

Thanks to their willingness to wait longer than workers, employers are stronger in individual bargaining.[92] Union action balances bargaining powers, because it (i) reduces competition among workers and (ii) allows workers not to be forced to accept the first offer from the firm, but to wait.[93] In the institutional context where unions are protected by the law, union action may succeed in raising wages over the minimum subsistence level prevailing in a deregulated labour market. In the Webbs' theoretical framework, since a negative relation between the unitary wage and employment (as in the case of the wages fund theory) is not admitted, the increase in wage (i) does not reduce employment and (ii) generates increases in productivity (for the reasons discussed later) and in demand. The rationale for the positive relation between wages and productivity is found in the following effects. An increase in wages increases the 'physical strength and mental training of the manual working class' (S. and Webb 1919b, p. 627 and also 1919a *passim*) and reduces the deterioration of the quality of the workforce (ibid., pp. 308 and 444); minimizes social conflict.

The Webbs also argue that high wages positively affect demand. The point is clearly emphasized, within the Fabian society, by Thomas Dickson

(1905, p. 7): 'For if wages are cut down, it means that the workers are able to buy still less; and if they demand still less woollens, and food, and coal, and boots, still fewer workers would be required to produce them'. Since it is socially rational to increase wages (as well as to improve workers' conditions in the workplace), the Webbs consistently advocate a policy of defence of union action. At this point, the ways in which unions can achieve their aim need to be analysed. The most effective way, in the Webbs' view, is through collective bargaining, described as follows:

> Instead of the employer making a series of separate contracts with isolated individuals, he meets with a collective will, and settles, in a single agreement, the principle upon which, for the time being, workmen of a particular group, or class, or grade, will be engaged.
>
> (S. and B. Webb 1919b, p. 173)

The state is in a 'position of arbitrator' (ibid., p. 596). Two advantages for the working class emerge from the adoption of this method: first, cohesion among workers, since minimizing competition and hence increasing worker bargaining power forces employers not to cut wages; second, workers' interests are defended by 'expert negotiatiors', namely, union leaders (ibid., p. 181). The main (intermediate) union aim is to obtain 'the standard rate' of wages, that is a 'moral' (S. Webb, 1906, p. 2) *minimum* wage level for any particular job (ibid., p. 279), in view of the 'principle of identical pay for identical effort' (ibid., p. 319),[94] and the final result of union action should be 'the greatest "National Dividend"' (ibid., p. 802).[95]

Furthermore, the minimum wage, in the Webbs' analysis, positively affects the level of employment. In fact, a wage increase will produce an increase in employment, due to both the supply-side effects described earlier and the increase in 'aggregate income' (ibid., p. 445).[96] As a result, in order to increase employment and efficiency for the whole system, 'To oppose such a disastrous irregularity of work is a fundamental principle of Trade Unionism' (ibid., p. 435).[97] In this context, economic policy is necessary in order to enhance union action, to settle the minimum wage, to reduce unemployment[98] (see S. and B. Webb 1898; Webb 1891, 1899, 1912b, 1912c, 1914a, 1923, 1927; Webb and Cox 1891).

According to this picture, while private (unscrupulous) entrepreneurs are interested in reducing money expenditure, the state aims at promoting an increase in social efficiency, mainly by promoting the adoption of codes of behaviour which lead firms to improve workers' conditions. (S. Webb 1906, p. 5).

It is quite plain that – in this theoretical framework – union action determines positive effects on 'National Dividend' (i.e. total output) *within a given range of wage increases*. However, the Webbs do not explicitly deal with this issue:[99] the model presented later will also set out to provide a solution to the question, that is, finding the value of wages which maximizes total output.

As Picchio (1993, p. 5) points out – referring to the article 'The English Poor Law: Will It Endure?' by Beatrice Webb:

> [she] analyzes the historical role of the state in the labour market, and stresses the necessity for a radical restructuring of social policy on employment,

minimum wages and living standards of the labouring population. She attributes the great increase of state social expenditure in the second half of the 19th century [...] to the lack of structural mechanisms for adjustment between supply and demand of labour. She argues, in terms of social ethics and efficiency, for the recognition of a normal and structural role for the state in the process of adjustment.

The Webbs' attention to the quality of labour relationships – and the ethical variables involved – casts some doubt on the interpretation suggested by Flanders (1968) that their theory of union action is a traditional theory which does not pay attention to non-economic aspects of bargaining. In contrast, Baglioni (1969, pp. 86 ff.) finds a significant break between the classical theory of unions and that of the Webbs, in the sense that they explicitly stress the role of unions in promoting economic development.

The transition to socialism

The basic assumption is that 'economic and social conditions can, by deliberate human intervention, be changed for the better' (ibid., p. 559). In stating this, the Webbs counter the (individualistic) 'Manchester School' view that any intentional change is 'artificial', that is, not 'natural', and, for this reason, ineffective or even counterproductive (S. and B. Webb 1898, p. 231 ff.). The social philosophy underlying this idea can be summarized as follows: social evolution is not a *continuous* process and its outcome is not necessarily beneficial to society as a whole. Rather, this process should be regarded as *discontinuous*, where relevant changes occur when a large class of people experience prolonged misery: when misery is no longer suffered, a (collective) reaction is to be expected, aiming at minimizing misery,[100] and the final result depends on the relative bargaining powers of the parties (in this case workers and employers).

In this line of thought, social evolution selected unions as the most efficient institutions in order to achieve the maximum well-being not only for workers but for society as a whole. In a parallel way, developed societies have selected political democracy as the best way to solve conflicts (ibid., p. 842) as well as to ensure liberty. Hence: What is liberty? They write (ibid., p. 847):

> We ourselves understand by the words 'Liberty' or 'Freedom', not any quantum of natural or inalienable rights, but such conditions of existence in the community as do, in practice, result in the utmost possible development of faculty in the individual human being.[101]

As political democracy ensures liberty in the political arena, so industrial democracy should ensure freedom in the economic field. Moreover, in the Webbs' view, 'political democracy will inevitably result in industrial democracy' (ibid., p. 842). Industrial democracy is conceived as a new institutional setting where workers directly manage firms, with two consequent beneficial outcomes: (i) the development of the workers' intellectual faculties and (ii) 'a great increase in capacity and efficiency', both the result of their responsibility for the firm's performance (ibid., pp. 848–849). Accordingly, the transition to socialism – identified here with industrial democracy – would lead to higher social justice and higher levels of efficiency;[102,103] what Cole (1933, p. 490) calls 'pragmatic socialism'.

Sidney Webb (1914b, p. 4) argues that social evolution is unavoidable and it tends to move according to 'deliberate attempts to readjust the social environment to suit man's real or fancied needs. It is therefore not a question of *whether* the existing social order shall be changed, but of *how* this inevitable change shall be made.' He also stresses that 'socialism is not a utopia'. This is because 'it is irrational to assume that the existing social order [...] is destined inevitably to endure in its main features unchanged and unchangeable' (ibid., p. 3). He adds that 'the production and distribution of wealth [...] needs to be organized and controlled for the benefit of [the] whole community' (ibid., p. 5), through a 'gradual expansion of the collective administration' (ibid., p. 18) which improves the standard life of citizens. The Webbs are not clear about the issue of collectivism. As Bevir (2002, p. 239) notes, 'sometimes [Sidney] Webb appears to suggest that collectivism involves extensive social control [but] his proposals remained modest'.

Trade unions play a significant role in promoting the transition to socialism. The Webbs see the evolution of unionism as associated with three doctrines: (i) the *Doctrine of Vested Interests*; (ii) the *Doctrine of Supply and Demand*, and (iii) the *Doctrine of a Living Wage* (Webb, S. and Webb, B. 1919b, pp. 809–816). As the authors point out, in the first doctrine the trade union must guarantee that no employment conditions are worsened, but this must occur without interference in the competitive working of the labour market (ibid., p. 562); all forms of resistance are admitted in opposing any worsening of employment conditions. In the second case, the activity of the trade union is compared with that of any other business; therefore the capacity to improve labour conditions is linked only to the market power of the trade union or of the industrial association (ibid., p. 572). Finally, in the third case, the authors emphasize the social role of the trade union: the state must allow it greater power in defining the best employment conditions because of the importance attached to the standard of living in the general social consciousness (ibid., p. 816). Among these doctrines, the Webbs assume that the latter is the only one that enhances the socialist programme.

In view of this reconstruction, the following main findings are worth noting. Their distinction between BEs and UEs leads to it being shown that – owing to competition in a deregulated labour market – the latter tend to prevail. This is also the result of the existence of asymmetric information. By assuming a positive relationship between wages and productivity, which acts as an externality and hence is not taken into account by the individual firm, this outcome generates a decrease in total output with respect to a labour market where BEs prevail. This therefore results in a coordination failure; a policy of regulation of the labour market (via union action) is socially rational.

These conclusions lead to the idea that, unlike the conventional wisdom (ethics *or* economics), the spread of moral codes is likely to produce an increase in efficiency and social welfare.

2 John Bates Clark

Moral norms and the labour market in neoclassical economics

2.1 Introduction

The idea that moral norms affect economic behaviour, widely accepted in classical political economy (see, among others, Porta *et al.* 2001), has been neglected for many years, and replaced (albeit implicitly) by the view that agents choose in an institutional *vacuum*. However, the simple standard picture of the neoclassical *homo oeconomicus* dates to more recent years; as a matter of fact, many early neoclassical writers emphasized the role of ethical factors in determining individual and collective choices.

Among the most significant examples of this line of thought are the works by John Bates Clark, whose research programme was to make (Christian) ethical prescriptions consistent with the neoclassical analytical framework. This particularly applies to the analysis of the functioning of the labour market, where Clark sets out to demonstrate that marginalist distributive rules satisfy both an efficiency and an 'equity' condition. This research programme is based largely on the influence that the Historical School (Knies above all) had on his scientific background, which is particularly reflected in his rejection of the reduction of human behaviour to that of a purely self-interested *homo oeconomicus*, and the consequent attempt to explore the relations between *homo oeconomicus* and *homo moralis*.[104]

The evolution of Clark's thought is the subject of a widespread debate.[105] On the one hand, some historians (see, in particular, Jalledau 1975) have presented it as discontinuous, in the sense that they stress the passage from a 'radical Christian' Clark to an 'analytical' Clark. According to this view, in the first phase, Clark was interested in the ethical foundation of market economies and called for a more anthropological approach to the study of human behaviour, while, in the second phase (corresponding to the publication of his best-known work: the *Distribution of Wealth*), he worked on a purely theoretical plane, in line with neoclassical theory. In a sense, the development of Clark's thought is seen as the 'conversion' from criticism of capitalism to its apotheosis. On the other hand (see Henry 1994; Maurandi 2001), it is argued that, first, the idea of Clark's 'conversion' is not supported by textual evidence and, second, the evolution of his thought is to be conceived as the passage from the study of methodological issues to the inquiry into purely theoretical questions. This latter view seems to be more convincing: the search for an ethical foundation of market economies is, in effect, a constant in the whole development of Clark's thought. This view underlies the arguments presented here.

This chapter sets out to provide an answer to the following main question: Does Clark succeed in achieving the results he expected, that is, is the neoclassical economic equilibrium (in the labour market) such that an exogenous ethical code is respected? In so doing, a preliminary critical reconstruction of his theoretical framework will be provided, with particular respect to (i) his peculiar idea of the 'synchronicity' of the production process and (ii) his theory of wages.

Furthermore, some theses by Clark – since they are included in the contemporary neoclassical framework – will be discussed in the light of the present debate, and also in the light of a different view of ethics and income distribution within the liberal approach, mainly based on the work of Friedrick von Hayek.

The chapter is organized as follows. In Section 2.2, Clark's analysis of the labour market is discussed and commented on; in Section 2.3, the compatibility between the marginal productivity principle and Clark's theory of the 'right wage' is tested; in Section 2.4, Clark's view on the evolution of moral norms is discussed. Appendix III provides a reconstruction of Hayek's theory of the labour market, aimed at emphasizing the differences and the similarities between the marginalist-Clarkian approach and the liberal view on the role of moral norms in affecting income distribution.

2.2 The equilibrium wage in a 'synchronized' production process

The starting point of Clark's analysis of the labour market is his rejection of the wages fund theory, and, particularly, the 'advance economics' connected with it (see Schumpeter 1954). In opposition to Sumner, he argues that wages are not paid from capital previously accumulated and that, on the contrary, 'Wages come from the direct product of the labor itself' (Clark 1883, p. 355). The reasoning behind this rejection is the following:

a   On the theoretical plane, Clark rejects the idea that the economic process is time-consuming, and replaces it with his peculiar view of 'synchronicity'. In the industrial sector, he argues, there is no need to start the production process at exogenously given moments (as happens in agriculture) and, as a result, there is no need to wait until the end of a production period for the beginning of a further production period. In this picture, capital is regarded as 'hydraulic capital' (Clark 1883, p. 357)[106] and the whole process of social production can be described by drawing an analogy with the working of an assembly line (see Graziani 1992, pp. 25–26).[107]

This approach gives rise to some observations.

  i   As Schumpeter (1934 [1912]) points out, while the approach can explain the working of the production process *once it has started*, it is unable to explain how this process might start.

   ii   Clark's argument refers to the industrial sector, *taken in isolation from the primary sector*. However, if one considers the links between agriculture and industry, his result is not tenable since the production process in agriculture is subject to a *natural timing* and the industrial sector – buying inputs from agriculture – has necessarily to wait until the agricultural production process is finished.

   iii Clark seems to identify a theoretical possibility with a practical necessity: while, as a matter of fact, capitalists can start the production process when they want, this does not imply that they do not always want to wait. In other words, Clark does not distinguish between a technical timing (i.e. the possibility of starting production at any moment) and a discretional timing (i.e. the decision to start production at a certain moment).

b   On the pre-analytical plane, and this is the most important point, Clark strongly opposes the (classical) thesis of the 'separation of wages and products', since this implies that workers are paid independently of their contribution to the production process. This remark is significant in Clark's framework, because it is the basis for his attempt to establish a link between the market wage and the 'just wage'.

The market wage is settled by competition and equals, in equilibrium, the marginal productivity of labour.[108] In this context, Clark's analysis aims to demonstrate that this equilibrium condition is such that 'exploitation' does not exist. The reasoning – which is found in the contemporary neoclassical picture of the working of a perfectly competitive labour market – can be summarized as follows. It is assumed that a fixed amount of capital is available for firms at a given moment. Capital consists of an 'instrument of production' (Clark 1965 [1899], ch. 9), so that it is conceived as *technical* capital independent of social relationships (i.e. to say that – as opposed to the classical approach – wages are not capital). Labour marginal productivity is assumed to be decreasing as the number of workers increases. The rationale for this assumption is found in the following passage, from the *Distribution of Wealth*, chapter XII.

Let the number of units of labor be measured, in [Figure 2.1], along the line AD. Let them be set working in a series, in connection with a fixed amount of capital. The product of the first unit of labor, as aided by all the capital, is measured by the line AB. What the second unit of labor adds to this product is the amount expressed by A^IB^I. The third unit enlarges the output by the amount $A^{II}B^{II}$, the next by $A^{III}B^{III}$, the next by $A^{IV}B^{IV}$ and the last by DC. DC measures the effective productivity of any unit of labor in the series and fixes the general rate of pay. If the first unit of labor claims more than the amount DC, employers will let it withdraw, and will substitute for it the last unit. What they lose by the withdrawal of any one unit in the entire force is the amount DC.

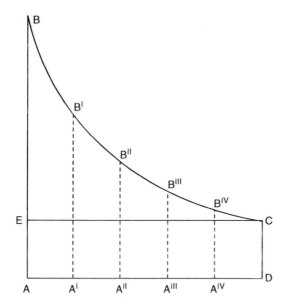

Figure 2.1 The marginal productivity assumption.

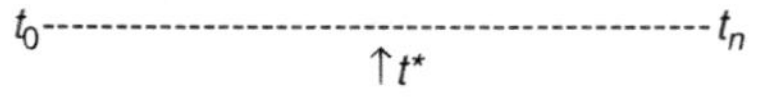

$$t_0\text{-----------------------------------}t_n$$
$$\uparrow t^*$$

Figure 2.2 The genesis of new capital.

In this scenario, workers are not exploited, based on the idea that the higher productivity of the first units depends on the availability of a greater quantity of capital: hence, the area ECB is *capital* marginal productivity.

The following statements summarize Clark's analysis:

a   Capital exists *before* firms employ labour.
b   The first unit of labour uses *all* the existing capital.
c   The use of all the capital makes the first unit of labour more productive than the second.[109,110]

Let us comment on these steps.

In the first passage, one can trace a theoretical problem, namely the 'problem of the genesis of new capital'. In Clark's view, in fact, (i) consumption goods come continuously into the market ('synchronicity'), (ii) capital is necessary to produce these goods and (iii) 'the *genesis of new capital* [...] requires abstinence', that is, waiting (Clark 1965 [1899], ch. IX). Figure 2.2 represents an interval when, at each moment, goods are sold for the entire economy.

In view of assumption (i) goods are sold at each moment between t_0 and t_n (t_0 and t_n included). Let us consider the case where capital must be replaced, for instance, in t^*, for a significant number of firms. In view of assumption (ii) a time-lag occurs for the genesis of new capital and, consequently, for the production of consumption goods. Consequently, in this interval, firms cannot sell goods. Basically, Clark's assumption (iii) refers to a condition which is in sharp contrast with the postulate of synchronicity, because he argues that the production process (of capital goods) is time-consuming, and requires 'waiting', and, at the same time, that goods are sold continuously.

A different line of critique of Clark's concept of capital, and his view of 'synchronicity', was put forward by Eugene Böhm-Bawerk. In *The Positive Theory of Capital*, he criticizes Clark's theory of capital on the basis of the following remarks:

a   According to Böhm-Bawerk's interpretation, Clark adopts a '*value concept of capital*', that is, the idea that capital is not a sum of *goods* but a sum of *values* and, at the same time, he refers to capital (defined as 'true capital') as an abstraction. The rationale of the 'value concept of capital' lies in the fact that, since capital goods are not homogeneous, it is impossibile to sum them in physical terms and, therefore, the sole possible device in order to *measure* capital is to sum their values. Böhm-Bawerk notes that this approach is quite confusing, because it is unclear whether capital *is* a value or *has* a value.[111] Moreover, the concept of 'true capital' appears a 'mystic' vision of the concept of capital, with no links with the current (i.e. practical) view of capital itself. In the light of the debate on capital between neoclassical and neo-Ricardian economists in the 1960s (see Harcourt 1972), one can argue that the 'value concept of capital' produces a relevant contradiction: capital cannot be measured in money terms because for the price of capital goods to be known it is necessary to know the (physical) productivity of capital, but – since capital goods cannot be measured in physical terms – the (physical) productivity of capital goods cannot be measured and, therefore, the price of capital goods is unknown (see Napoleoni 1982, p. 182).

b   Böhm-Bawerk also stresses that the production process requires *time* and that, as a result, Clark's 'synchronicity' approach lacks realism and should be regarded as an axiom. Moreover, even if one considers that – following Clark – both logical and historical time is irrelevant, as shown earlier, the production of new capital goods is not 'automatic' (see Blaug 1985) and this affects both the length and the efficiency of the production process (because, following Böhm-Bawerk, the increase in the intensity of capital determines an increase in the efficiency of the production process) and the availability of consumption goods at a given time (because more consumption goods *will be* produced and sold once the new capital goods are in operation).

c   Böhm-Bawerk emphasizes that the economic process is dynamic, so that agents also take future events into account when they choose. The preference for present consumption and the increase in technical efficiency owing to the extension of the period of production (with more capital-using methods) are the main aspects of a dynamic economy. As a result, Clark's picture of the labour market suffers from a failure to consider its dynamic nature. In particular, Böhm-Bawerk maintains that (i) labour demand is generated by the existing wage fund at the beginning of each production period;[112] (ii) bargaining over wages and employment is affected by agents' intertemporal discount rate. In particular, and following Blaug's (1985) reconstruction, Böhm-Bawerk's model leads to the conclusion that the equilibrium wage is equal to $w = f(t) - tf''(t)$, that is, the difference between total output in a working year and interest on the product over the same period, where $f''(t)$ is the marginal productivity of the expansion of the period of production – contrary to Clark's static view.[113]

2.3 Marginal productivity of labour and the 'right wage'

After having demonstrated that the equality between marginal productivity and the real wage is a condition of efficiency, Clark goes on to try to show that this is *also* (and above all) a condition of justice.

The first step in his reasoning is the definition of a standard of justice. Clark provides two standards of justice, one referring to the *micro* plane, the other to the *macro* plane.

a *The micro plane.* Here, the standard of justice is given in *The Distribution of Wealth*, chapter II, where it says that a just distribution is achieved when 'it gives to every man his own'. Hence, in Clark's view, since exploitation does not occur in a competitive labour market, every worker receives exactly what she/he produces,[114] so that the marginalist rule is both efficient and just. In this context, justice is linked to *merit*, on the basis of the rule 'to each what he creates'.

b *The macro plane.* Clark's 'social teleology' lays down that

> the ultimate end of political economy is not, as is generally assumed, the mere quantitative increase of wealth. Society, as an organic unit, has a higher economic end. That end is the attainment of the greatest quantity, the highest quality, and *the most just distribution of wealth*.
>
> (Clark 1882, p. 838, italics added)

It is important to stress that Clark does not refer to a standard of *equity* in distribution – which implies a comparison between profits and wages – but to a standard of *justice*, which, as Henry (1994, pp. 111–112) clarifies, is based on the criterion of 'equal exchange' resulting from 'the normal action of demand and supply in an open market', and 'limited to *individual* relationships'. Therefore, the most just distribution of wealth is achieved when market exchanges occur in a context where both parties have the same bargaining power.

As we know, contemporary neoclassical thought takes no interest in normative matters. In studies in the history of economic thought, the issue of whether

Clark's theoretical model should be considered highly questionable or whether it should be regarded as an exercise working along a different line of inquiry with respect to the contemporary framework is a matter of debate.

According to this latter view (cf. Stigler 1946 [1941]), it is argued that the normative issues involving Clark's arguments are strictly linked to his economic policy and, hence, that his pure economics and his reflections on ethics should be regarded as being on different planes of analysis. This argument is reinforced by the reflections on Clark's post-*Distribution of Wealth* writings. Prasch (2002, p. 444) – rereading the later publications and manuscripts – rejects the idea that Clark was 'simply another apologist for business interests' and maintains that he was a supporter of labour legislation. In effect, Clark considered unions as essential bargaining agents for workers in an age of trusts and monopolies, although he also wished to check the power of unions.

The opposite interpretation sustains that Clark's attempt to make the neoclassical theory of the labour market consistent with a theory of the 'just' wage is highly questionable. This interpretation – which appears more convincing than that discussed earlier– runs along the following lines.

a   Clark does not consider a low wages equilibrium as a condition of injustice, if wages are linked to labour marginal productivity. More generally, he does not fix a relationship between the market wage and the 'subsistence' wage, however it is defined. Hence, *it may occur that the unitary wage is below what is necessary for workers' survival, but – if this depends on low marginal productivity – the consequent equilibrium is to be considered just.* Furthermore, note that this argument is based on *what Clark (not necessarily society) considers 'just'*: consequently, his theory of the just wage should be regarded not as a positive, but rather as a normative theory, aiming at per-suading the working class that there is no scientific basis for social conflict (see Section 2.4).

b   As Veblen (1972, p. 175) points out, Clark's attempt to establish a 'natural' standard of justice is misleading, since – in his view – justice is, by itself, a *relative* concept, depending on the dominant culture:

> The equity, or 'natural justice' claimed for it is evidently just and equitable only in so far as the conventions of ownership on which it rests continue to be a secure integral part of the institutional furniture of the community; that is to say, so long as these conventions are part and parcel of the habits of thought of the community.[115]

It should be pointed out that Veblen and Clark support very different views on the nature and the genesis of ethical codes (see Chapter 3). While Veblen believes that standards of justice are produced by the ruling classes or are sub-ject to bargaining (that is why they are assumed to change over time and from society to society), Clark's position seems close to the contemporary 'con-tractualist' approach: justice is mutual advantage, it is impartiality, and hence, because market exchanges usually generate this outcome, where market exchanges occur, an objective standard of justice can be traced (on these issues, see Hausman and McPherson (1984), and Chapter 3).

c   As Pullen (2001, p. 7) argues, if one recognizes that labour and capital act in combination, 'The marginal product is labour-correlated, but not, in a mono-casual sense, labour-created' (so the author suggests using the term 'marginal productivity after labour'), and, as a result, it is nonsensical to interpret the marginal productivity theory in a normative sense.

d   Clark's effort to show that ethical validity of income distribution according to the individual contributions was strongly criticized also by Frank Knight. In his *Ethics of Competition*, he denied the validity of the 'productivity ethics' on the basis of two remarks:

    i   The equalization of marginal productivity to the average wage is neither possible nor a criterion of morality. It is impossible because of the fact that – in normal conditions – incomes tend to be very unstable over time and man cannot 'live on average'. Furthermore, it is not a criterion of morality because

> the income does not go to the 'factors' but to the owners, and can in no case have more ethical justification than has the fact of owner-ship. The ownership of personal or material productive capacity is based upon a complex mixture of inheritance, luck, and effort, probably in that order of importance.

However, only effort can have 'ethical validity' and 'from the standpoint of absolute ethics most persons will probably agree that inherited capac-ity represents an obligation to the world rather than a claim upon it' (Knight 1951, p. 56);

    ii   He also maintains that – contrary to Clark's picture – perfect competition is not the normal condition, since the 'workings of competition educate men progressively for monopoly' (Knight 1951, p. 52) and the rise of monopolies generates concentration of economic power and unequal income distribution: two outcomes that are ethically unacceptable.

Nevertheless, the next step of Clark's argument is to show that – as a result of the gradual passage from 'unlimited' to fair competition – workers' standards of living tend to grow, and social conflict to disappear, so that social justice will result from the spontaneous spread of moral codes.

This argument will be discussed in the following section.

2.4   The genesis and the spread of moral norms

Clark firmly believes that competition tends to be transformed over time, becoming less aggressive. The competition that characterized the early stages of capitalism was 'unrestricted' or 'abnormal', while later it necessarily undergoes a process of gradual moderation by the powerful action of moral norms.

Unrestricted competition is a condition where moral norms play no role in constraining corporate behaviour. Clark (1879, p. 159) maintains that – in its crude form – it never existed because 'a rude perception of right and wrong' has always existed, and competition is a historical constant (Henry 1994, p. 110). However, in the course of history, moral codes spread, from the family to the neighbourhood to the whole society. The reason why this happens is not very clear in Clark's works, but some passages can help to reconstruct his (albeit largely implicit) assumptions.[116] Clark seems to provide two different theories on the spread of moral norms, which will be discussed in the following paragraphs (cases I and II).

Case I – moral norms and collusion

Here, the starting point of Clark's analysis lies in his rejection of the following argument by Henry Adams:

> Suppose that of ten manufacturers nine have a keen appreciation of the evils that flow from protracted labor on the part of women and children [...] But the tenth man has no such apprehensions [...] The nine men will be forced to conform to the methods adopted by the one. Their goods come into competition with his goods, and we who purchase do not inquire under what condition they were manufactured. In this manner it is that men of the lowest character have it in their power to give the moral tone to the entire business community.

In other words, competition forces the 'good' entrepreneur[117] to act immorally, in order to prevent the competitors from taking away his market share, thus reducing his/her profits, *even if the 'bad' entrepreneurs are few in number*. Clark criticizes this argument, arguing that 'The nine men may reduce wages reluctantly and only at the last moment' because acting without respecting moral codes 'will react detrimentally on their principles' (Clark 1887, pp. 54–55). Hence, Clark's assumption is that the *market cannot modify moral norms* once they have been consolidated in the individual conscience. Rejection of moral norms may occur *temporarily*, only when market conditions make it impossible not to do so, namely when – by respecting them – a firm risks bankruptcy.

Clark also stresses that 'good' entrepreneurs react to the rapacity of their competitors by moving into 'solidarism', which, in turn, modifies the industrial structure from intense competition among *small* firms into 'consolidation' and trusts (Clark 1887).[118] Otherwise, 'These monopolies are more apparent than real', because – after a 'Darwinian struggle for existence' – they do not eliminate competition, but moderate it.

At the same time, workers too tend towards solidarity, via unions. These act as a balancing force with respect to employers' superior bargaining power. The emergence of unions is seen as a positive phenomenon,[119] if they help to set up 'equal exchanges' in the labour market, that is, if they do not claim wage increases over labour productivity (see Maurandi 2001, p. 151).

Sequence 2.1 summarizes these arguments. Let A be good employers, B bad employers, P their profits, BP their relative bargaining powers.

Sequence 2.1 Competition and social justice

> unrestricted competition $\rightarrow BP_B > BP_A \rightarrow P_B > P_A \rightarrow$ solidarity among A/among workers $\rightarrow$ trusts/unions $\rightarrow BP_A > BP_B \rightarrow P_A > P_B \rightarrow A > B$ (social justice).

Note that, for sequence 2.1 to hold, it is necessary to assume that type-A employers, initially weaker than B, find it easier to cooperate than type-B employers. It would be reasonable to argue that this occurs *because they are used to competing in a less aggressive way*.[120,121] In this situation, moral norms basically arise from collusion, which, in turn, is the outcome of the profitability for groups of non purely selfish entrepreneurs of defending themselves from the predatory behaviour of their competitors.[122]

Case II – moral norms, economic development and the scale of wants

In the *Distribution of Wealth*, chapter XXXV.5, Clark emphasizes that

> Five general changes are, as we said at the outset, continually going on: population is increasing, capital is increasing, industrial methods are changing, the modes of organizing labor and capital for productive purposes are changing, human wants are multiplying and refining. Every one of these changes, moreover, results from a perfectly normal cause, and it is wholly in accordance with nature that they should all go on together.

Capitalism is seen here as a dynamic system, which *spontaneously* tends to produce wealth and redistribute it according to the standard of equity given by the payment of inputs and according to their contribution to the production process. Furthermore, Clark (1880, p. 310) also argues that men's wants 'arrange themselves in a scale in the order of their intensity', from bare necessity to superfluities or 'spiritual' needs. Putting these arguments together, one reaches the conclusion that *moral norms may emerge as the outcome of economic development*, in the sense that, as income increases, people tend to satisfy higher wants, and possibly to begin acting under the constraints of moral codes.[123] In other words, it is the gradual reduction in the degree of scarcity of resources which *may* allow agents to behave less competitively.

In view of this reconstruction, two remarks are worth making.

a   On the theoretical plane, Clark provides an optimistic view of the dynamics of capitalism. Market forces – without external intervention – *spontaneously* spread moral norms. Capitalism tends to become a social system where both efficiency in production and justice in distribution are achieved. In some respects, this seems to reflect a normative programme, devoted to persuading the working class that socialism (the 'true' socialism, i.e. cooperation) does not need social conflict or revolution to be achieved. This programme is widely debated in the article 'How to Deal with Communism' where Clark strongly criticizes the classical–Ricardian idea that capitalism is based on (and tends to generate) class antagonism.

b   On the methodological plane, his analysis is very close to contemporary reflections on the links between ethics and economics, on the multidimensional nature of human behaviour in society, and on the debate on social responsibility of firms. However, as shown earlier, Clark's arguments are not always clear and mutually consistent. This may depend on a methodological bias: while – following Knies and the Historical School – he emphasizes the existence of the *many and changing* motives underlying human action (for instance, altruism, the desire for cooperation), and the fact that these motives may change from one agent to another (which leads him to explain the genesis and the spread of moral norms), when following the neoclassical framework, on the other hand, he is forced to assume that agents are purely self-interested, and that they choose independently of the social, institutional and historical context in which they act. Clark's contradictions can also be regarded as his merit in the history of economics: his attempt to reconcile ethics and economics has led to the recognition that this is difficult if not impossible within the neoclassical framework, and has at the same time led many contemporary economists to explore this relationship in a different theoretical framework, rejecting the rational choice hypothesis and the self-interest axiom.

Appendix III

The conception of justice in the liberal tradition: Hayek's theory of the labour market

Clark's theory of income distribution is the basis of the contemporary neoclassical approach to the issue, although contemporary neoclassical economists do not insert ethical consideration into their models. A different line of thought, within the liberal paradigm, starts from Hayek's contribution and develops a picture of the functioning of the labour market where (i) the marginal productivity assumption is not considered as a necessary assumption in order to demonstrate that an efficient income distribution must rely on the rewards according to individual merit, (ii) the neoclassical axiom of instrumental rationality is rejected[124] and (iii) ethical considerations are taken into consideration in order to show that – contrary to Clark's approach – it is actually *ethics* which can determine *inefficient* outcomes. More precisely, as Ralf Eriksson (1997, p. 124) emphasizes, Hayek distinguishes between three kinds of morals: 'innate morality', which is typical of primitive societies and takes the form of solidarity and altruism; 'systems of morals', which will be shown to produce a destructive impact on the spontaneous order; and 'evolved morality' 'that stands between instinct and reason [and] is supposed to "tie together" – in the evolutionary process – the primitive and the modern man'.

In what follows, Hayek's theory of the labour market will be discussed (with particular reference to the work *The Constitution of Liberty*) as the major representative scientific effort to provide a picture of the rules governing income distribution within the liberal view of the functioning of a market economy, and outside the standard neoclassical (and Clarkian) approach.[125]

The starting point of Hayek's analysis lies in the remark that in a 'free society', the labour market (like the market for goods) is the place where agents experience mutual advantage from exchange:

> That the freedom of the employed depends upon the existence of a great number and variety of employers is clear when we consider the situation that would exist if there were only one employer – namely, the state – and if taking employment were the only permitted means of livelihood.
>
> (Hayek 1960, p. 121)

The argument runs as follows. (i) Employers need workers in the same way as workers need employers. (ii) The opportunity to choose increases as the number of employers increases (with respect to labour supply) in a competitive market. Hence the sole condition where workers are at the mercy of employers is when unemployment exists (Hayek 1960). Note that, in contrast to the case of the state as the sole employer, Hayek implicitly assumes that the increase in the number of entrepreneurs implies the increase in the degree of *heterogeneity* of wages and working conditions; that is, this degree is minimum when monopsony exists. However, it should be pointed out that these assumptions do not necessarily rest on a logical necessity: as a matter of fact, both in the case of numerous employers and in the case of the state as the sole employer, wages and working conditions may have the same degree of heterogeneity. On the one hand, proposition (ii) does not imply that the quantity of employers results in a difference in the quality of what they offer; on the other hand, it is quite plain that the state, although under monopsony, is very likely to require workers for different tasks, with different wages and different working conditions. In other words, *the increasing number of agents does not necessarily imply their increasing heterogeneity*: and, if heterogeneity of what is offered is not a necessary outcome, the range of opportunities – if conceived, as Hayek conceives it, as the availability to choose among different offers – does not increase as the number of employers increases.

Furthermore, the number of employers is treated by Hayek as an exogenous variable, depending on individual propensity to risk. Although a 'free society' gives anyone the chance to become an independent worker, the number of independent workers does not depend on the simple fact that anyone is formally free to choose where to work. In a free society with low individual propensity to risk, the number of employers would be small, because *freedom to choose does not imply that the individual choice is free.*

In Hayek's view (pp. 267 ff.), unemployment, in turn, depends on union action. Union leaders use their persuasive power in order to induce workers to think that wage claims will be effective. This strategy, insofar as workers follow their leaders, is successful in increasing membership and hence in increasing union bargaining power. However, the increase in wage above its market level generates unemployment, involving a distributional conflict between those who are employed (the 'insiders') and the unemployed workers (the 'outsiders'):

> The interest of those who will get employment at the higher wage will therefore always be opposed to the interest of those who, in consequence, will find employment only in the less highly paid jobs or who will not be employed at all.
>
> (Hayek 1960, p. 270)

In other words, unions 'serve only sectional interest even when [they] obtain the support of all' (Hayek 1960), via the use of coercive power, such as the picket line (ibid., p. 274). A further negative effect of union action is inflation: the continuous and progressive increase in the price level – Hayek argues – is ultimately due to the pressure on money wages, but it is favoured by monetary policies, for if the supply of money were not expanded, the wage increases would solely determine unemployment (Hayek 1960, p. 281).[126] However, when the wage–price spiral is in operation, the workers' 'illusion' that their income is increasing cannot go on indefinitely without their realizing that it must be stopped: inflation is, as a result, 'politically and socially fatal' (ibid., p. 282).

This picture of the working of the labour market raises the following remarks.

a   The negative relationship between the unitary wage and the level of employment is *an assumption* and, if so, it is not necessarily tenable. However, Hayek shows that union action produces only negative outcomes in view of this assumption, which – if relaxed – would obviously generate very different, if not diametrically opposed, results. More important is the union leaders' view of the functioning of the labour market. Hayek (ibid., p. 282) maintains that unions 'see wages determined by some conception of "justice", rather than by the forces of the market'. Hence, *the search for distributive justice produces inefficiency* and *inefficiency produces injustice* (i.e. unemployment and/or decline in real wages). Insofar as union leaders' aim is to achieve social justice – however defined (see the following text) – and provided that their action generates inefficiency and injustice, it is unclear why (i) they continue claiming wage rises and (ii) workers continue joining unions. Two possible answers are in order. First, neither leaders nor membership believe that unemployment is the result of the increase in wages and that it depends on variables they cannot manage. Second, the pursuit of social justice is a *strong belief*, unchangeable even if it is proven to be counterproductive. In both cases, unions' mistakes do not lead to a process of learning and hence do not force leaders and membership to change their behaviour over time.

b   If union leaders aim to increase wages not at the expense of employment, but if – as in Hayek's thought – they never achieve this result, a continuous vicious circle is likely to occur, setting up a *hysteresis* effect. Suppose that unions obtain a wage rise (w_t) in period t and that this determines unemployment (UN_t); in the ensuing period, they will obtain a further wage rise ($w_t + 1$) with higher unemployment, and so on. Reasonably, the employment rate will not tend to zero, because firms will stop this process by exploiting their increasing bargaining power. The key point is that if union leaders do not learn from their mistakes, unemployment will increase almost indefinitely, as long as union leaders are successful in exercising their persuasive power over membership.

c   Just like union leaders, workers – in Hayek's view – do not learn from their own and their leaders' mistakes. They continue to join the union even if they risk unemployment and, more important, in so doing they continue not to exploit their whole range of liberty, by leaving others to decide on their wages and employment contracts. The individual freedom to bargain without intermediaries is voluntarily limited by accepting the coercive power of the organization they choose to join. This argument also applies to the choice of being employed, which involves the great majority of people. The voluntary limitation of the individual range of liberty is likely to depend on the tendency to miminize risks or – in a sense the same thing – to bear the lower degree of individual *responsibility*.

It is worth noting that Hayek's view on the effect of union action is not the widespread view in the history of neoclassical economics. Within these theoretical positions, that of Pareto – particularly in the *Cours d'économie politique* – appears highly significant. He strongly supported union action, maintaining that employers have greater bargaining power because – owing to workers' lower income – they can wait longer than workers (Pareto 1964, p. 183). Hence, without union action, there is no competition and wages are fixed by firms at the lowest possible level. Unions can balance bargaining powers mainly via the *bourses du travail*, that is by offering their members a subsistence income necessary to enable them to wait for the labour contract to be signed. By ensuring that conditions for competition are effective, unions promote the maximum well-being (*maximum d'ophélimité*) for society as a whole. Pareto's theory of the labour market seems to suffer from significant flaws. Above all, it is hard to maintain that union action ensures free competition: as a matter of fact, the existence of unions generates a monopoly over labour supply.[127] Therefore, if firms too tend to collude, a bilateral monopoly arises and the level of wages depends on the relative bargaining powers. Pareto himself seems to hint at this situation when he concludes that there are no definite economic 'laws' with regard to wages (Pareto 1964, p. 183), as if wage bargaining were indeed ruled by bilateral monopoly. Yet, one can argue that the quasi-equalization of the bargaining powers of firms and workers can generate an increase in ophelimity insofar as this strategy changes the market structure and makes it closer to a perfect competition configuration, where the degree of ophelimity is at a maximum. Accordingly, Pareto seems to look at political support for union action as a necessary step to reach a labour market configuration where – in the course of social evolution – symmetry in bargaining powers will be reached without external interventions. According to this interpretation, the initial increase in wages – due to union action – can determine the increase in savings on the part of workers and, in a dynamic framework, an increase in their bargaining power over time: the workers' advantage is therefore just temporary. In view of these remarks, it is not easy to find the rationale for Pareto's support of union action *on the theoretical plane*. Hence, one has to turn to the philosophical and political background of his theory (see Bruni 2002). Chapter I, book II, of the *Cours d'économie politique* deals with 'social evolution' and establishes the philosophical bases of Pareto's view of the dynamics of capital–labour relations, and of the genesis and the role of institutions. Pareto maintains that – even if social evolution is gradual and discontinuous – society tends spontaneously to select, in every period, the most efficient available institutions. In some cases, present institutions are similar to institutions existing in the past (and this is the case with unions), but there is no reason to oppose the setting-up of institutions when they spontaneously arise from social interaction. On this level, one can interpret Pareto's support of unions as the acceptance of a social institution which has been selected in historical evolution as an efficient institution, overcoming the resistance which always opposes social innovations (Pareto 1964, book II, p. 9). Pareto's support of unions therefore has to be interpreted *on the political plane*. His position can be seen as the outcome of a political device aimed at preventing the socialist programme for revolution. As a matter of fact, the improvement in workers' living standards – as a result of union action – would produce their progressive disaffection from this prospect. In effect, it is not surprising – as Romani (2003) notes – that most of the Italian economists of the period advocated a policy of high wages: some (the liberals) to avoid the socialist solution; others (the moderate socialists and the radicals) to improve workers' conditions, in view of a gradual transition to socialism, where the evolution of the unions is subject to the 'law of shifting elites'.[128]

Turning back to Hayek's view, the argument presented earlier – that social justice is a strong belief (determining the demand for 'just wages') – is explicitly taken into consideration in his works. The widespread ideas related to the possibility of achieving social justice and to the meaning society attaches to the concept are propelled by two forces: envy and the employee status of the majority of people.

a   *The demand for social justice.* Hayek (1960, p. 93) argues that 'most of the strictly egalitarian demands are based on nothing better than envy'. Envy, in turn, arises from the idea that the rich are not rich because of any merit of their own, and – as Hayek recognizes – merit is both a vague and a misleading concept. Accordingly, merit should be conceived as *assessable merit* (p. 94), that is, 'merit that other people can recognize and agree upon and not merit merely in the sight of some higher power'.[129] Success is the result of merit and/or of luck, and – in Hayek's view – the credit that society gives an individual refers solely to cases where success has been achieved thanks to circumstances within his/her control: in Hayek's words (p. 95), 'merit is not a matter of the objective outcome but of subjective effort'. This leads to the distinction between merit and individual value: merit involves individual effort, while individual value, although it may be completely independent of merit, is the ability to (unintentionally) improve one's social standing (p. 98). Hayek's argument runs as follows. It is sometimes impossible to reward individuals according to their merit and, above all, this policy is undesirable: it is not merit but value which should be rewarded, in order to increase the incentive to act. Accident is likely to produce an increase in wealth and the person who has produced an efficient outcome, albeit by chance, should be rewarded according to what his/her services are worth to society. Therefore, 'the question as to whether the resulting distribution of income is just has no meaning' and, more important, the pursuit of social justice inevitably leads to the control of rewards on the part of the state, disincentives to work and further demand for state intervention (p. 100).

The conception of social justice, Hayek continues, derives from the status of the majority of people, that is, the status of employee. Justice is conceived as based on their needs, and this conception largely drives economic policy: high levels of taxation and the 'paternalistic provisions' of social services (p. 123). Since the preference for being an employee depends on the desire not to bear responsibility, the condition of a dependent worker is almost naturally connected with the idea that failures and economic misfortune are the result of others' actions: they are simply the 'victims' of somebody else's mistakes. Moreover, their successful claim for legislation protecting them generates negative effects, insofar as it makes the economic environment less favourable to the independent (ibid.).

b   *Intellectual leadership and the ethical codes.* In the *Constitution of Liberty*, Hayek (pp. 126 ff.) argues that ethical codes emerge because of the existence of 'a group of idle rich', acting as pioneers, whose aim is not material gain but – *just because they do not work for money rewards* – the improvement of the 'public conscience', including the abolition of slavery, the prevention of cruelty and a more humane treatment of the insane. This argument raises some comments.[130] First, even if these pioneers – the intellectual leadership – are engaged in persuading public opinion on the wisdom of acting according to ethical codes, what is it that enables them to reach their objective? Second, what is the meaning of 'cruelty', 'humane treatment' and so on (i.e. what Hayek conceives as morality) in a theoretical context where only market forces appear to be able to establish efficient codes of behaviour?

Moreover, Hayek (pp. 127–130) maintains that intellectual leaders help to promote material as well as spiritual growth. This idea appears questionable *prima facie*, in view of the following points. First, one can object that the moral values which the intellectual leadership supplies – instilled through education – do not necessarily contrast with the moral values society has independently adopted. Second, given the simple fact that intellectual leaders are not pressed by the necessity for monetary rewards, it is unclear why they should put forward theories on how to improve the material and spiritual condition of the whole society.[131] This is what Eriksson (1997, p. 114) names the 'Hayek problem of the evolution of human culture', which can be applied to the whole of Hayek's thought on the subject – that is, the transition – in an evolutionary perspective – from primitive man (a social altruistic creature) to modern economic man (a self-interested agent). Eriksson tries to solve this problem by constructing 'functional cycles', based on cultural – non-genetic – changes. In particular, 'evolved morality' is supposedly the outcome of the institution of private property and hence of self-interest and the market. Economizing is not an inborn attitude, but a learned characteristic. Accordingly, the tendency to save, to respect private property, to be honest – as dimensions of the morality of modern economic man – can be conceived as the result of the long-term process of learning the most convenient codes of behaviour. They are convenient on the microeconomic plane and – in the context of the Hayekian spontaneous order (i.e. the spontaneous process of coordination between the actions of agents in the market)[132] – they are also profitable for society as a whole.

3   Thorstein Veblen

The institutionalist approach
to income distribution and
ethical codes

3.1   Introduction

The work of Thorstein Bunde Veblen[133] is not easy to classify, since it involves economic, sociological, anthropological and psychological reflections.[134] This 'eclecticism' may be seen both as the main cause of the long-term devaluation (if not oblivion) of his thought[135] and, by contrast, as the principal reason for the interest that his reflections may hold for many contemporary economists. His profound analysis of the role of social norms in orienting agents' behaviour is of major importance in interpreting the functioning of market economies, where this interpretation is based on the idea that markets do not work in an institutional *vacuum*; basically in line with the methodological bases of New Institutionalism.[136,137]

Institutions are defined by Veblen as 'prevalent habits of thought with respect to particular relations and particular functions of the individual and of the community' (Veblen 1975 [1899], p. 190). They are selected in the process of social evolution, according to the principle of the 'selective conservation of favourable variations' (i.e. natural selection), and, in turn, they affect the habits and customs of the community where they are accepted:

> Institutions are not only themselves the result of a selective and adaptive process which shapes the prevailing or dominant types of spiritual attitude and aptitudes; they are at the same time special methods of life and of human relations, and are therefore in their turn efficient factors of selection.
>
> (Ibid., p. 188)

In Geoffrey M. Hodgson's interpretation (in Davis *et al.* 2004, p. 87), this means that 'there is both upward and downward causation; individuals create and change institutions, just as institutions mould and constrain individuals' and – more generally – 'Institutionalism is not necessarily confined to the "top down" cultural and institutional determinism with which it is sometimes associated.' In Veblen's view, the principle of selective conservation of favourable variations is at the basis of the genesis of institutions, according to two main mechanisms:

a   'The development of [the] institutions is the development of society' (ibid., p. 190), because individuals – and hence society – tend to change their habits of thought as well as their behavioural models in response to the stimuli that external changes provide. This mechanism favours the emergence of new institutions.

b   By contrast, social and psychological inertia favours conservatism, therefore generating a twofold effect: (i) slowing the process of institutional change and (ii) amplifying the gap between present institutions and present wide-spread mental attitudes. In Veblen's words: 'Institutions are products of the past process, are adapted to past circumstances, and are therefore never in full accord with the requirements of the present' (ibid., p. 191).

Inertia is seen both as a psychological and as a social phenomenon. In the first case, Veblen refers to an 'instinctive resistance' to change (ibid., p. 203). In the second case, inertia arises from the *non-convenience* (on the part of the leisure class) and *non-possibility* (on the part of the lower class) of trying to modify the present institutional profile. The 'leisure class' is a class which is 'by custom exempt or excluded from industrial occupations, and reserved for certain employ-ments to which a degree of honour attaches' (ibid., p. 1). By contrast, the lower class is employed in industrial occupations. In Veblen's view, the privileges enjoyed by the leisure class act as an obstacle to social change, while the lack of 'mental effort' and 'nervous energy' does not allow the lower class to promote institutional innovations. Furthermore, the convenience of maintaining the existing institutions for the leisure class favours the widespread view that innovations imply chaos and social disorder (ibid., pp. 202–203).

On this basis, two main questions are in order:

a   Who – which class – establishes the prevalent habits of thought and the consequent codes of behaviour, and how?
b   Which forces can drive institutional and social changes, opposing the inhibitory effect of psychological and social inertia?

The following paragraphs will be devoted to providing answers to these ques-tions, and the focus will be particularly on *The Theory of the Leisure Class*. Although Veblen's thought changed over time, the attempt of this chapter is to 'isolate' an analytical core which can be representative enough of his whole reflection. The exposition is organized as follows. Section 3.2 explores the dif-ference between what Veblen calls 'the struggle for survival' and 'the struggle to excel', in order to understand how moral and social norms are produced and what their contents are; Section 3.3 deals with Veblen's theory of income distribution and Section 3.4 concludes, providing a comparison between Clark's and Veblen's views on income distribution and the way morality affects it.

3.2   The struggle to excel versus the struggle for survival: waste or efficiency as values

The concepts of conspicuous consumption, invidious comparison and the instinct of workmanship are at the basis of Veblen's theoretical framework.

Conspicuous consumption

Veblen argues that the primary motive for consumption, apart from the consumption devoted to satisfying basic needs, is *ostentation*. This particularly affects the leisure class – whose main aim is to preserve its *reputation*, as well as to keep the gap between its own living standard and that of the lower class[138] almost constant – and, as regards the class of goods, to preserve 'the more desiderable things', such as 'rare articles of adornment' (ibid., p. 69). These goods (the so called 'Veblen goods') are not desired (only) for their intrinsic utility, insofar as they serve no other purpose apart from ostentation. They are desired *prima facie* because they are scarce, and, in the second place, because they fit the prevailing norms of taste (ibid., ch. VI).[139] Furthermore, a Veblen good is a good for which the quantity demanded rises when its price rises: 'The consumption of expensive goods is meritorious, and the goods which contain an appreciable element of cost in excess of what goes to give them serviceability for their ostensible mechanical purpose are honorific' (ibid., pp. 154–155). It is worth noting that Veblen goods do not rest on the contemporary idea that a positive price–quantity ratio is likely to occur in cases of asymmetric information problems (see, among others, Akerlof 1970). They do not presuppose that the quality of the product is unknown to the buyer. Accordingly, Veblen goods are such that a high price is per se a mark of *beauty* (see Edgell 1999).[140]

Moreover, ostentation involves waste (in Veblen's terms, this is 'the law of conspicuous waste'). In *The Theory of the Leisure Class*, waste is defined as 'usefulness as seen from the point of view of the generically human'. As a matter of fact, this definition is rather ambiguous insofar as what 'generically human' means is not further clarified by the author. In reviewing *The Theory of the Leisure Class*, Cummings (1899) criticizes Veblen since 'The economist accepts individual wants uncritically, and considers that expenditure economic which is directly to their satisfaction, that wasted which is not directed.' Cummings is right if one accepts (as opposed to Veblen's view) the methodological viewpoint of the neoclassical approach (individualism); that is, preferences are assumed to be exogenous and agents' choices are perfectly rational.[141] Otherwise, by accepting Veblen's holistic methodology Cummings's critique is nonsensical: *from the point of view of society as a whole*, conspicuous consumption is waste because it prevents some resources from being used in a *more efficient way*. As Bush (1999, p. 136) remarks, 'the notion of the "generically human" simply has no synonym in the classical/neoclassical lexicon. It is a notion that smacks of some sort of social conception of usefulness, which is beyond the reach of orthodox methodological individualism'.

The invidious comparison

In *The Theory of the Leisure Class*, Veblen refers to envy as a strong motive to strive for success:

> The term [invidious] is used in a technical sense as describing a comparison of persons with a view to rating and grading them in respect of relative worth

of value – in an aesthetic or moral sense – and so awarding and defining the relative degrees of complacency with which they may legitimately be contemplated by themselves and by others. *An invidious comparison is a process of valuation of persons in respect of worth.*

(Veblen 1975, p. 34, italics added)

Accordingly, the accumulation of wealth, and its consequent ostentation, is not the result of the purpose of satisfying needs, via consumption; it is an intermediate goal in order to gain reputation, esteem and respect within a given social group.[142] In other words, consumption is not an end in itself, as in the standard neoclassical view: it is, above all, a *means to excel*.

Two considerations are worth noting. First, as opposed to the dominant view, competition is not a 'struggle for survival', but – at least within the leisure class – it is solely a *struggle to excel*: 'the struggle is substantially a race of reputability on the basis of invidious comparison' (Veblen 1975, p. 32). Second, by developing Veblen's argument, *competitive consumption does not produce economic growth*.[143] Let us suppose individuals A and B are engaged in a struggle to excel and – because of their affiliation to the leisure class – they are not producers. At a given moment, the available surplus is a given. If A obtains a higher level of consumption than B, A finds it profitable that the economic growth rate is low, while B's probability of obtaining a higher level of consumption than A increases as economic growth becomes higher. However, since B is not a producer she/he cannot directly contribute to increasing aggregate output and the ultimate result is a zero-sum game, where the higher A's consumption is, the lower B's is.

The instinct of workmanship

This is typical of agents who are outside the leisure class, and – particularly – of those who are engaged in generating new knowledge. In Veblen's words (1975, p. 15): 'As a matter of selective necessity, man is an agent [...] He has a sense of the merit of serviceability or efficiency and of the demerit of futility, waste, or incapacity. This aptitude or propensity may be called the instinct of workmanship,' and 'idle curiosity' ultimately supports it. The instinct of workmanship involves the pleasure in useful work, the dislike of waste and the adoption of a way of thinking based on mechanical sequences.[144,145] In this case, esteem is not gained via ostentation of consumption, but 'by putting one's efficiency in evidence' (Veblen 1975, p. 16). O'Hara (1999, p. 163) shows that the instinct of workmanship falls within the Veblenian category of 'good instincts', that is instincts which 'promote the collective welfare or collective life process of the global society'. Similarly, Asso and Fiorito (2004, p. 448) distinguished between 'other-regarding and self-regarding instincts. The former have as their aim the welfare of the family, clan or group, while the latter find expression in aggression, predation, and domination'. Good instincts include 'parental bent' and 'idle curiosity'. The first is related to care of other people (i.e. altruism, *lato sensu*), while the second – strictly connected to the instinct of workmanship – concerns the desire for knowledge and, when in operation and in the long term, produces 'the most substantial achievement of the race – its systematized knowledge and quasi-knowledge of things' (Veblen 1964 [1914], p. 87).

On the basis of the habits described before, Veblen analyses the functioning of a capitalistic economy by assuming the existence of four macro-agents:

- the leisure class, whose aim is conspicuous consumption:
- businessmen, interested in making profits;
- technicians, who are engaged in producing new knowledge;
- workers, whose aim is to obtain a wage level that ensures a desired standard of living, which, in turn, depends on the level of consumption they consider 'fair' in given historical contexts.

The perception of a *decent* living standard is largely affected by the ruling class: 'It is for this class to determine, in general outline, what scheme of life the community shall accept as decent or honorific' (Veblen 1975, p. 104).[146,147] A *decent* standard of living is what is permitted by the subsistence wage, which – in Veblen's words (1975, p. 107) – is 'of course not a rigidly determined allowance of goods, definite and invariable in kind and quantity [...] This minimum, it may be assumed, is ordinarily given up last in case of a progressive retrenchment of expenditure.'

Conflict among these classes appears to be the main feature of Veblen's picture, with particular reference to the conflict between (a) technicians and businessmen and (b) ruling classes and workers. Let us now consider the nature and the effect of these conflicts.

a *Businessmen versus technicians*. Following the interpretation of Griffin and Karayiannis (2002), Veblen proposes two theories of entrepreneurship, applied to two different phases of the development of the capitalist system. In the first stage,[148] entrepreneurs contributed to economic growth mainly because they were real innovators, assuming the risks of their pioneering activity, in a context where the entrepreneur was at the same time proprietor and manager of the firm. In this sense, Griffin and Karayiannis (2002, p. 62) argue that (i) the Veblenian 'old type entrepreneur' is similar to the Schumpeterian entrepreneur and (ii) profits were 'a fair and justifiable reward'.[149] Two basic factors determine the movement towards a new type of entrepreneurship. First, the exogenous increase in population – and the consequent increase in demand – pushed firms to increase production and, as a result, 'personal supervision of the work by the owners was no longer practicable' (Veblen 1964 [1923], p. 105). Second, in this new condition, not only can profits be obtained even without introducing innovations, but innovations – insofar as they increase output – are useless or even dangerous when generating overproduction. Hence, the old-type entrepreneur becomes a businessman mainly interested in *financial* transactions: the transformation of the 'captain of industry' into the 'captain of solvency' (Veblen 1964 [1923], p. 208). Moreover, as Kenneth J. Arrow ([1975], in Tilman 2003, vol. II, p. 47) stresses: 'their search for individual profit maximization may prevent the realization of economies of scale'. These effects occur in a market configuration where the firm is not a price-taker, but – following Arrow's interpretation (ibid., pp. 47–48) – operates in a context of 'what we would now call monopolistic competition, a recognition by one seller of imperfect substitute of his product', which implies that advertising is a 'significant element of competition' and can be regarded as 'waste'. In a similar vein, in rereading Veblen's *Theory of Business Enterprise*, Chypher ([1988] in Tilman 2003, vol. II, p. 78) argues that 'Veblen drew a distinction between competitive capitalism and finance-driven, monopoly/oligopoly/trust form of economic organizations which came to dominate the US economy from the 1870s onward'. This process – according to Chypher's interpretation – was analysed by Veblen in the following works, and particularly in *Absentee Ownership* [1923], where 'the Veblenian dichotomy of "industry" and "business" which might be found in his earlier distinction between the "Captains of industry" and the "Captains of Finance" no longer existed' because 'Investment bankers who dominated the financial sphere intermingled with those who operated the key industries.'

In Veblen's basic theoretical framework, technicians are engaged in producing knowledge. The conflict between businessmen and technicians is based on the two different and opposed goals they pursue and, as a result, on their different and incompatible habits of thought: that is, the search for money profits versus the pursuit of knowledge. In other words, a conflict arises between the industrial way of thinking (*to make goods*) and the pecuniary way of thinking (*to make money*).[150] These different habits of thought produce two major economic effects: first, owing to the effort of technicians and the support of the banking system, competition leads to the bankruptcy of smaller firms and, hence, to a movement towards a market configuration where monopolistic positions prevail; second, the financial control of firms by businessmen involves a policy of 'sabotage', that is, 'a deliberate restriction of the productivity of capital and labor in order to keep prices and profits higher' (Hobson [1937] in Tilman 2003, vol. II, p. 34). The technicians' aim of increasing productivity, via the use of new knowledge, and thus expanding production is in conflict with the businessmen's purpose of obtaining money profits.

According to this view, the firm appears as a pure bureaucratic structure which is able to produce only because of its exploitation of common 'industrial knowledge'. Knowledge is a public good which is appropriated by firms via legal rights, what Veblen calls 'sabotage'. In his own words:

> It appears [...] that the prime creative factor in human industry is the state of the industrial arts; that is to say, the determining fact which enables human work to turn out a useful product is the accumulated knowledge, skill and judgement that goes into work [...] For the transient time being, therefore, any person who has a legal right to withhold any part of the necessary industrial apparatus or materials from current use will be in a position to impose terms and exact obedience, on pain of rendering the community's joint stock of technology inoperative to that extent.
>
> (Veblen 1994 [1923], vol. IX, pp. 62–65)

The notion of 'sabotage' is linked to the propensity to 'predatory behaviours'. In *The Theory of the Leisure Class*, Veblen (1975, pp. 12–13, italics added) writes:

> Industry is effort that goes to create a new thing, with a new purpose given it by the fashioning hand of its maker out of passive ('brute') material; while *exploit, so far as it results in an outcome useful to the agent, is the conversion to his own ends of energies previously directed to some other end by another agent.*

This passage poses two questions. How is community knowledge generated? And, what makes it possible for firms to 'sabotage' these immaterial resources?

Veblen is unclear on these issues or, as Clarence Ayres ([1960] in Tilman 2003, vol. III, p. 109) remarks, he is 'confused by his adoption of the scientist's pose of lofty superiority of moral judgements'. The criticism by Frank H. Knight (1935) focuses on this point: the Veblenian idea that the 'instinct of workmanship' is the ultimate driving force of economic development is, in his evaluation, 'inscrutable' and leaves no space to analyse the *economic* mechanisms underlying the production of knowledge. In mainstream economics, economic growth is known to be mainly driven by the accumulation of savings, since savings – via the intermediation of the banking system – are a precondition for investments. In more recent times, the neoclassical growth theory has been largely based on the Solow model (Solow 1956), where – however – variations in savings *do not* affect 'steady-state' growth; technical progress is the key variable in explaining economic growth and it is exogenous. Knowledge (i.e. human capital) enters the new neoclassical models of economic growth only at the end of the 1980s, by means of the endogenous growth theory (see Lucas 1988; Romer 1989), where the increase in the propensity to save affects the increase in the accumulation of human capital[151] and – by assuming that human capital positively affects productivity – this produces an increase in aggregate output (see Serrano and Cesaratto 2002). The basic difference between the mainstream and the Veblenian/ Institutionalist approach to the genesis of technical advancement lies in what follows: in both cases it is an exogenous variable, but in the neoclassical Solow model it is simply not explained (it is a sort of 'engineer's gift' or 'manna from heaven'), and in Veblen's theoretical framework it depends on *institutional* variables, that is, the peculiar habits of thought of technicians. On the methodological plane, Knight's critique is questionable, insofar as a model aimed at explaining economic growth on institutional bases may be convincing and realistic once one admits that (i) not all economic phenomena find their causes in purely economic variables and (ii) institutions affect the operation of a market economy. In a sense, this issue involves the definition itself – or, more properly, the field of investigation – of political economy. Clarence E. Ayres ([1960] in Tilman 2003, vol. III, p. 112) approaches the issues in the following terms:

> The main outlines of institutionalist theory correspond exactly to these questions. What determines how well-off any whole community is, is the degree of technological advancement which that community has been able to

obtain; and what determines that some members of the community shall be better off than others, and who those some shall be, is the institutional structure of that society. These answers are directly contrary to those of classical price theory.

On these grounds, Ayres concludes – as opposed to Knight's view – that there is nothing 'inscrutable' in the Veblenian/Institutionalist approach to economic growth: anthropology and psychology – within the Institutionalist framework – can help economists to a better understanding of the processes they are called upon to interpret or explain.

In contemporary terms, knowledge – insofar as it is transferable – can be defined as a public good (see, among others, Schultz 1961). As seen earlier, owing to the property rights on capital, entrepreneurs are able to exercise 'sabotage', that is, to obtain immaterial resources via predatory behaviours.[152] In Veblen's thought, predatory attitudes emerge in the course of socio-historical and cultural evolution, assuming that the 'initial stage' is characterized by 'peaceable life' (Veblen 1975, p. 19). Accordingly:

> The transition from peace to predation [...] depends on the growth of technical knowledge and the use of tools. A predatory culture is similarly impracticable in early times, until weapons have been developed to such a point as to make man a formidable animal.

Otherwise, contemporary societies rest on 'the survival of archaic traits of human nature under the modern culture' (ibid., pp. 20–21). The appropriation of the surplus generated by the increase in knowledge is made possible by the fact that entrepreneurs are the proprietors of firms. Of course, new technology will be introduced only if entrepreneurs perceive or foresee their positive effects on profits. Their monetary habit of thought leads them to take interest in *price*-setting, for the sake of profits, in a context of asymmetric *bargaining powers* between them and technicians or skilled workers. It is what J. A. Banks ([1959] in Tilman 2003, vol. III, p. 243) defines as 'the approach of the absentee businessmen'. Absence derives from the functional separation between the owners and management, where management is ultimately under the command of the owners.[153] According to Banks (ibid., p. 243), the role of management appears to be ambiguous:

> where a manager's relationship with those under his command is couched chiefly in terms of wages and cost accounting his habitual thinking will be pecuniary, whereas if the relationship is for the purpose of getting goods produced according to a time schedule his attitude will be industrial.

Moreover, the conflict between businessmen and technicians or skilled workers – at the core of Veblen's picture of industrial relations – has two main dimensions: on purely economic grounds, it is a conflict over income distribution (i.e. profits versus wages); on the psychological plane, it is a fundamental miscomprehension or uncommunicability relating to very different habits of thought. 'The two classes' – Veblen (1904, p. 318) writes – 'come to have an increasing difficulty in understanding one another and appreciating one another's convictions, ideals, capacities and shortcomings.'[154]

b *Ruling classes versus workers.* As O'Hara (1999, italics added) maintains, 'An important aspect of Veblen's theory of social wealth is the notion of *institutional exploitation.*' The idea is that human labour and knowledge (also 'incorporated' into labour) are the main inputs for the production of social wealth. Wages are at the subsistence level and the surplus results in profits and rents, and – as seen earlier – profits derive from 'predatory behaviours'. The existence of predatory behaviours as well as the possibility of exerting them is explained by Veblen in historical terms. Stephen Edgell ([1992] in Tilman 2003, vol. I, p. 207) provides a useful synthesis of Veblen's view of this issue: 'technological advance and the growth of an economic surplus coincided with the beginning of ownership, encouraged predation, and downgraded the status of labor which acquired the "character of irksomeness"'. The continuous production of surplus – over subsistence wages – and the establishment of the institution of property rights made the economic system class based and allowed 'parasitism' in favour of a 'leisure class'. Moreover, freed from productive labour, the leisure class became the *ruling class*: 'The upper classes' – Veblen (1975, p. 1) writes – 'are by custom exempt or excluded from industrial occupations, and are reserved for certain employment to which a degree of honour attaches. Chief among the honourable employments in any feudal community is warfare; and priestly office is commonly second to warfare.' And, in the course of historical evolution, when the exercise of physical power lost importance, politicians became the most important part of the 'upper classes'.

Of course, the leisure class is interested in preserving its standard of living and privileges, and it is consequently interested in preserving the *status quo*. In order to achieve this end, two main devices are used:

i   *Controlling education.* The ruling class is able to minimize possible worker discontent – and thus possible social conflict – by controlling the education system. In Veblen's view, the management of schooling by the ruling classes is a powerful institutional strategy for the purpose of transmitting habits of thought functional to the preservation of the existing socio-economic order. Hence, 'schools [...] are shaped by and rest upon a leisure-class culture', based on humanities and erudition (Veblen 1975, p. 391).

ii *Controlling income distribution.* The ruling classes are also interested in keeping wages at the lowest level, or – according to Veblen – an unequal distribution of wealth is necessary (Veblen 1975, p. 205). The rationale for this thesis can be found in three points. First, for a given output, the greater the surplus available for conspicuous consumption (and for a given level of profits), the lower the wages obviously are. Second, the greater the difference between the consumption of the leisure class and that of other classes, the more intense is the effect of ostentation on the aggregate plane. Third, the lower the workers' consumption level,[155] the lower their 'available energy' to promote social conflict. This is a typical Veblenian theme in *The Theory of the Leisure Class* and will be the subject of the following section.

3.3   Income distribution

This picture, in which ruling classes are able to control workers' possible tendency to conflict, is a picture of a stationary economy and a stationary society, where conservative interests prevail. Veblen's main interest lies in his explaining institutional change 'upon the materialistic framework to such an extent that the role of technology, economic action and institutions are to the forefront of all his major studies' (Edgell [1975] in Tilman 2003, vol. I, p. 104).

For the reasons discussed earlier, it is technical advancement which ultimately promotes economic growth. This is not (only) because technical progress – as in the neoclassical model – determines an increase in productivity without causing unemployment, but mainly because it can modify the prevalent habits of thought with particular regard to workers, also affecting income distribution.

Veblen's argument on this issue is unclear, and many interpretations have been put forward. On the one hand, Donald A. Walker (1977, p. 220) maintains that Veblen's 'central thesis' is

> that new habits of thought result from the emergence of new ways of making a living, which are in turn the result of technological change. Institutions are static and resist change; new institutions are formed as the result of the dynamic impact of technology.

Hence, a direct causal link is found, where technical change determines changes in habits of thought, while the role of institutions is conservative. On the other hand, Malcom Rutherford ([1984] in Tilman 2003, vol. I, pp. 121–122) argues that Veblen's 'system involves a *sequence* of change which involves institutions affecting technology and technology affecting institutions'. Accordingly, a sort of feedback effect involving technology and institutions appears to be traceable in Veblen's work, following this interpretation.

Rutherford (ibid., p. 127) also stresses that – in Veblen's thought – 'there is [. . .] a dialectic reminiscent of Marx: the internal logic of a system giving rise to contradictions that create its own transformation'. The interpretation of Veblen's view of institutional change that will be proposed in what follows starts from this point.

The rereading of Veblen's theory of institutional change proposed here is based on the idea that social and cultural evolution as well as economic growth are the outcome of the dynamics of income distribution.[156] The basic assumption is that the subsistence wage is not a purely economic variable, insofar as it involves *value judgements* on the part of workers and society as a whole, at least in the sense that not all the values of the subsistence wage are *perceived as fair*.[157] In the case where the current wage is perceived as *unfair*, conflict is likely to be in operation, owing to what Veblen calls 'social odium' (Veblen 1975, p. 372),[158] the reaction to income differences which are perceived as not *economically nor morally justifiable*. Of course, for the conflict to be in operation, a radical modification in the habits of thought on the part of workers is a necessary condition: what was considered 'normal', that is, economically and morally justifiable, is now considered 'abnormal' and therefore unacceptable, on both the economic and moral plane. In a sense, envy may ultimately support the possible reaction.

Given these assumptions, two main theoretical schemes can provide an interpretation of the *mechanisms* which give rise to institutional change, in a Veblenian perspective, and on condition that workers' habits of thought have been changed. This latter argument will be approached below.

a *Institutional change drives economic growth*. As seen in the previous section, the basic dichotomy with regard to *values* involves *waste versus efficiency*. In the case where workers internalize codes of behaviour oriented to efficiency, waste on the part of the leisure class becomes unacceptable, both on economic and on moral grounds. As a result, social conflict is likely to occur. Although Veblen does not explicitly refer to social conflict, he maintains that institutional change finds its 'inhibitory effect' in the existing unequal income distribution:

> the institution of a leisure class acts to make the lower class conservative by withdrawing from them as much as it may of the means of sustenance, and so reducing their consumption, and consequently their *available energy*, to such a point as to make them incapable of the effort required for the learning and the adoption of new habits of thought.
>
> (Veblen 1975, p. 204, italics added)

Note that the category of conflict – which will be used in what follows – is not outside Veblen's discourse. In the work *The Engineers and the Price System* of 1921, he remarks that under the existing *status quo*, one would reasonably expect reactions on the part of workers. Veblen notes this effect in opposing the widespread view (supported, at that time, by Herbert Spencer, in *From Freedom to Bondage* 1891) that the increase in workers' discontent does not find any justification, since wages have increased. However, because of his focus on American society, he believes that Americans have such high esteem of their ruling classes that conflicts are – *in that context and in that period* – to be excluded. Apart from the contingency, therefore, it appears legitimate to reread Veblen's contribution by taking social conflict into consideration.

Let w be the current (subsistence) wage, Cl conspicuous consumption, I investments and Q the aggregate output; assume that all variables are in real terms. Sequence 3.1 holds

Sequence 3.1 Conflict and growth

$$\uparrow w \rightarrow \downarrow Cl \rightarrow \uparrow I \rightarrow \uparrow Q$$

For a given output, the increase in wages owing to a successful conflict – *if* it affects (negatively) leisure class consumption – determines a reduction of 'waste' and therefore allows firms to have more resources for *productive* investments, which, in turn, result in an increase in output. In other words, following Veblen's argument, one can argue that the increase in wages at the expense of the income of the leisure class determines a reduction in the demand for 'futile' goods and, as a result, an increase in production of 'useful' goods, because of the increase in worker demand.[159] In this context, the positive effect of conflict on the growth rate is mainly due to the increase in the production of goods which can be used in order to further expand production, thus reducing waste. This argument represents an extension of Veblen's principle of 'invidious consumption', since comparison is now not *within* a class but *between* classes. In the first case, Veblen links high levels of consumption to the desire to obtain the *respect* of individuals who form the leisure class and hence self-respect: 'A certain standard of wealth' – he writes (Veblen 1975, pp. 30–31) – 'in the one case, and prowess in the other, is a necessary condition of reputability, and anything in excess of this normal amount is meritorious,' producing envy; it is, and it is less and less meritorious the more the accumulated wealth is inherited. And: 'So soon as the possession of property becomes the basis of popular esteem, therefore, it becomes also a requisite to that complacency which we call self-respect.' Although these considerations refer to the leisure class, Veblen (ibid., p. 36) recognizes that 'certain secondary features of the emulative process, yet to be spoken of, come in to very materially circumscribe and modify emulation in these directions among the pecuniarly inferior classes as well as among the superior class'. The fundamental distinction, in this case, is that individuals of the inferior classes can increase consumption (also for ostentative purposes) only by means of 'efficiency and thrift', while for members of the superior class the 'taboo on labour' holds. In this case, as Bowles and Park (2002) stress, one reaches the conclusion that working hours go up as the degree of inequality of income distribution increases. This may occur because the desire to emulate the standard of consumption of the rich influences workers' allocation of time between labour and leisure. In view of sequence 3.1, however, the increase in wages is not due to the increase in workers' efficiency nor to the increase in working hours, because – approaching the issue in a different way with respect to Bowles and Park's contribution – it is here assumed that the changed habits of thought of workers lead them to oppose the existing social order. In this case, invidious comparison involves a *moral judgement* on income distribution which, in turn, gives workers no incentive to be more efficient to try to reach the standards of consumption of the leisure class, but instead encourages them to try to reduce leisure class consumption, insofar as its level is perceived as 'too high'. In a similar line of thought, Rutherford ([1984] in Tilman 2003, vol. I, p. 130, italics added) argues that, in Veblen's analysis, 'Changes of the base occur when *anomalies* build up as a result of the prevailing system becoming out of touch with the habits of life and thought of some significant portion of population'. On the basis of the interpretation proposed here, 'anomalies' result in the unequal income distribution ultimately generated by the leisure class, for the purpose of preserving the existing order and its privileges. Edgell ([1992] in Tilman 2003, p. 385) also remarks that conspicuous consumption produces the negative result of 'inhibited productive work (i.e. conspicuous abstentation from useful effort)'. The reduction of the difference between leisure class and worker consumption – hence *an increase in the degree of equality in income distribution* – implies an *increase in productive efficiency*, in sharp contrast with the neoclassical view that efficiency is rather a precondition (via the increase of output) of higher worker living standards. Moreover, conflict is a means to propagate ethical codes contrasting waste and oriented to efficiency, thus reducing exploitation. This, in turn, affects the degree of fairness in social relations. As Lutz and Lux (1988, p. 122) point out: 'In exploitation one agent is taking advantage of another or others [...] Unfairness, then, is the existence of exploitation, and fairness is its opposite – non exploitation.' Institutional change – as described here – is based on the perception of unfairness or, more precisely, on the perception that income distribution does not respond to economic or moral criteria.[160] Marc R. Tool ([1977] in Tilman 2003, vol. I, p. 823) remarks that the emergence of institutionalism can be seen in connection with the fact that 'economics of allocation is gradually replaced or succeeded by economics of valuation' and that 'neoinstitutionalists recognize that there is no way to avoid value judgement in economic analysis'.

Rereading Veblen in the light of the theoretical category of *social conflict* poses the problem of the similarity and the differences between Veblen and Marx. Edgell and Townshend ([1993] in Tilman 2003, vol. I, p. 313) stress that 'Veblen's theory of increasing status competition, expressed in terms of a "struggle to keep up appearances" represents an alternative to Marx's theory of increasing class conflict'. In effect, and in line with the interpretation proposed here, Veblen's theory of evolutionary change differs from Marx's view in at least two respects: (i) conflict concerns workers against the leisure class (or even technicians and businessmen), not – as in Marx – labour versus capital; (ii) conflict is driven by changes of habits of thought on the part of workers, also involving value judgements on the existing income distribution, without reference to the 'material' (structural) foundation of Marxian class conflict.[161]

b *Institutional change without economic growth.* Particularly in *The Theory of Business Enterprise* of 1904, Veblen approaches the issue of the increase in expenditure for advertising, and its effect on institutional change. The starting point is the observation that, in the course of social evolution, firms tend to become larger and larger. At the same time, a significant shift from competition to monopolies occurs and, as a result, the phenomenon of the uniform rate of profits tends to disappear. In Veblen's view, firms aim at obtaining a 'normal' rate of profit, where 'normal' means reasonable and, at the same time, habitual. It is the 'common sense' prevailing within the community of businessmen, which leads them to consider a given rate of profit normal or abnormal. Furthermore, businessmen are interested in *money* profits and, for this very reason, they oppose monetary policies which can generate modifications in the price level.

The increase in firm size occurs above all because of technical advancement, which – insofar as it produces economies of scale – allows the processes of mergers and acquisitions, affecting industrial concentration ratios. The pursuit of money profits, and the growing connections between industry and finance, lead, in Veblen's view and in normal conditions, to a kind of competition based on the artificial and intentional movement towards instability. Phillip A. O'Hara ([1993] in Tilman 2003, vol. III, pp. 270 ff.) describes the process of instability in the following way. The increase in industrial efficiency – owing to the effort of technicians – leads to overproduction, which, in turn, determines a reduction of prices and profits. Moreover, 'in a cyclical fashion, expectations may improve and innovation, capacity utilization and productivity may be given a boost, along with business profits, as new firms start to expand and governments spend on armaments and the like'. Thus, while the tendency to depression is likely to increase efficiency, the tendency to expansion derives from the improvement in corporate expectations also promoted by external intervention. Nayaradou (2004) interprets Veblen's theory of business cycle as driven by money supply, new technologies and expectations and involving hysteresis effects: Veblen's approach, according to this interpretation, is based on microeconomic arguments.

In normal conditions, the private interest of the businessman contrasts with the interests of the society as a whole. However, Veblen recognizes that 'ethical codes' (such as the voluntary limitation of the production of pollution) drive the behaviour of *some* entrepreneurs, who are generally few in number and who in this way risk bankruptcy. Apart from these cases, the reduction in costs resulting from technical advancement allows firms to increase their expenditure on advertising. Otherwise, advertising is necessary for the individual firm in order to establish 'differential monopolies': the increase in the market share of the individual firm is strictly linked to its expenditure on advertising and, insofar as this applies to all firms, advertising does not produce beneficial results for consumers, nor for firms as a whole. In saying this, Veblen opposes the dominant view that advertising is useful because it provides information to consumers: by contrast, and on the macroeconomic plane, it is a waste. Kenneth J. Arrow ([1975] in Tilman 2003, vol. II, pp. 47–48, italics added) provides the following reconstruction of Veblen's theoretical approach to advertising:

> Veblen [...] recognizes what we would now call monopolistic competition, a recognition by one seller of imperfect substitutes of his product [...] Indeed, Veblen puts great stress on product differentiation as an economic strategy and recognizes that trademarks, brand loyalty, advertising and other selling costs are significant elements of competition. These expenditures, of course, can be regarded as *wastes: they yield indeed a competitive advantage but no social advantage.*

Furthermore, according to Veblen, advertising acts as a stimulus to productivity on the part of workers. This occurs because advertising creates *new needs* and, in order to satisfy them, workers are induced to work more and/or more efficiently.

This determines an increase in output that allows 'parasitic' activity (such as advertising) to persist over time. However, Veblen's analysis can give rise to a different conclusion, once the category of conflict is inserted into his theoretical framework.

Let w^* be the desired wage, that is, the level of wage that allows workers to obtain the level of consumption induced by advertising, A the total expenditure on advertising, P profits. Sequence 3.2 describes a process of institutional change driven by social conflict.

Sequence 3.2 Advertising and institutional change

$$\uparrow A \rightarrow \uparrow w^* \rightarrow \downarrow P \rightarrow \uparrow A \rightarrow \uparrow w^*$$

The increase in expenditure on advertising, insofar as it induces workers to desire more consumption goods, leads to an increasing difference between the actual real wage and the desired real wage. This, in turn, produces a tendency to conflict and, if it is successful, an increase in wages. The consequent decrease in profits encourages firms – the individual firm and firms as a whole – to increase expenditure on advertising, in order to gain (or not lose) market shares, in a context where, owing to the fall in profits, it becomes more and more difficult to increase this spending. In this picture, institutional change – driven by conflict – produces the opposite result with respect to sequence 3.1, that is, *prima facie* a progressive fall of profits. This is because it is reasonable to assume that advertising leads workers to emulate upper-class consumption and, hence, social conflict is directed against firms. However, recalling Veblen's theory of the firm, firms are likely to react by collusion, which allows them to exploit scale and scope economies, hence reducing costs and possibly increasing prices. Moreover, also in this case (as mentioned earlier), social conflict – if successful – reduces the degree of institutional exploitation and, as a result, shifts the economy to a higher standard of 'morality'. The links between the industrial system and the finance sector may reinforce the bargaining power of firms. In *The Theory of Business Enterprise* (ch. five), Veblen deals with these links and notes that in normal situations and for the purpose of obtaining normal profits, firms need finance from the banking system. However, no relation between the accumulation of *money* capital and the accumulation of *physical* capital exists and, therefore, in Veblen's view, finance does not affect production. Money capital serves only the purpose of *controlling* the production process, mainly by means of transactions in the financial market.[162] Donald R. Stabile ([1988] in Tilman, 2003, pp. 32 ff., italics added) interprets Veblen's theory of income distribution in a very similar way. He starts by arguing that 'all classes, including workers, emulate the leisure class'. As a result: 'Workers who lost the status accorded to them as skilled craftsmen might indeed have grown restless. They might even have displayed their *dissatisfaction by voting for socialist candidates as a form of protest*.' They claim high wages for the purpose of 'meeting the standards of consumption set by leisure-class values'. The ordinary device in order to reach this goal is to 'remain loyal to their union if they had one, or form one if they did not'. Stabile also deals with the Veblenian view of the nature and the role of unionism and remarks that: (i) 'He never saw, as happened in the 1930s, that unions could improve their legal status within the system' and (ii) the levels of membership vary significantly among countries as a result of different cultural patterns. So, for instance, while German workers were conditioned by imperialism, American patriotism acted as a powerful obstacle to the rise of strong unionism. Social conflict occurs, in this interpretation, via workers' choice to join the union and/or via the political arena, by voting for parties which oppose the existing system.

Moreover, according to Stabile, the rise of unionism, as well as 'radicalism', is strictly linked to technical advances, because of 'the values inculcated by the machine process'. He notes that 'Veblen had earlier argued that even the industrial workforce could be affected by business values of making money, leisure class values of emulation, and patriotism, all of which countered the influence of the machine process' (ibid., p. 34). Whatever the mechanisms inducing institutional change may be, the interpretation put forward by Rick Tilman ([1972] in Tilman 2003, vol. III, p. 16) is quite convincing:

> there is Veblen's preference for technological values as opposed to ceremonial values, and his assumption that the former cannot function effectively except in an 'open society' while the latter are characteristic of a 'closed society' usually dominated by respective elites or traditions which inhibit the exercise of civil liberties.

Rejecting the interpretations of the Veblenian political ideal as 'technocratic managerialism' (Dobriansky 1957), Tilman ([1972] in Tilman 2003, vol. III, p. 16) emphasizes Veblen's 'sympathy for syndicalism, especially the American variant found in the Industrial Workers of the World'. This is because 'Syndicalism, particularly in its American form, repudiates elitist control of industry, whether technocratic or not, in favour of worker's control of industry.'

The key question is now: what mechanisms, albeit in the long run, can induce workers to modify their habits of thought and therefore to promote institutional change?

Two main interpretations are possible.

a   *On the psychological plane*, as Walker (in Tilman 2003, vol. II, pp. 68–69) emphasizes

> The immediate consequence of the adoption of mechanistic logic for the economic organization of society is that the domination of the natural rights philosophy is weakened. Although the technicians do not react by opposing their masters, the workers begin to question the traditional metaphysical bases of justification of economic institutions. They become critical of specific economic and social arrangements, such as the distribution of income, the existence of privileged classes, the

economic and legal domination of businessmen and, Veblen insisted, the desirability of thrift and even the family.

In other words, the relationships which occur within the firm between technicians and workers are able to 'convert' workers, in the sense of giving them a chance to internalize values oriented to efficiency and opposing waste. 'The mode of production' – Cutrona (2003, p. 62) underlines – 'that marks modern capitalism is characterized by mechanical processes. They transform the archetypal working man and consequently imply deep changes in the ways men think.' As a result: 'The man who uses machinery devices on a daily basis develops the mental habit of speaking in terms of cause and effect, by which he means the close connection among the process phases.'

b   *On economic and institutional grounds*, and following the interpretation earlier, the change in workers' habits of thought may be due to the gap between the desired real wage and the current real wage or, more generally, to the perception that the existing income distribution satisfies neither economic nor moral criteria. This, in turn, may depend on the processes of induced consumption on the part of firms (mainly via advertising), or on the dissatisfaction deriving from a wage level which does not allow workers to consume in an ostentatious way, or on the gradual internalization of codes of behaviour oriented to efficiency – by means of the adoption of a *forma mentis* directed to 'mechanical sequences' – and opposing waste.[163]

Moreover, social conflict may – if successful – generate an increase in wages. This, in turn, is likely to produce two effects: (i) if workers' consumption is largely affected by the desire for ostentation, the increase in their living standard leads to a parallel increase in their *desired* living standard (Veblen 1994, vol. VIII, p. 395); (ii) the possible increase in wages positively affects the 'available energy' to promote conflict,[164] deriving from workers' discontent with the current income distribution ('social odium' in Veblen's words [Veblen 1975, p. 352]). Technical progress – under the constraint of corporate policies directed to reducing production for the purpose of increasing prices and profits – may produce an increase in the 'subsistence wage'[165] and may significantly affect customary habits of thought. In particular, effect (i) is in operation when workers are under the control of the leisure class, while effect (ii) is likely to occur when workers – in firms governed by technicians – internalize the moral values typical of the management technicians. As a result, the value of *waste* – typical of the leisure class – is overshadowed by the value of *efficiency*, which characterizes the productive class.

Schooling is also a key factor in this picture. Veblen maintains that the leisure class is able to control workers by managing the educational processes: 'schools [...] are shaped by and rest upon a leisure-class culture', based on the humanities and erudition (Veblen 1975, p. 391). Chapter XIV of *The Theory of the Leisure Class* is devoted entirely to the topic 'The higher learning as an expression of the pecuniary culture', and the starting point of Veblen's (ibid., p. 365) reflection is the following:

> The habits of thought which are so formed under the guidance of teachers and scholastic traditions have an economic value – a value of affecting the serviceability of the individual – no less real than the similar economic value of the habits of thought formed without such guidance under the discipline of everyday life.

Veblen distinguishes between two types of knowledge: esoteric and exoteric knowledge (Veblen 1975, p. 367). In his own words:

> As the body of systematised knowledge increased, there presently arose a distinction, traceable very far back in the history of education, between esoteric and exoteric knowledge; the former – so far as there is a substantial difference between the two – comprising such knowledge as is primarily of no economic or industrial effect, and the latter comprising chiefly knowledge of industrial processes and of natural phenomena which were habitually turned to account for the material purposes of life.

Therefore, one can argue that schooling does not necessarily propagate the habits of thought of the leisure class and serve to preserve its interests. On the one hand, 'esoteric knowledge', based on erudition and 'placed primarily in the higher, liberal and classic institutions and grades of learning' (ibid., p. 369) tends to 'lower rather than to heighten the industrial efficiency of the community' (ibid., p. 382). On the other hand, 'exoteric knowledge' – based on cognitive interest for 'casual sequence in phenomena which makes the content of a science' (ibid., p. 384) – appears to be a useful instrument to propagate codes of behaviour oriented to efficiency and thus capable of helping to expand production, favouring – albeit in the long term – institutional change.

3.4   Concluding remarks: T. B. Veblen and J. B. Clark – a comparison

This chapter has dealt with Veblen's analysis of institutional change, interpreting it in the light of the dynamics of income distribution. In particular, after having reconstructed Veblen's theory of instincts – where instincts are conceived as historically and socially affected and do not rest on purely biological grounds – it is argued that his picture of the working of the capitalist system presents two main features: the capitalist system is, by its very nature, (i) based on conflicts among different economic interests as well as on different habits of thought among classes and (ii) intrinsically dynamic.

Conflicts mainly involve technicians versus businessmen and ruling classes versus workers. In the first case, the opposing aims are to expand production, via the use of new knowledge and the consequent possible increase in productivity, and to reduce production, thus increasing prices and profits. In the second case, the dispute is over income distribution: the ruling classes (i.e. the 'leisure class') need the most unequal income distribution in order to preserve their standard of living, while workers – *once they become aware of the 'injustice'* – aim at increasing their wages, both as an end in itself and for emulative purposes. It has been maintained that – given the lack of clarity in Veblen's approach on this question and the consequent possible interpretations – the category of social conflict may help to explain institutional change. Basically, it derives from the processes of induced consumption (i.e. advertising by firms), which generates a gap between the desired real wage and the current real wage. According to this view, social conflict proves to be the driving force of the (gradual) modification of the existing order, although it may be governed or even stopped by the control exercised by the leisure class over education.

The interpretation of Clark's and Veblen's approaches to income distribution and the role of morality in affecting it gives the opportunity for a comparison, which can be made on two distinct levels:

a   *On the methodological plane*, Clark's model is based on methodological individualism: in the labour market, just as in the market for goods, agents bargain in an 'atomistic' way, that is, without the mediation of unions or representation of firms, in a conception of the labour market as a perfectly competitive market. Social classes are not taken into consideration and agents enjoy the same bargaining powers. Moreover, although Clark also considers other models of behaviour (which can be explained by his early studies in the German Historical School), his basic argument is founded on the rational choice paradigm. In contrast, Veblen's approach is based on what can be called the 'macrofoundation of microeconomics': agents' behaviour is profoundly affected by their affiliation to a particular social class and, as a result, the rational choice paradigm cannot apply. Instincts, habits, customs and power relationships structure individual behaviour, according to a 'norm-driven' perspective.

b   *On the analytical plane*, Clark reaches the conclusion that the spontaneous operation of market mechanisms, insofar as it ensures the equalization of the marginal productivity of labour and the real wage, determines a 'just' income distribution: incomes are related to individual merits and, for this very reason, no form of exploitation can occur in perfectly competitive labour markets. Moreover, by assuming that individual needs change when incomes increase, Clark also reaches the conclusion that – even in dynamic terms – a market economy generates efficient and 'just' outcomes: an increase in income leads to the emergence of needs oriented to 'solidarity' and – when these needs become demands – they orient production on the part of firms, giving rise to a phenomenon of economic growth driving 'moral' growth. Veblen criticizes Clark's idea that wages, in competitive markets, are 'right', on the grounds that the standards of morality for workers (and for society as a whole) are ultimately established by the ruling classes ('the leisure class') in their own interests. He also criticizes the idea that wages are fixed according to the marginal productivity of labour, due to the fact that workers and employers have different degrees of bargaining power. As a result, there is no spontaneous mechanism to ensure that income distribution is 'right', according to any criterion of morality at all. The prevalent morality is established by the ruling classes and preserved mainly via education, and institutional changes are possible only by means of social conflict.

4 Ethical codes and income distribution in the neoclassical and institutionalist theoretical frameworks

4.1 Introduction

There is no unanimous consensus on what the basic features of either the neoclassical or institutional theoretical frameworks are.

On the one hand, the neoclassical approach can be seen in at least two different perspectives: (i) the Walrasian approach and thus the idea that perfectly competitive markets via price fluctuations, are able, to achieve equilibrium, so that external interventions are counterproductive for the purpose of obtaining a Pareto-efficient allocation of resources;[166] (ii) the so-called neoclassical synthesis, based on the idea that inefficient outcomes depend on market imperfections (such as incomplete information) and that the Keynesian view of the functioning of a market economy is simply a 'special case' of the neoclassical picture.[167] In both cases, the following basic assumptions hold: (i) agents are rational, in the specific sense that they maximize a utility function – given their exogenous preferences – under the budget constraint (see Robbins 1932); (ii) market economies are not affected by uncertainty, and culture, instincts, habits and customs do not enter the analysis; (iii) scarcity of *all* resources affects agents' behaviour, and it is because resources are scarce that agents have the incentive to use them more efficiently; (iv) individualism is accepted both on the methodological plane, – that is, individuals choose independently of the 'social class' they belong to – and on the moral plane (see later). For these reasons, one can consider the neoclassical view of economics to be *axiomatic*: agents behave in a similar way independently of the historical, social and institutional settings in which they live, consume, produce and save. Pier Luigi Porta and Roberto Scazzieri (2001, p. 10) see the neoclassical approach as 'a pure *logic of choice*':

> following [the] dominant view, economics comes to distinguish itself [...] among the social sciences not for its subject matter but for its *approach*. It is straightforward to see that Robbins's definition may in principle be suitable in describing *any* kind of human choice problem, whether economic or not.

But in a sense, the neoclassical criterion of rationality makes the question of what a pure *economic* problem is, nonsensical. The obvious implication is that economists should be able to study *any* problem of choice or even to deal with issues traditionally left to other sciences, approaching them with the rational choice criterion (i.e. so-called imperialism). These considerations largely apply to the neoclassical synthesis as well. Although in this theoretical framework, the idea that markets spontaneously reach the optimal allocation of resources is rejected, the basic assumptions of the neoclassical–Walrasian approach still hold. Nevertheless, the question of the continuity between the Marshallian paradigm and Keynes' thought is still open. Patinkin (1956, 1987), among others, maintains that Keynes' works before the *General Theory* (hereafter *GT*) are in line with the neoclassical–Marshallian tradition, and that it was only with the *GT* that Keynes (1973 [1936]) developed his idea of revolutionizing economic theory essentially by rejecting Say's law (it was now aggregate demand that determined aggregate supply). This reading of Keynes' whole contribution is known to have been the starting point for a far-reaching cultural-theoretical campaign which convincingly argued that the *GT* model is nothing but a very special case of the general economic equilibrium model. In Hicks and Hansen's theory, in fact, the *GT* model is seen as the 'case of crisis' (the liquidity trap). Later literature then showed that the *IS–LM* model is in turn a special case (the case of perfectly adjusting supply) of a model of aggregate demand–supply, and that this model in turn is a special case of the model of aggregate supply–demand with expectations (the case of adaptive expectations). By contrast, other scholars, such as Graziani (1991), Fodor (1983) and Meltzer (1988), stress that – for many relevant reasons – this is an extremely reductive interpretation of Keynes' work. In particular, the endogenous theory of money,[168] the idea that market economies work under structural uncertainty, the view of the functioning of the labour market as a 'residual market' and thus the demonstration that unemployment depends on lack of effective demand – not on wage rigidity – are not taken into account in the Hicks–Patinkin rereading of Keynes.[169]

On the other hand, institutionalism is often regarded in the light of the distinction between old and new institutionalism, in economics as well as in sociology and political science (see Immergut 1998; Scott 1995). Hodgson (1998) compared the two theoretical frameworks, reaching the conclusion that 'there is no unanimity, even among its adherents, as to what is precisely to be included in the "new" variety' (ibid., p. 175). In his interpretation, 'new' institutionalism mainly focuses on agency and change, assuming that agents are rational actors, and explores the ways institutional change can occur. By contrast, the 'old' institutionalism is based on the idea that *habits* play a crucial role in affecting behaviours, that rational choices may derive from habits and, finally, that habits are 'regarded as crucial to the formation and sustenance of institutions' (ibid., p. 180). Hirsch (1997) stresses the importance of the focus on cognitive processes in the 'new' institutionalism and, similarly, Powell and DiMaggio (1991, p. 15) maintain:

> Not norms and values but taken-for-granted scripts, rules, and classifications are the stuff of which institutions are made. Rather than concrete organizations eliciting affective commitment, institutions are macrolevel abstractions, [...] independent of any particular entity to which moral allegiance might be owed.

Neoinstitutionalists [...] prefer cooler implicit psychologies: cognitive models in which schemas and scripts lead decision makers to resist new evidence [...]; learning theories that emphasize how individuals organize information with the assistance of social categories [...]; and attribution theory, where actors infer motives post hoc from menus of legitimate accounts.

Tagashi Negishi (1989, p. 20) – following Blaug (1985) – interprets institutionalism (in its broader meaning) in the light of the following features:

(1) dissatisfaction with neo-classical economics, which is abstract, static and based on hedonistic and atomistic conceptions of human nature, (2) a demand for the integration of economics with other social sciences, such as sociology, psychology, anthropology and legal studies, or what might be described as a faith in the advantages of the interdisciplinary approach, (3) discontent with the casual empiricism of classical and neoclassical economics, expressed in the proposal to pursue detailed quantitative investigations, and (4) the plea for more social control of business, in other words, a favorable attitude to state intervention.

The search for integration with other disciplines appears to be the common basic feature of 'old' and 'new' institutionalism, while the main difference appears to be in the emphasis on habits, in the first case, and on rational choice,[170] in the second case.

Lilia Costabile (1998) approaches the issue from a different perspective and in quite a convincing way. In dealing with the new institutionalism, she distinguishes between a 'dichotomic' and a 'non-dichotomic' analysis of the private sphere versus institutions. Starting from the consideration that institutions are social devices to solve (or, more reasonably, to reduce) conflicts, adherents to the first approach argue that market mechanisms are the only institutional device able to solve conflicts, thus achieving a 'spontaneous order', while the political arena is invariably subject to pressure from lobbies which promote sub-optimal solutions. The private sphere is thus in contrast with the public sphere. By contrast, adherents to an alternative approach argue that conflicts are sometimes reduced by means of public intervention, while the market may, in some cases, fail to deliver optimal solutions. In this sense, there is no dichotomy between the private and the public spheres. This is labelled the 'negotiated order' approach.

The fundamental contribution of Douglass C. North (1990) can help to identify the basic notions which characterize contemporary studies within the institutional framework. He points out (ibid., p. 3) that

Institutions are the rules of the game in a society, or, more formally, are the humanly devised constraints that shape human interaction. In consequence they structure incentives in human exchange, whether political, social, or economic. Institutional change shapes the way societies evolve through time and hence is the key to understanding historical change.

This chapter deals with the ethical foundations of neoclassical and institutionalist approaches, and with the implications for the analysis of income distribution. They will be considered as *contrasting* views of the functioning of a market economy and reference will be made particularly to the Walrasian model, in the first case, and to the 'old' (or non-neoclassical) institutionalism, in the second case. The exposition is organized as follows. Section 4.2 deals with ethical issues in the neoclassical framework; Section 4.3 approaches the same issue within the Institutionalist view; Section 4.4 explores the differences in the analyses of income distribution with particular regard to the contrasting views on the effects of labour market deregulation.

4.2 Ethics and neoclassical economics

The question of the ethical foundation of neoclassical economics can be approached by considering that: (i) in the neoclassical model, preferences are assumed to be exogenous; (ii) the 'invisible hand' theorem (the pursuit of self-interest *unintentionally* produces beneficial social effects) generates policy prescriptions oriented to minimizing the role of the state and is ultimately supported by *liberal ethics*. Let us now deal with these propositions.

The axiom of exogenous preferences

In the neoclassical view, preferences are assumed to be exogenous and they are represented by a utility function. The rational choice paradigm establishes that a rational choice is one that maximizes this function, given the constraints – typically a budget constraint and a time constraint. This criterion is called instrumental rationality and can be regarded as the process of choosing the most efficient means to reach the given goals. Instrumental rationality can be seen as tautological: if one assumes that agents are rational, therefore – observed *ex post* – every choice is necessarily rational, or – in other words – considering *de facto* behaviour as the outcome of revealed preferences, *de facto* behaviour cannot be anything but rational.[171]

By interpreting this criterion as an analytical tool (thus, not as tautological), the following preconditions must hold in order to allow agents to exercise a rational choice: (i) preferences must be well ordered (Varian 1992); (ii) information must be processed without costs; (iii) agents must be *free to choose* and (iv) resources must be scarce. Let us now focus on points (iii) and (iv). Freedom to choose is clearly a precondition for a rational choice: no external intervention, no social pressure, no power relationships and no instincts, habits or customs must be in operation, since – if so – the individual agent would choose according to the preferences of *other* agents or according to his/her *past* preferences.[172] The scarcity of resources is the basic axiom of the neoclassical theoretical framework. Choices could not be rational if resources were not scarce, because – in the opposite case – agents would simply not face any problem of choice. Therefore, *it is because resources are scarce that agents are rational*, and – insofar as rationality leads to efficient outcomes – *it is because resources are scarce that agents behave in an efficient way.*

The main feature of the rational choice paradigm, if one seeks its ethical foundation, lies in the (implicit) assumption that ends are exogenous – in the sense that they are freely selected by agents – and that there is no space for a 'scientific' inquiry into their legitimacy. Thus, they can be 'stupid' or not, just as they can be 'moral' or not. The 'rational fool' case (Sen 1977) is a very useful tool to explore the methodological foundations of the rational choice paradigm. The story runs as follows. Consider a group of racists confronting some immigrants and assume that the risk of being caught by the police is negligible in the case of an attack by the first group. In this context, Sen shows that violence is rational and that the gain, in terms of total utility, for the racists is greater than the loss of utility for the immigrants.[173] Violence may be rational, although it may be 'stupid' – in the sense that there may exist other and *more reasonable* forms of protecting themselves from a perceived danger, or in the sense that it is myopic (the immigrants could react violently when they have reached a 'critical mass') – and it is 'immoral' insofar as it violates the existing formal rules. As a result, one may argue that – *since the neoclassical criterion of rationality is instrumental* – rational choices can be moral or immoral without altering the validity of the criterion itself.[174] As Skorupski (1999, p. 85) points out: if 'the epistemological thesis that all practical reasoning must be instrumental' is accepted, then 'the question always arises why a player should obey a rule when it does not advantage him to do so'. Furthermore, Sen (1987a) distinguishes between rationality as consistency (i.e. instrumental rationality) and rationality as the pursuit of self-interest:[175] in the first case, he maintains that consistency in choosing depends on the *interpretation* of the choices and that, in any case, internal consistency cannot be conceived as a *sufficient* condition for classifying an action as rational. Shaun P. Hargreaves Heap (in Davis *et al.* 2004, p. 42) points out that the philosophical roots of the criterion of instrumental rationality 'go back to Hume and it quite naturally sits within the wider tradition in political theory of liberal individualism'.

The criterion of instrumental rationality also gives rise to some paradoxical results. Among these: in applying the rational choice paradigm to the analysis of voting, one reaches the conclusion that – if costs are sufficiently high – voting behaviour must be explained in the light of variables which do not enter the individual's cost–benefit analysis, since the individual's contribution to the result of the election (and hence his/her direct benefit) is approximately nil. A rational agent would not vote, although we never observe a condition where all agents do not vote (see Mueller 1989). It is also argued (see Schumpeter 1950, p. 27) that – since the collection of information is costly in the case of elections, and the expected benefit for the individual voter is approximately nil – voters tend to behave as 'rationally ignorant': it is profitable *not* to acquire information, in the cases where, as the information set (and hence its cost) increases, the outcome of a rational choice does not change. Moreover, in the consumption theory, a condition may occur where – for perfectly substitutable goods – the ratio between the marginal utility of two goods is *always* equal to the ratio of their respective prices (in graphical terms, this means that the slope of the indifference curve is equal to the slope of the budget constraint). In this situation, a rational consumer would be simply incapable of choosing, so rationality would imply inertia. In more general terms, Shaun P. Hargreaves Heap (in Davis *et al.* 2004, p. 45) points out that

> the paradox of rational choice [...] forms the basis for the Hobbesian argument for the creation of the State. To obtain the superior outcome where there is a system of law and order, we have to give up the freedom to contract in or out. We simply have to accept the authority of the State and surrender some of the freedom that we would otherwise enjoy.

Zamagni (in Sacco and Zamagni (2002), pp. 10 ff.) maintains that the rational choice paradigm suffers from a major methodological weakness: its actual philosophical foundation – in his interpretation – rests on 'axiological individualism', and the widespread idea that the rational choice paradigm is a useful analytical tool to analyse economic behaviour is not a convincing argument for supporting it, since it should be justified on *philosophical grounds*. In particular, Zamagni argues that the existential dimension – which is no doubt a basic dimension of human life – cannot enter the rational choice paradigm, where solely the acquisitive dimension is taken into consideration.

Liberal ethics

Many variants of liberal ethics exist. John Skorupski (1999) provided critical reconstruction of the debate within the liberal framework. In his interpretation, the basic feature of liberalism is *equal respect*, that is, the idea of the 'ethical equality of human beings' (ibid., p. 241). He distinguishes between classical liberalism, moralistic or idealist liberalism, modernist or populist liberalism and, finally, value-pluralist liberalism. He sees classical liberalism (associated with the liberal thinkers of the first half of the nineteenth century) as a critical response to Kantian ethics and a revival of Hellenism (ibid., p. 236). John Stuart Mill, in his work *On Liberty*, is one of the major representatives within this line of thought, re-proposing the Greek ideal of self-development. In that period, the emphasis on freedom for individuals to 'develop in full diversity' leads to 'a new faith in the historical progressiveness of human nature and society' (ibid., p. 239). The liberal-communitarian view is labelled as moralistic or idealist liberalism. The most representative scholar is T. H. Green, whose basic idea is that 'selfhood is realized through pursuit of the "common good"' (ibid., p. 243). By re-proposing a Kantian view, Green stresses that the participation of the working class in the life of a 'moral community' is an educational device in order to allow workers to obtain full autonomy. Moreover, he also maintains that individual capacity to act rationally is the precondition for *moral growth*. Thus a link between *rationality*, conceived as the capacity to make a rational plan of life, and *morality* is established. In Skorupski's reconstruction, Karl Popper's work represents the culmination of contemporary 'modernist liberalism', which can be summarized by the idea that the *open society* is a unique society which allows 'critical rationalism'. The search for truth – also in an epistemological meaning – is left to the spontaneous interaction of individuals with different views. Objectivity can be reached by overcoming flawed arguments and by gradual approximation to consensus, in a never-ending process. He insists on the 'dualism of facts and decisions', and, in Skorupski's interpretation, this separation is 'an essential bulwark against authoritarianism' (ibid., p. 247). Finally, value-pluralist liberalism (associated here with Isaiah Berlin) emphasizes the idea that 'there are incompatible systems of value which can be put onto a single-scale' and that 'objectivism about values leads to authoritarianism in politics' (ibid., p. 248).

Although these views do not directly enter neoclassical economics, it seems that the concepts of *equal respect*, on the one side, and of *diversity*, on the other side, can be taken into consideration.

The interpretation of the neoclassical analysis of income distribution proposed here is based on these two concepts. It may be argued that – when the notion of equal respect is included in the economic discourse – it leads to the idea that bargaining involves agents with *equal* powers. This idea, in turn, may be seen both as the ethical foundation of the neoclassical analysis and as its normative aspect. In the first case, it pertains to the neoclassical picture of a market economy where no class distinctions exist and every agent is free to choose whether to be an entrepreneur or a worker (see, among others, Graziani 2003, pp. 18 ff.). Moreover, with particular regard to the labour market, the assumption of atomistic bargaining, combined with the idea that full employment exists, leads to the conclusion that no party has superior bargaining power. In the second case, the normative aspect of the argument concerns the view that external interventions are counterproductive insofar as markets are spontaneously able to reach equilibrium (i.e. the optimal allocation of resources) and that – if it is to be admitted – external intervention should solely aim at reducing the possible conditions of superior bargaining power on the part of some agents. The cases of 'market failure' (with particular regard to the production of public goods) legitimate external intervention, and hence the substitution of state command for spontaneous exchanges via market mechanisms.

The notion of diversity concerns a different aspect of the neoclassical approach. It may be argued that, within this theoretical framework, agents have identical bargaining powers and, at the same time, because of their different attitudes (basically reflected in their different preferences) and owing to the freedom they enjoy, they are able to assume any social position they want – given their constraints. In other words, the joint notions of equal respect and diversity fit the neoclassical picture of the market economy, where *bargaining powers are identical from individual to individual and, at the same time, social mobility is fully allowed*. Furthermore, as seen in Chapter 2, insofar as marginalist distributive rules are based on the idea that wages are linked to productivity, they may be interpreted as the analytical confirmation of the ethical principle of diversity: the higher a worker's ability, the higher his/her wage. In this specific sense, the ethical criterion of diversity leads to a distribution of income based on individual *merits*.

One can object that labour productivity – in the basic neoclassical picture of the labour market – depends on the available capital and that all workers have the same productivity, under the assumption of decreasing marginal returns. However, by removing the simplifying assumption that workers are homogeneous, wage differentials have to be explained by taking other variables into account (not only the stock of capital per worker), and these variables – individual propensity to risk, human capital, effort – basically reflect the *single* worker's 'ability'. This consideration leads to the question of whether abilities are partially 'innate', partially 'acquired' (i.e. the result of the effort of the *single* worker) or 'inherited', the result of the joint efforts of the single workers and his/her family and/or his/her social background). It is clear that, while – in the first case – merit is purely individual, in the second case, the individuation of the individual merit is unclear or ambiguous. The problem arises, in particular, in the case where ability is developed through education.

The contemporary mainstream literature on human capital – that is, the stock of knowledge that individuals have accumulated via learning by schooling and learning by doing – emphasizes the idea that wage differentials, as well as the probability of finding a job corresponding to the expected status, depends on private investment in education. Since the labour contract is affected by asymmetric information problems, firms are likely to find it profitable to avoid (or to minimize) the costs of selection and to consider formal education as a 'signal' of the real productivity of workers (see Salop and Salop 1976). Moreover, since it is assumed that human capital accumulation increases labour productivity, it ultimately drives economic growth: the so-called endogenous growth theory (see Lucas 1988; Romer 1989). In this theoretical context, the choice of investing in human capital is left to a unit (the family) which acts rationally, without conditions deriving from its background and – in the normal case – with the opportunity to finance this investment via perfectly competitive credit markets. The opposite view (see Bowles and Gintis 1976) states that social networks widely affect both the choice of investment in human capital (in quantitative and qualitative terms) and – above all – the opportunity to find a job corresponding to the expected status. In other words, the higher the level of family income and social rank, the greater the accumulation of human capital and the better the chance of finding a good job. A 'crowding out' effect is likely to occur: the richer agents (who are not necessarily the more meritorious) find the best jobs only because they are rich and, as a result, the low-income individuals (although they may be more meritorious and even if they have the same education) find the worst jobs. In contexts where labour demand for highly skilled workers does not increase significantly, the increase in the individual and aggregate stock of human capital only produces *over-education*. The reason why individuals choose, if they can, to increase their human capital even if they know that labour demand will not increase can be explained by the search for 'competitive advantage' with respect to other workers (see Thurow 1975). In fact, if the increase in human capital on the microeconomic plane is perceived as an effective way of obtaining a job (whatever it is), then all agents who can, will choose this strategy and the overall result will be an excess of human capital supply over demand, and a low 'social return' of human capital accumulation.

To conclude, it is necessary to stress that – contrary to John Bates Clark (see Chapter 2) – contemporary neoclassical economists do not take ethical considerations into account, nor do they think that their theoretical framework rests on a definite philosophical background. However, in the light of the earlier discussion, one can conclude that neoclassical *methodological individualism* is linked to *ethical individualism*. This appears particularly clear in approaching the issue of exogenous preferences and, with reference to income distribution, the stress on freedom (in the descriptive as well as in the normative sense) as a precondition for rational choice leads to a picture of the working of a market economy where individual pursuit of self-interest – no matter whether 'moral' or 'immoral' – unintentionally generates the maximum social welfare. As Lionel Robbins (1932) wrote: 'So far as we are concerned, our economic subjects can be pure egoists, pure altruists, pure ascetics, pure sensualists or – which is more likely – bundles of all those impulses.' Note that the fact that individual choices may be moral or not is irrelevant only because it is *implicitly* assumed that agents do not violate (at least) the existing set of formal norms, or – in other words – that 'social capital' is a given.[176] The paradox of the single-spot interaction (see Chapter 1) is simply solved by *implicitly* assuming that all agents are honest: they pay even when it is rational not to pay *if* legal rules prescribe payment.

4.3   Ethics and institutional economics

As seen in Chapter 3, institutional economics (at least the so-called old institutionalism) rests on the idea that the functioning of market economies – contrary to the neoclassical picture – does not rest on *natural* constants of human nature but is deeply affected by a set of formal, social and moral norms, which, in turn, have a *historical* dimension and evolve through institutional change.

This view is linked to a very different approach both to the criterion of rationality (and the nature of individual and social preferences) and to the ethical discourse, with respect to the neoclassical approach. These topics are discussed in what follows.

Institutional rationality

Vanberg (1993) points out that the neoclassical criterion of rationality should be rejected in an institutionalist theoretical framework on the grounds that its methodology emphasizes the *realism* of assumptions and does not aim at building an *axiomatic* model.[177] Therefore, the criterion of rationality must be revised in the light of the following evidence: (i) history matters, and hence present decisions are affected by past decisions, via learning; (ii) uncertainty exists, and therefore agents try to adapt their behaviour to changing circumstances, by adopting a 'rule-following behaviour', that is, by forming categories of situations perceived as similar and responding to changes in the light of these categories. Norms and 'rules of thumb' also help agents to face uncertainty;[178] (iii) social structure affects, although it does not determine, individual behaviour and preferences, via the operation of culture, traditions, habits, customs and power relationships. More generally, it is maintained that the neoclassical consumption theory relies on a very naive psychological theoretical framework. Many researches – both theoretical and empirical – have shown that emotions, impulses and instincts play a crucial role in orienting consumption. Within this line of thought, 'cognitive dissonance' is a relevant issue. It has been shown that consumers aim at preserving above all their 'mental health' and, for this purpose, they select only the information which makes their past choices consistent with their past convictions, avoiding information which could produce regret. In so doing, and particularly for consumption associated with 'high' expenses, they persuade themselves that their past choices were 'right'. Albert O. Hirschman (1982) suggested considering *delusion* as one of the key variables in explaining consumption choices. Delusion occurs when agents experience cognitive dissonance and cognitive dissonance, in turn, leads them first to regret and then to modify their plan of consumption, via a psychologically costly learning process. Therefore, for the purpose of minimizing these costs (deriving from the gap between the expected result and the actual result), agents tend to choose strategies of 'repeated consumption'; that is, they tend not to modify the basket of goods acquired. Hirschman also stresses that present consumption depends on past consumption and – more generally – that delusion may produce in someone the desire to prove his/her worth. On the macroeconomic plane, this effect is able to explain individual participation in collective actions, overcoming free-riding problems. The neoclassical assumptions of non-satiation and of the indifference of the utility of gains and losses are also questionable. Camerer (1997) has found that New York City cab drivers work shorter hours on good days and that they have *income goals*, so that when they reach their goal they stop. Marglin (1974) interprets the emergence of the capitalist production process as a device to prevent workers from choosing the length of their working week. Kahneman and Tversky (1979) found experimental evidence that the value function is not symmetrical over gains and losses: a dollar loss is psychologically more costly than the increase of utility deriving from a dollar gain. The so-called Ellsberg paradox adds a further empirical argument against the rational choice paradigm: experiments show that people give the highest probability to the event they face first, even though the first event does not necessarily have the maximum probability of occurring. This can be interpreted as the preference for risk and aversion to uncertainty.

'Failures of rationality' also arise in cases where the occurrence of an event modifies the *perceived* probability of its recurrence or – more generally – modifies individual beliefs. As Reisman (2002, p. 54) remarks, 'People overestimate the statistical probabilities when a disastrous airplane crash is prominently reported in the news. They vote for more policemen and tougher sentencing when a personal friend becomes the victim of an accident or crime.' Moreover, non-rational attitudes can also derive from the worry about the possible changes of some economic variables. Following Reisman (2002, p. 57), this is the case of workers, who, though 'unwilling to countenance cuts in their money wages, will be more accepting of price rises [...]: the reason is not money illusion but the attachment to an established value'. Moreover, the Walrasian model only takes private (i.e. rival) goods into consideration, so that human relationships are set aside not only because – owing to the existence of the 'auctioneer' – agents can avoid meeting, but also in the sense that a set of existing goods (think, for instance, of the e-mail or the telephone) needs human relationships in order to be consumed. These are what can be defined as *socially complementary goods* deriving from network externalities (see Varian 1996). Human relationships are even more important in the case of the so-called socio-emotional goods, such as the care for children, since such 'goods and services cannot be separated from the "producer" without changing their character [...]. Depending on social relationship, the physical good or service symbolizes the feeling between the producer and the recipient' (Schmid 2004, p. 133).

In the institutional theoretical framework, no unique motivation of human behaviour is assumed: on the contrary, it is recognized that a variety of motives underlie individual decisions. Therefore, following Vanberg, 'institutional rationality' differs from the neoclassical criterion because it is based on the idea that agents behave according to *principles*, not in view of the *maximization* of their utility function. In a sense, as Vanberg argues, a criterion of rationality is not essential in institutional economics.

Some institutional economists suggest adopting a criterion of *pragmatic rationality*, or what Van Staveren (2001) labels 'meaningful rationality', following John Dewey's pragmatist philosophy. Human 'vulnerability' is the key issue in this line of thought, involving uncertainty with regard to both economic variables and social relationships. It is pointed out that – in a world where uncertainty is pervasive – the most reasonable procedure for making choices is to follow some shared values in society, even when this implies 'tragic' choices. Rationality is pragmatic in the specific sense that it is based on the suggestion that the individual agent is engaged in continuous relationships with other agents who share a similar set of values, for the sake of reducing the risk of erroneous choices in a world of structural uncertainty.

In the institutional approach to rationality, two basic remarks can be made:

i   the economic problem is not a problem of allocation of scarce resources among different exogenous uses. This statement finds its rationale in the idea that resources are not *exogenously* scarce, that is, they are not scarce for *natural* constraints, but they are scarce because of the peculiar institutional context in which individuals make their choices. In particular, since corporate price policies determine the available resources affecting income distribution, scarcity should be seen as *endogenous*, that is, deriving from market structures which do not allow the maximum level of production.[179] This does not imply that a *natural* scarcity never exists, but that – *if the postulate of unlimited needs is accepted* (and hence saturation in consumption is not admitted) – 'relative' scarcity (i.e. the gap between needs and the availability of goods) is affected by both exogenous and endogenous constraints. The rise of monopolies, for instance, generates an endogenous increase in the degree of scarcity, through the increase in prices. Hyman P. Minsky (1996, p. 365) has put forward a similar argument:

> Our rich economy has ample available resources for investment in people and in the material infrastructure of society. The question is not whether resources are available, but of the willingness to mobilize these resources by taxing and borrowing for public projects.

In other words, and within a post-Keynesian and institutional theoretical framework,[180] scarcity of resources ultimately depends on the degree of 'willingness' (or the convenience) on the part of firms and of the banking sector to make resources available to consumers. More generally, scarcity is likely to be affected by power relationships, and not only via price and wage setting on the part of the firm. Power can be defined as the possibility for A to force B to do something that B does not want to to, or to impede B from doing what she/he wants to do. In a similar fashion, Allan Schmid (2004, p. 22) points out that 'the relationship between A's opportunity and B's exposure and obligation define their relative power', adding that 'Market power or the ability to affect price in exchange is only one dimension of power'. Moreover, scarcity is linked to power relationships insofar as 'In a world of scarcity and interdependence, a transaction is necessarily a matter of mutual coercion' (ibid., p. 71). In a more sophisticated way, Jack Knight (1992, p. 41) proposes the following definition: 'To exercise power over someone or some groups is to affect by some means the alternatives available to that person or group. To use more formal language, power relates to the ability to affect one's feasible set.'

ii   One can distinguish between *relevant* and *irrelevant* situations (or – more reasonably – between situations of varying degrees of relevance) in studying the process of individual choices, by defining the 'degree of relevance' in relation to the opportunity cost in terms of income (or even of utility) of erroneous choices. In other words, it seems quite reasonable to assume that *not all* situations have the same importance for individuals (the choice of labour is certainly more important than the choice between a cup of coffee or a cup of tea), that the loss – in terms of income and/or utility – caused by the erroneous choice in the case of a relevant situation is higher. Therefore, individuals tend to behave in a rational way (at least in the sense that they tend to calculate, even under uncertainty) when choices pertain to relevant events, and, in contrast, they tend to behave according to habit in the event of less relevant outcomes. The level of income available at the moment of the choice is likely to affect the judgement of the relevance of the events, in the sense that the lower the income, the higher the number of relevant events. This is due to the higher opportunity cost for a large number of possible erroneous choices.[181]

Note that, in the institutionalist approach described here, methodological individualism is rejected and, above all, preferences are not exogenously given.

Therefore, contrary to the neoclassical approach, ethical codes affect behaviour at least in the sense that when agents choose they take into account the set of norms prevalent in society (or in specific groups).

Ethics and institutions

In view of all this, it can be said that the issue of ethics is strictly linked with purely economic inquiry in the institutionalist approach. This particularly applies to the analysis of the functioning of the market in a capitalist economy and to the approach to income distribution (see Section 4.4). The first issue will be discussed in the following paragraphs.

On the methodological plane, as argued earlier, the basic difference between the neoclassical and the institutional paradigm lies in the fact that the first conceives economic analysis from a *formalist* point of view, while the second approaches economic issues on the grounds of what is called 'pragmatic realism', involving the constant attention to economic facts and to the peculiarities of different economic systems according to their history and the cultural framework within which they operate. The description of the functioning of a market economy which follows from this methodological point of view differs widely from the neoclassical approach. In particular, while neoclassical economists see the market as a *natural locus* (reflecting the supposed constants of human behaviour) and identifies the market with the economy as a whole, institutionalist economists stress the idea that the market is a *social and historical construct*. In other words, neoclassical economists conceive the working of markets under the following assumptions: (i) preferences are given; (ii) all resources are scarce; (iii) perfect competition is the normal condition. The supply–demand mechanism ensures that – without external intervention – equilibrium is reached in all markets, and equilibrium identifies with the optimal allocation of resources. Therefore, no assumption on the formal/legal status of the economy is needed, and institutions – where they are assumed to exist – generate counterproductive effects. On the other hand, institutional economics approaches the issue by considering that (i) the market cannot be identified with the whole economy, at least in the sense that exchange is not the sole field of inquiry of economics and that – as a matter of fact – some economic outcomes derive from transactions which do not pass through the market (for instance, they enter the political arena); (ii) competition is an 'artificial' process, resulting from the specificity of the economic system being studied, and – above all – formal, social and moral norms are at the basis of its operation.

In the formalist view, the assumption of equal bargaining powers among agents in all markets is fully justified, if the purpose is to build a perfectly consistent model. This is not the case where economics is conceived according to the methodology of realism. Institutional economics is based on the assumption that *power relationships* are an essential feature of capitalism and that – when they are put to the test in the marketplace – perfect competition is nothing but an 'ideal': the existence of different degrees of bargaining power among agents is the normal condition. Allan Schmid (2004, pp. 22–23) points out that

> The point of power is that the rich have other options and command over other resources that they can deny those with little to offer in exchange. Economic power is an input into political power to alter rights and vice versa.

A's possibility of forcing *B* to do (or not to do) something is – more generally – what constitutes a power relation. More generally, North (1990, p. 16) emphasizes that 'Institutions are not necessarily or even usually created to be socially efficient; rather they, or at least the formal rules, are created to serve the interests of those with the bargaining power to devise new rules.'

Given this theoretical framework, what are the possible links between ethical codes and institutions?

In answering this question, Argandoña (2002) – in a quite convincing approach – starts from two basic assumptions: (i) institutions are 'regularities of behaviour' and (ii) ethics is not an arbitrary and abstract construction but what guarantees the equilibrium condition in the economic, social and political arenas. He maintains that ethics cannot be conceived as a class of social institutions: ethics is a 'meta-institution' or a 'higher-order' institution. This thesis rests on the following arguments. First, the identification of some ethical criterion with an existing institution would make it *contingent* and *relative*, which is unacceptable if one regards ethics as what guides agents' behaviour. Second, the strength of an ethical prescription does not derive from *social* sanctions but from *inner* convictions. Third, ethical prescriptions must apply to non-recurrent situations and – while institutions are subject to change – ethical principles should be independent of changes in the environment in which they operate. In other words, ethical principles are *general*, while institutions, as well as social norms, are *specific* to a peculiar historical context. As a result, ethics is needed not for the purpose of covering a class of institution, but in order to express value judgement on existing institutions and their changes, and, in this respect, ethics can be regarded as a 'meta-institution'. Argandoña (2002) also emphasizes the view that the judgements deriving from ethics and applied to institutions must be oriented to establishing whether the existing institutional framework – as well as its possible changes – is able to guarantee an 'optimum', not (only) in economic terms, but – above all – in terms of a wider notion of human well-being and human development. Following this line of thought, the rules of ethics ultimately rest on reason, in the sense that although reason is unable to design a social setting, it can help us to understand which elements of ethical prescription can promote human development in the event of institutional changes. In other words, reason is able to identify the actions and institutions which are potentially harmful for individual agents and for society as a whole. In this process, ethics can provide the necessary tools in order to judge not only the existing institutional framework but also the possible institutional changes.

In dealing with Veblen's thought (see Chapter 3), it has been argued that – although his inquiry aims at providing a *scientific* analysis of contemporary economics (where value judgements have no place) – the basic distinction he traces is between *good* and *bad* instincts. In view of this, two dimensions of Veblen's ethics can be traced.

The first dimension pertains to 'bad and good' and involves value judgements *on the existing institutional framework* (as well as on its possible changes) based on ethical criteria. In particular, it can be argued that good instincts are those that allow institutional changes which promote a reduction of waste. The reduction of waste – in the Veblenian meaning – generates, in turn, a higher level of production and a more equal income distribution. In this peculiar meaning, *good* is linked both to *efficiency* and to *equity*, and, as a result, institutional changes are ethically admissible insofar as they promote an increase in the standard of living of the working class, by reducing the (wasteful) consumption of the leisure class. A second dimension of Veblen's ethics can be traced in his conflictual view of the functioning of a market economy, in the sense that conflict arises in cases where the existing *status quo* (above all, in terms of the present income distribution) is inconsistent with the commonly held (above all, by workers) sense of justice. This second dimension of Veblenian ethics is not purely normative: it is based on the idea that people express value judgements, deriving from their inner convictions, on economic variables. This particularly applies to judgements on income distribution; this topic will be examined in what follows.

4.4   Contrasting views on income distribution

The neoclassical approach is based on the idea that income distribution reflects the marginal productivity of inputs – namely, labour, capital and land – and that the marginal productivity of all inputs decreases when the amount of an input (given the amount of the others) increases. The theorem of the 'exhaustion of the product' allows exploitation to be excluded, in the sense that it is shown that when markets are perfectly competitive, all inputs receive a reward which is the measure of their marginal contribution to the whole product, and the whole product is distributed to the inputs which contributed to create it: no 'residue' – that is, no share of output which cannot be 'explained' – exists (see Flux 1894). Furthermore, it can be demonstrated that the equality between marginal productivity of input L and its rewards w is a necessary condition for an *efficient* outcome: profits are at a maximum, as is total worker utility, and – since these conditions come about when labour demand equals labour supply – a full employment equilibrium occurs.[182]

The main policy prescription deriving from this view is deregulation of the labour market in the event of involuntary unemployment, since unemployment depends on 'rigidities' of the labour market (see Layard *et al.* 1994).[183] Deregulation involves two aspects: deregulation of the labour *market*, and hence policies devoted to reducing union bargaining power (and, consequently, to reducing the average real wage), and deregulation of the labour *contract*, and hence policies designed to give the firm more freedom of hiring and firing. The rationale of this suggestion can be found in the following arguments.

a   *The effects of labour market deregulation on the capital/labour ratio*. In the basic neoclassical theoretical framework, the individual firm faces the problem of the choice of techniques under two assumptions: (i) in the labour market, firms and workers bargain over the real wage and (ii) given the other inputs, capital and labour are partially substitutable. The equilibrium condition is reached when the ratio between the marginal productivity of inputs (MPL/MPK) equals their prices (w/p_k), where w is the unitary real wage and p_k is the price of capital goods, L is labour and k is capital. Insofar as deregulation implies a decrease in the unitary real wage (say, from w to w'), it allows firms to reach a new equilibrium (MPL$'$/MPK$' = w'/p_k$), with a lower value of *MPL* and hence – owing to the assumption of decreasing returns – a higher value of L. As a result, labour market deregulation is an effective way to increase employment, because it is assumed that firms operate with a technology which allows the substitution of inputs, and – for the sake of maximizing profits – that firms find it profitable to choose labour-intensive arrangements.

b   *Labour market deregulation and economic growth.* If labour market deregulation implies a reduction of union bargaining power and, therefore, a reduction of the average real wage, this produces positive effects on profits. The increase in profits, in turn, allows firms to increase their investments (via self-financing); the increase in investments determines an increase both in aggregate output and in employment, provided that technological unemployment is not likely to occur.[184] Moreover, one can argue that a similar mechanism can be in operation in an open economy. The reduction of the average real wage allows firms to cut prices and, as a result, to increase their exports. This, in turn, determines an increase in profits, investments, growth and employment in the area where policies of deregulation have been implemented. A positive outcome is also due to the reduction of unemployment benefits, insofar as they discourage job hunting and – by reducing the opportunity cost of low effort on the part of the employed – they reduce labour productivity. Therefore, it is maintained that a reduction of the so-called replacement ratio (unitary unemployment benefit/unitary wage) can increase both labour supply and labour productivity. The rationale for this argument is that unemployment benefits discourage job search (because – by assuming that work is only disutility – individuals would prefer paid leisure to work) and that the higher they are, the lower the effort of the employed workers will be, because of the lower opportunity cost of being fired. In contrast, one can argue that unemployment benefits allow workers to carry out their job hunting more carefully, thus determining a more efficient allocation of the labour force.[185]

c   *Deregulation of the labour contract: the 'discipline device'.* In the neoclassical theoretical framework, it is also maintained that the increase in corporate freedom to hire and fire – which is the main, though not the only, dimension of labour contract deregulation – generates positive effects both on profits and on employment. This occurs because the more firms can freely fire, the more credible is the threat of dismissal and the more workers are forced to increase their effort; which is called the 'discipline device' (see Shapiro and

Stiglitz 1984). The increase in effort, in turn, positively affects labour productivity and hence – on the macroeconomic plane – economic growth. Finally, economic growth determines an increase in employment. The underlying assumption is that workers perceive labour only as disutility and, therefore, when it is possible, they tend to 'shirk'. The more rigid the labour contract, that is the longer its duration, the greater the likelihood of shirking. Note that this effect crucially depends on the probability – perceived by workers – that the contract will be renewed. In fact, the more workers perceive (or know) that the labour contract is temporary, the more they will rationally tend to reduce their effort, since even if they do provide their maximum effort, they will nevertheless be sacked when it expires. Moreover, it is argued that freedom to fire workers is an incentive to hire, or – in other words – that firms' *availability* to hire basically depends on their *capability* to fire.

This (dominant) view has been the object of numerous critiques. The Sraffian, the Keynesian and the institutional approaches to the question will be discussed in what follows.

Critiques on the neoclassical value theory: the Sraffian view

Sraffa's well-known critique of the law of diminishing returns (Sraffa 1926) represents one of the most significant attacks on the internal consistency of the neoclassical model. The interdependence of markets – that is, the fact that variations of prices and/or quantities in a single market affect the equilibrium conditions in other markets – makes this law unacceptable on the logical plane. 'The really serious difficulties', Sraffa (1926) writes,

> make their appearance when it is considered to what extent the supply curves based on the law of returns satisfy the conditions necessary to enable them to be employed in the study of the equilibrium value of single commodities produced under competitive conditions. This point of view assumes that the conditions of production and the demand for a commodity can be considered, in respect to small variations, as being practically independent, both in regard to each other and in relation to the supply and demand of all other commodities.

Since this assumption is clearly rejected by evidence, it is impossible to find the equilibrium conditions in a single market in a static domain. The relevance of this argument to the present discussion lies in the fact that when diminishing returns are not in operation and when this particularly applies to labour, deregulation does not produce the effects foreseen in the neoclassical approach. Consider the case of fixed technical coefficients: given the stock of physical capital available for the individual firm, a reduction in the unitary wage does not modify the technical configuration. The marginalist distributive rules cannot be applied and, more important, the production function becomes useless as an analytical tool. The Sraffian view is also worth noting for having emphasized the socio-political nature of wage bargaining. In the work *Production of Commodities by Means of Commodities* of 1960, Sraffa – by rereading classical political economy – provides a theoretical framework where the distribution of the social product in wages and profits ultimately depends on the relative bargaining power of workers and firms, in the marketplace as well as in the socio-political arena. In politics, this idea has been translated into the notion of the wage as an 'independent variable'. In this context, policies of labour market deregulation affect only income distribution, without increasing employment, mainly because the assumption of a negative relationship between the unitary wage and employment is not tenable (see Garegnani 1984; Pasinetti 1974; Roncaglia 1993).

Critiques on the functioning of the labour market: the Keynesian view

Schematically, and only for the purpose of the issue approached here, the Keynesian model can be summarized by starting from the following assumptions: (i) Owing to uncertainty, workers and firms bargain over the *money* wage; (ii) the level of employment positively depends on effective demand, so that the labour market is a 'residual' market. The wage is both a component of production costs and a component of effective demand, via worker consumption. It is common knowledge that in *GT*, Keynes shows that a policy of wage reduction, causing a reduction in consumption and effective demand, is an ineffective strategy for increasing employment: 'There is [...] no ground for the belief that a flexible wage policy is capable of maintaining a state of continuous full employment' (Keynes 1973 [1936], p. 267). While it is reasonable to expect that – on the micro-economic plane – the individual firm can obtain higher profits via labour market deregulation and the consequent reduction of costs, the aggregate result of this policy is a decline in consumption and, hence, in effective demand and employment. A similar outcome is likely to occur when labour contract deregulation is considered. The argument runs as follows. Assume that (i) deregulation increases uncertainty and that workers aim at enjoying a constant level of consumption over time; (ii) the 'discipline' effect is in operation. Under these assumptions, one can show (see Forges Davanzati and Realfonzo 2004) that policies of deregulation of the labour contract determine an increase in the propensity to save and, hence, a reduction of consumption, effective demand and employment. The fall of the employment level is amplified by the increase in labour productivity as a result of the 'discipline' effect. In fact, firms face a lower level of demand while their productive capacity is higher: the only solution in order to avoid overproduction and the reduction of profits is to fire workers and/or not to hire them. In this case, too, while deregulation may be perceived as profitable for the individual firm, it is counterproductive for the purpose of increasing employment when the macroeconomic picture is considered.

Critiques from the institutional theoretical framework

In view of the earlier discussion, the institutionalist critiques of the neoclassical model rely on a methodological view which emphasizes realism in contrast to the conception of economics as an axiomatic science. The main points of divergence are

a In the neoclassical picture, because of the supply–demand mechanism in the labour market, the average real wage can be set at absolutely any value, so no link between the market wage (w^0) and the subsistence wage (w^*) exists. However, to approach the question from a realistic point of view, it is clear that an economy where $w^0 < w^*$ is an economy where workers are unable to live and work (if the market wage is below the purely biological subsistence wage) and/or social conflict is very likely to occur (in the more plausible case where subsistence is historically and socially determined). However, the neoclassical idea that wages vary in response to variations of labour demand and labour supply is also open to dispute in terms of logic. Nobody can deny that, in industrialized countries, the average family possesses (at least) one television set and that the television set is *permanently* in the basket of goods consumed by the family in question. Hence, a significant reduction of its income should lead the family to sell its television set in order to acquire more necessary consumption goods, but this is sharply in contrast with evidence. In other words, the neoclassical view would imply that – because of wage fluctuations – durable consumption goods cannot necessarily enter the workers' basket of goods, if wage fluctuations affect the available income of the employed workers.

b It is also stressed that – contrary to the standard neoclassical approach – labour is not a good like all the other goods. The rationale for this argument, which is obvious *prima facie*, is that those who acquire labour must establish *continuous* relationships with this peculiar good. This is not the case for, say, oranges or lemons. Furthermore, these relationships are *social* relationships, that is, relationships between *human* agents and not between human agents and *things*. This remark *may* have normative aspects, although they are not strictly implied: according to Guy Standing (1999, p. 4), 'workers should not be subject to "market forces" in the same way as oranges and lemons, and [...] they should have rights, forms of security and forms of social protection'.

The definition of labour is strictly linked to this issue. Early marginalist economists – W. S. Jevons, among others – opposed the classical distinction between productive and unproductive labour and proposed the idea that labour is, by definition, 'any painful exertion of mind or body undergone partly or wholly with a view to future goods' (Jevons 1879 [1871], p. 183). In elaborating his theory of individual labour supply, Jevons extends this definition to include three elements: (i) labour is disutility; (ii) utility comes after the exertion; (iii) labour demands calculation. Of course, his aim is to exclude leisure from this definition, inactivity being represented – in his own example – by a walk or a game of cricket (of course, not played by a professional). However, Jevons' definition appears questionable, since it is possible to show that, say, a walk contains all the elements of his definition: it implies effort, utility may come after the effort (think, for instance, of the case where one walks to improve one's health) and, finally, it may also demand calculation (see Forges Davanzati 1995). G. J. Stigler (1946 [1941] p. 98) correctly points out that 'the attempt to differentiate labor from play on the basis of the futurity remuneration is unsound [...] labor cannot be defined except in terms of its demand'. Recently, in an attempt to overcome the problem of the lack of realism of the basic neoclassical theory of the labour market, Solow (1990) suggested treating labour as a *peculiar* commodity, stressing the idea that the labour market is a *social institution*. In particular, he dealt with phenomena of wage rigidity arising from the specific nature of competition among workers, especially in the segments of the labour market where reputation plays a significant role. In so doing, he found a 'no undercutting' mechanism, according to which the individual worker finds it unprofitable to compete with the other workers by accepting a lower wage in order not to lose her/his reputation. Solow's contribution aims at providing a further explanation of wage rigidities on the microeconomic plane and under the assumption of rational choice, and it falls within the neoclassical theoretical framework and, in particular, within the search for the microfoundations of macroeconomics. The idea that labour is not a good like all the other goods and that it is not necessarily a source of disutility can be expanded by considering that labour activity is strictly linked to the construction of man's *identity:* therefore, it is not only a means of survival, but also an end itself. Moreover, the view that work and leisure must be separated is also questionable (see Schmid 2004, p. 86), if one conceives the workplace also as a place for socialization. Not surprisingly, Warr (1999) finds that being unemployed is a major cause of unhappiness.

Institutional economics also conceives the market (and especially the labour market) as a social construct, but – differently from Solow's approach – the working of market mechanisms is seen as based on not purely rational choices, and income distribution does not reflect the marginal productivity of inputs. In contrast to the basic neoclassical model, it is assumed that agents have different bargaining powers, resulting from their different position in the social hierarchy. Moreover, in view of the 'old institutionalism' (Veblen, above all), not all activities are seen as productive, and 'predatory behaviours' are taken into account. Philip A. O'Hara ([1993], in Tilman 2003, vol. III, pp. 263–287) provided a rereading of Veblen's theory of income distribution based on the distinction between productive and unproductive labour. Unproductive activities (such as sales personnel, bankers and accountants) are defined in terms of their nil contribution to the production of social wealth. O'Hara develops a formal model where corn is both an input in every production process and the sole output. Wages are fixed in real terms and the surplus is generated via the operation of 'workmanship'. No 'economic law' is assumed in order to establish criteria for income distribution, and income distribution – wages apart – reflects the relative bargaining powers of bankers, businessmen and technicians. Since economic growth is driven by 'workmanship', a redistribution in favour of unproductive activities reduces the available surplus. Moreover, O'Hara (1999) shows that the higher the ratio of income from unproductive activities to productive activities is, the less inclined productive workers are to produce.

In this context, policies of labour market deregulation can produce the following effects: (i) social conflict, if – in view of the discussion in Chapter 3 – the real wage is settled above what is perceived as a *fair* wage; (ii) no changes in the employment level, since firms are interested in obtaining profits via increased prices and not via increased production; (iii) an increase in the available surplus, with ambiguous outcomes for economic growth depending on the way it is distributed between productive and unproductive activities. The policy prescriptions deriving from this model are the following:

i   The deregulation of the *market for goods*, instead of the labour market, is an effective strategy for attaining increased output and employment. In the Veblenian–institutional framework, in fact, firms tend to collude and, at the same time, to adopt strategies of monopoly pricing. As a result, output is lower than it is in a context of competition and so is employment. It is worth noting that – in this theoretical context – and as noted earlier – *scarcity of resources is not a natural phenomenon*, but – insofar as it depends on corporate strategies – it has an *institutional dimension*.

ii   The *increase* in wages, combined with a more severe regulation of the labour contract (i.e. a reduction in freedom to fire), would lead entrepreneurs to increase the available stock of capital and/or to introduce innovations, in order to obtain their 'normal' profits. In the history of economic thought, and particularly at the end of the nineteenth century in non-marginalist approaches – the 'German School' above all, and also some Italian economists (Francesco Saverio Nitti, for instance) – it is possible to find explicit references to this idea.[186] Labour market deregulation allows firms to obtain high profits by cutting wages, and policies of 'low' wages are possible as a result of the superior bargaining power of entrepreneurs. By assuming that economic growth is mainly driven by capital accumulation and innovation, this strategy is counterproductive for this purpose. By contrast, an exogenous increase in wages, determining an increase in costs and a reduction of profits, acts as an incentive for entrepreneurs to increase their effort in order to obtain at least the previous level of profits; and, in so doing, they can exploit the whole available stock of capital and/or they can introduce innovations (see Rees 1973). The first device is consistent with the Veblenian theory of the firm, where – owing to the conflict between businessmen and technicians, with the former in a position to manage pricing policies – firms obtain their normal profits via monopoly pricing, refraining from exploiting the production capacity which the existing stock of knowledge generates. Accordingly, institutional economics does not propose a scheme of income distribution where inputs are allocated efficiently. Douglass C. North (1990, p. 21) remarks, 'Efficiency [. . .] does not necessarily have the nice properties that economists give the term, but frequently is associated with group dominance at the expense of others.' Moreover, as Frank Wilkinson (1998, p. 30) observes, 'Long term costs [of deregulation] include the detrimental effects on productivity and employee commitment that accompanies increased insecurity, low morale and the creation of antagonistic, non co-operative and low trust employment system.' Deregulation can also produce an increase in social conflict, in contexts where unions are strong enough to oppose these policies (insofar as they reject them), and – as a result – it can determine a reduction in output and employment. Accordingly, while deregulation can be profitable for the *individual* firm (particularly in the case of small firms) – since the wage reductions and/or the adoption of temporary contracts do not generate conflicts in the socio-political arena (e.g. general strikes or voting against the government that supports policies of deregulation) – the overall result, in the case where *all* firms follow this strategy, is likely to be a reduction of output (and profits) deriving from strikes. Workers' (and unions') opposition to policies of labour market deregulation can be explained in view of two considerations: (i) high wages and job security are typically their main aims when bargaining with firms, and deregulation is typically seen as producing the opposite effects; (ii) deregulation can

> face fierce opposition from large or powerful sectors of society. Opposition is made worse by the recognition that the orthodox recipes ultimately call into question the social model as a whole, implying that unemployment can be cured only at the cost of a radical change.
>
> (Saint-Paul 2000, p. 1)

iii   Policies of labour market deregulation – with particular regard to flexibility of labour contracts – also involve ethical issues. This view is in sharp contrast with the neoclassical argument, based on the idea that – as seen earlier – not only do ethical issues not enter the economic discourse but it is even counterproductive to conceive economic policy on the grounds of ethical principles. While the first statement falls within methological inquiry, the second proposition pertains to the question discussed here. In the neoclassical model, and for the thesis laid out here, deregulation promotes an increase in employment and economic growth. Moreover, the Pareto optimality criterion can also apply to the case. Since deregulation increases employment, and since the increase in employment implies an increase in the utility of hired workers, it generates an improvement in the conditions of part of the population while nobody loses: thus, policies of deregulation involve a Pareto improvement.

By contrast, within the institutional theoretical framework and as shown earlier, the idea that labour is a commodity just like all other commodities is rejected and replaced by the view that labour is actually a very peculiar input owing to the very fact that it is performed by *people*. Following this line of thought, Argandoña (2002) argues that institutional changes are ethically admissible if they promote human development (see earlier discussion), and the notion of human development, in turn, is multidimensional. Guy Standing (1999, p. 376) emphasizes the following topics as the most important dimensions of corporate or government policies devoted to human development: skill reproduction security; social equity; work security (health and safety); economic equity (income security); democracy (representation security). These dimensions are, at the same time, to be respected on the microeconomic plane as well as on the social plane. He also maintains: 'Reasonable security is a necessary condition for real freedom and autonomy. Insecurity is a form of injustice and a source of it. *The distribution of security, just as much as the distribution of income, is thus an ethical issue*' (Guy Standing 1999, p. 38, italics added). The ethical aspect of lack of security emerges if one considers that job security is a precondition for human development for at least two reasons. First, temporary jobs place the individual worker under pressure of threat of dismissal, thus increasing the uncertainty about her/his future and therefore reducing the possibility of satisfying high-order needs, which is the ultimate goal of the life plan of the worker as a *person*. Second, evidence shows that job insecurity negatively affects health, and these effects seem to be more severe in a state of unemployment. Domenighetti *et al.* (2000), in particular, show that the psychosocial stress induced by job insecurity (i.e. fear of unemployment) has a negative effect on the most significant health indicators. Accordingly, not only is the possibility of human development denied, but perverse economic outcomes may result, in view of the consequent increase in public expenditure for medical care.

The 'human development' approach, initially proposed by Sen (1999) and Nussbaum (1992), mainly focuses on normative needs analysis, in view of the idea that it is possible 'to suggest minima and types of access or opportunity which each citizen must have, that can be acceptable to and/or obligatory upon any social philosophy, but beyond which they are free to differ' (Gasper 1996, p. 2). This minimum set of needs are *basic* needs and are conceived as the fundamental prerequisite for human development (see Chapter 1). Basic needs ethics, Gasper (1996, p. 24) suggests

> simply seek to establish a minimum level of capability to which all community members have claim; beyond that level basic needs ethics hand over to other types of ethic. They are deliberately restricted in scope, in order to obtain sufficient consensus in a plural society.

The set of *basic* needs includes access to safe water, health service use, education and a reasonable life expectancy. These dimensions are conceived as preconditions to allow people to reach their goals, and their goals are not included in the (neoclassical) utility function but related to a more general final end, that is, happiness. Easterlin (1995) shows that – above a given level – the increase in income determines a reduction in an index of 'happiness', and this paradox is reasonably solved by considering that high incomes are generally associated with 'relational poverty', that is, with scarce or bad social relationships. 'Relational poverty', in turn, and the consequent search for increase in personal income crucially depends on comparison with the income of others.

Moreover, one can argue that the increase in job insecurity affects competition *among workers*: the more the individual worker perceives as credible the threat of dismissal, the more she/he will tend to compete with his/her colleagues in order to reach a level of productivity which will reduce the probability of being fired[187]

(see Pacella 2005). This is a virtuous effect of deregulation on the purely economic level, insofar as it increases labour productivity. However, provided that
productivity crucially depends on teamwork, the individual's willingness to cooperate is the key variable in order to obtain high profits and a high level of growth
(see, among others, Sen [1985] in Zamagni 1995, p. 86 ff.). It also seems reasonable to expect that conflict among co-workers acts as an incentive to 'jockey for
position' within a team of workers, which, in turn, may result in 'horizontal'
mobbing activities (i.e. among co-workers). Of course, the shift from 'fair' competition to 'unfair' competition crucially depends on the individual propensity to
act 'immorally'. If one assumes that 'morality' is linked to economic and institutional variables, job insecurity is likely to 'convert' workers, giving rise to unfair
behaviour: in other words, changes in the rules governing the labour contract may
produce changes in workers' attitude towards moral values. In this case, the
'conversion effect' can be conceived as the abandoning of individual moral
beliefs in order to cope with an increase in the intensity of competition in the
event of changes of economic and institutional variables.[188]

4.5   Concluding remarks

This chapter has provided a comparison between the neoclassical and institutionalist approaches on the methodological and analytical plane and in view of their
different ethical foundations. It has been argued that the neoclassical approach
rests on the idea that agents behave rationally and freely choose their goal.
This does not mean that ethical considerations are excluded, though, implicitly,
they support the analysis on the grounds of *ethical individualism*. In contrast,
institutional economics is based on the idea that (i) ethical convictions – both for
the individual and for groups – affect economic behaviour (on the descriptive
plane) and (ii) ethics can and, as a matter of fact, do modify it (on the normative plane).

These opposed views generate contrasting analyses of the mechanisms which
underlie income distribution. In the neoclassical picture, the reward of inputs is
the outcome of a pure technical consideration, related to their supposed decreasing marginal productivity. By contrast, institutional economists emphasize the
different bargaining degrees of power of different agents and, as a consequence,
they maintain that income distribution ultimately depends on economic and political power. With particular regard to the policies of labour market deregulation, it
has been argued that the fundamental factor distinguishing the neoclassical from
the institutional analysis lies in the contrasting views on the nature of labour:
a commodity like all the others in the first case; a very peculiar input, where
psychological and ethical aspects are to be considered, in the second case. After
discussing the neoclassical policy prescription (deregulation of both the labour
market and the labour contract, in order to increase employment), and the
critiques from the Sraffian and Keynesian points of view, the institutionalist

approach to the issue is examined. By assuming the 'human development' approach as its ethical foundation, it has been argued that policies devoted to increasing job insecurity violate the fundamental principles deriving from this moral view and, moreover, may produce negative effects also in terms of efficiency – on the macroeconomic plane.

Conclusions

Does 'morality' affect income distribution? And, if so, what are the effects of the widespread adoption of ethical codes on the functioning of the labour market? Starting from these questions, this book has explored two contrasting views in the history of economic thought and in the contemporary debate: what we have called the inside-the-market and the outside-the-market approaches. They can be connected – as has been shown – with the neoclassical and the institutional theoretical frameworks, respectively, and their major (although obviously not the sole) adherents in the history of economic thought are John Bates Clark and Thorstein Veblen.

The neoclassical approach proposes the idea that (i) ethical codes are spontaneously generated and propagated via the operation of market mechanisms and (ii) economic growth produces 'moral growth'. In the absence of external interventions, this generates both an increase in income and an improvement in the 'degree of morality' (at least in the form of increasing propensity towards cooperation and solidarity) to the advantage of all agents. John Bates Clark adds the idea that, in a static economy also where markets are perfectly competitive, 'morality' (in the form of payment of 'right' wages) is spontaneously guaranteed by the corporate convenience of equalizing the average real wage to labour marginal productivity and, since marginal productivity reflects workers' *merit*, income distribution is *just*: no case of exploitation can occur. A more radical argument, within the liberal tradition, has been put forward by Hayek: the concept of social justice itself is nonsensical and it is only the search for efficiency which can promote an increase in incomes, also – although not intentionally – favouring the workers, and, – above all, favouring them more than in the event of union action.

By contrast, the institutional approach – conceived here as a line of thought opposing 'mainstream' economics – puts forward the idea that (i) ethical codes are generated through bargaining in the socio-political arena and (ii) they are established to the advantage of groups who enjoy superior bargaining power. Social conflict is likely to play a crucial role in driving institutional changes. The rereading of Veblen's contribution provided here suggests the idea that the ruling class (i.e. the 'leisure class') is able to preserve its privileges insofar as the moral and social 'value' attached to waste is accepted by workers. Efficiency – conceived as the opposite of waste – can become a socially accepted 'value' thanks to the operation of technicians and, once workers have overcome the traditional habits of thought, they can react to the existing institutional equilibrium via social conflict.

The final chapter of this book has been devoted to comparing the neoclassical and the institutional theoretical frameworks, in the light of the contrasting views on the role of ethics, rationality and income distribution. In line with the comparison between the works of John Bates Clark and Thorstein Veblen, it has been found – with particular reference to three main issues – that significant divergences exist. Schematically, they can be summarized as follows. First, the neoclassical approach is based on the rational choice paradigm, while institutional economists place great emphasis on the role of instincts, habits, customs and power relationships in determining human behaviour. Second, neoclassical economics excludes the ethical dimension from the economic discourse and – above all – rules out the possibility of stating whether the existing distribution is just or not, according to any criterion of justice at all. By contrast, the issue of justice, with particular reference to income distribution, plays a crucial role within the institutional theoretical framework, both 'from outside' (judgements expressed by external observers) and 'from inside' (judgements expressed by economic agents). Third, neoclassical and institutional economists have very different views on the effects of labour market deregulation. In the first case, this policy is conceived as effective in increasing employment, mainly because of the higher incentive for firms to hire workers at lower cost and with more freedom to fire; in the second case, it is argued that flexibility increases uncertainty and insecurity with a twofold negative effect: (i) on the ethical plane, it is argued that insecurity makes it impossible for workers to fully develop their potentiality (according to the human development approach), while also determining a reduction in their chance to increase their human capital and affecting their health; (ii) on the economic plane, and in line with the Keynesian model, it is maintained that the increase in the degree of uncertainty is likely to determine a reduction in the propensity to consume (for the sake of keeping consumption almost constant, even in the event of firing) and hence in effective demand and employment.

Notes

1 The genesis and the spread of ethical codes: the inside-the-market versus the outside-the-market approach

1 A similar case is described by Khalil (2003) in dealing with altruism: 'Why would an agent help others, when he knows that he will not meet them again or that it will not help his reputational capital?'

2 Probably the best known solution to this paradox – in the history of economic ideas – can be found in Adam Smith's *The Theory of Moral Sentiments*. As Khalil (2003) points out,

> to Smith, the reason why one acts justly is not primarily because of sympathy with the other; otherwise, one would behave unjustly because one is usually more sympathetic with his own needs. Rather, the agent acts justly mainly because of self-integrity.

Moreover, it should be noted that this paradox does not hold within a Walrasian world, where it is assumed that agents agree *ex ante* on all the relevant variables and, as a result, time is basically irrelevant.

3 A recent detailed critical reconstruction of the contemporary debate within moral philosophy has been made by Cremaschi (2005).

4 Critics of the utilitarian approach (also in the ranks of liberal scholars) emphasize that it 'overlooks the fact that the freedom to perform an act is meaningless unless the subject is in possession of the requisite means of action, and that the pratical question is one of power rather than formal freedom' (Knight 1929, p. 133).

5 The attempt to reconcile the paradigm of instrumental rationality (in the sense of utility maximization given the budget constraint, or of cost minimization given total utility) with the undeniable existence of the solidarity motive in social action is frequently made in utilitarianism (see Viano in Viano 1990, pp. 42 ff.). According to Viano (ibid., p. 43), this attempt – provided, among others, by Sidgwick (1907 [1874]) – is, however, destined to fail. This is mainly due to the fact that since Pareto optimality – accepted by Sidgwick – sets the condition that there will be an increase in social welfare only if at least one individual increases his utility without any other individual suffering a reduction in his own utility, it is based on a philosophical anthropology which, as such, rules out the possibility of goods (and/or utility) being transferred without payment. Sidgwick's theoretical operation therefore falls into an inherent contradiction, since it is logically impossible to reconcile Pareto optimality with considerations of distributive justice. See Appendix I.

6 Yeager (2001, pp. 154–155) maintains that the distinction between rule and act utilitarianism is not convincing, since – in both cases – 'results are what count'. And, in both perspectives, 'the issue is whether good results are best pursued afresh case

by case. Rules are recommended not for their own sake – not as fetishes – but for their usual good results.'

7 The principle that between two alternatives it is rational to choose the one whose worst possible outcome is better than the best possible outcome of the other.

8 To be exact, according to the so-called principle of difference, distribution differences are admitted only if they are to the advantage of less advantaged individuals.

9 It is worth noting that – in so doing – libertarians violate the principle (widely accepted, see Sumner 1984) that rights must arise *within* an ethical theory and hence cannot serve as its foundation. In other words, the statement '*A*'s rights finish when *B*'s rights start' presupposes that the intersections between *A*'s and *B*'s constitute the theoretical foundation of ethics, while rights should be defined *before* individuals interact according to ethical prescriptions or constraints.

10 In Nozick's view, this does not imply that freedom is justified on the ground of pro-ductivity, in the sense that the rights to non-aggression and non-interference pertain to every individual *independently of his/her contribution to production*. I thank Dr Francesco Biondo for this useful specification. Among economists, the idea that 'the chooser knows best', or – in different words – that the individual *alone* can estab-lish what is 'good', is mainly supported, in recent debate, by Milton Friedman (1962, p. 12): 'As liberals' – he emphasizes – 'we take freedom of the individual, or perhaps the family, as our ultimate goal in judging social arrangements [...]. Freedom has nothing to say about what an individual does with his freedom.'

11 I thank Prof. Sergio Cremaschi for this clarification. In a similar vein, Marc Fleurbaey (in Davis *et al.* 2004, p. 138) observes that 'Nozick allows for a minimal state [...], but other libertarians are more radical and would trust the market even in the presence of public goods effects such as in law and order issues'. A more complete discussion of liberal ethics will be provided in Chapter 4. Note that the emphasis on freedom is also present in the so-called capabilities approach, put forward by Amartya Sen (see, in particular, Sen 1979), whose contribution will be discussed.

12 One can argue that Christian ethics – if not ethics as a whole – finds its own founda-tions in ethics itself, or – in other words – Christian (and Catholic) ethics does not need a *speculative* theoretical background. I thank Prof. Mario Signore for this suggestion.

13 A distinct line of thought within Christian ethics is the so-called economy of com-munion project, which proposes a model of the firm with a double commitment: profit-sharing; careful management in favour of customers, workers and stakeholders ('The new horizons of economy of communion' International Convention – September 10–12, 2004). To understand how these enterprises see moral acts in the economy we can refer to three dimensions of Ricoeur's moral theory: the first dimen-sion connects everyone with their fellow 'him' or 'her', the faceless other, through innumerable links in the society where we live. In this dimension, which is not of great relevance to the economy, there is *efficiency* (a morally important goal) and *justice*. The second dimension is connected to 'you', the other with a face. Here, the climate of dialogue, respect, listening, care and sympathy is very important in work-ing activity. The third dimension is connected to 'myself'; everyone has a natural moral responsibility towards themselves. Great attention to the dimensions of 'you' and 'myself' is very important if the right personal relations are to be set up in working activities, to increase the efficiency of the production process. To understand this moral position, reference should be briefly made to the philosophical movement of Personalism, well-known in the 1950s thanks to Emmanuel Mounier. The central concept of this movement is the *Person*, analysed in all structures of the personal universe: corporeal existence (the person is body and spirit); comunication (essential experience of the person); deep conversion (the person is subjectivity, interior life); facing up (the person faces up to life to overcome the negative); freedom in all aspects of human life (freedom is affirmation of the person); supreme dignity (relation

between the person and trascendence, reason of valorization and growth of the person); commitment (the act is the person's freedom and it is identified with the economic aspect of the personal universe). Mounier maintains that the primacy of the economic dimension is a historically anomalous situation from which it is necessary to emerge: it is impossible to solve economic problems by means of economic policy *alone*. Personalism meets Marxism on this critical point: the person under liberal democracy is the subject in the political sphere, but she/he remains an object in the economic sphere. A socialist world must replace capitalism, if by socialism one means substitution of what is conceived as an anarchical economy, based on profits, with an economy based on the person's perspectives; socialization of production; development of trade-union life; the person's dignity as a worker; no division into classes according to working activity and personal income. A renewed, democratic socialism is necessary in a perspective where organizational matters and human matters are inseparable.

14 A crucial question arises in this context, that is – according to Kamenka (1972, pp. 97–98):

> What, then, can a determinist make of freedom? The young Marx, following a line laid down in Spinoza and Hegel, treats freedom as self-determination [...]. The difficulty here strikes at the very heart of Marx's position. The self-determined can have neither history nor environment [...]. To speak of self-determined is to assert that the effect was its own cause; that is, to say that there has been no 'change'.

15 A similar thesis was put forward by the so-called Ricardian (or anti-Ricardian) socialists: Ravenstone, Hodgskin, Gray, Bray among others (see Lowenthal, 1911). By opposing the Ricardian idea that profits, wages and rents would tend, in the long run, to their 'natural' rate, they maintained that the 'best' distribution of income occurs when workers receive the whole social product. The rationale for this argument lies in the conviction that human labour is the *only* producer of value. Hence, the labour theory of value generates the normative argument that – because only labour produces wealth – it is *just* that the whole product is devoted to labour. Zagari (1991, p. 289) emphasizes the relevance of the contribution of the (anti)Ricardian socialists on purely economic grounds, with particular reference to their analysis of the role of 'aggregate demand' in generating increase in employment, but also notes that – at least in some cases – they tend to justify their policy prescription on 'giusnaturalistic' grounds.

16 David A. Collard ([1983] in Zamagni 1995, p. 234) expands this argument within the economic discourse by emphasizing that 'In economics we may say that an individual's strategy follows the Kantian rule if, when also adopted by others in relevant groups, it may be expected to lead to a preferred social state.'

17 Critiques of Kantian approaches, with particular reference to his supposed confusion between instrumental and ultimate ends, have been put forward, among others, by Hazlitt (1964, ch. 16).

18 This view has been strongly criticized, among others, by T. W. Adorno (see text), in *Negative Dialektik* (1966), particularly on the success of moral will and Kantian optimism towards the supremacy of ethics of decision: according to Adorno 'the survival principle', 'the vital impetus' and 'the death fear' play a different role from the role shown in Kant's example (in his *Kritik der praktischen Vernunft*) where he maintains that a moral man prefers to die rather than accuse an honest man unjustly. This behaviour follows from freedom, unknown for Kantian man without moral law. In contrast, Adorno affirms that the moral *ego* cannot rule the psychological *ego*.

19 The idea that moral norms reflect social interaction, involving the sense of duty, has been proposed by Andreoni (1990). He argues that actions which involve costs and apparently do not generate utility can be explained by a 'warm-glowing' effect, that is, the utility individuals enjoy by respecting their sense of duty. The notion of 'warm glow' can be used to explain the theoretical problem of why, in some circumstances,

agents do not act as 'free-riders' and, hence, they do not behave in an opportunistic way, although they could. According to Khalil (2003), however, this explanation cannot show the right thing to do because 'warm glow' is a *by-product* of doing the right thing.

20 The issue is extensively explored in Porta *et al.* (2001), among others.

21 A variant of this approach is the so-called gift-exchange scheme (see Akerlof and Yellen 1986). It is argued that, in some circumstances and with particular reference to labour relationships, agents who feel grateful for a gift received tend to reciprocate. This behaviour involves a moral code, insofar as each agent bears a cost without the expectation of a benefit. In the wide debate on this topic, two main theoretical problems are (i) What ensures that agents *want* to reciprocate? and (ii) What ensures that – even if they want to – they *can* reciprocate? See, among others, Zamagni (1995).

22 The idea that moral norms have a social dimension has been recently re-proposed by Fisscher *et al.* (2003). By contrast, Gick (2003) – following Hayek (1952) – derives moral codes from the evolution and change of 'individual perception' and 'action'. In particular, in response to a stimulus the individual carries out an action; if the action leads to the expected result, the stimulus will be repeated, as will the action. Finally, if this feedback continues positively for some time, the individual will produce a *private* moral rule.

23 The main objection to this view is based on an argument proposed by Ruse (1990, p. 65), which states that *has evolved* does not mean or imply *is good*. In other words, ethical values cannot be derived from evolution and hence the concept of civilization should be regarded – for this purpose – as nonsensical.

24 The debate on the nature of *moral* norms is also linked to the debate on the effects of *religion* on economic development. The theories of Max Weber and Michael Novak will be summarized in what follows. In *Die Protestantische Ethik und der Geist des Kapitalismus* (1904–05) Max Weber maintains that capitalism owes its driving force, the pursuit of profits independent of personal utility, and the conscience of professional as well as moral duty, to Calvinistic ethics. He contrasts 'responsibility ethics' – interested in future acts – to Kantian ethics of intention, but neither can this moral theory see its way clear in political struggle, where there is an entrenched clash of values. The pursuit of profits is not an end in itself, but a means by which to serve God. Capitalism identifies itself with the pursuit of profits; the typical mindset in the capitalist system drives individuals (i.e. entrepreneurs) to pursue profits. According to Weber economic development is guaranteed by the diffusion of Protestant ethics, closer than Catholic ethics to materialistic attitudes; however, it is impossible to affirm that capitalistic economic development follows solely religious factors. Weber, 'the Marx of the Middle class', maintains the importance of the middle class to the development of modern capitalism. A very important concept is that of the Calling (*Beruf*), which means that, for humanity to earn God's blessing, it must not overindulge in mystical monastic practice, but must perform intra-worldly duties typical of the individual professions. Protestant intra-worldly mystical practice violently opposes the carefree pleasure of possession, restricts luxury consumption and rids money-making activity of the inhibitions of traditionalist ethics. The 'rational' use of resources is, therefore, conceived as the opposite of avidity, and excludes love of possessions and working to earn. A different view on this topic has been put forward by Michael Novak. In his *Catholic Ethic and the Spirit of Capitalism* (1993), he affirms that the foundation of a capitalistic society is a moral, spiritual and religious foundation. In 1904 Max Weber tried to draw attention to this matter but – according to Novak – Weber's treatment fails to capture the very nature of modern capitalism and to formulate the Catholic Ethic. According to Novak, although Weber has correctly emphasized the religious and moral dimension of man and has identified the cause of Marxism's failure in its materialistic approach, his thesis has numerous weak points. First and foremost, Weber's definition of the Protestant ethic is not expounded clearly and bases itself on a common opinion of the European situation at the end of the nineteenth century, when Protestant countries of northern Europe had

a high level of industrialization and prosperity. With the term 'Protestant' Weber does not refer to the Anglican or Lutheran tradition: with this term he means 'Calvinist' or more exactly 'puritan'. In conclusion, according to Novak, Weber sets out to affirm an anti-Christian attitude: to tend to an accumulation of goods not as a means to attain other ends, but as an end itself, like the discipline of abnegation. Moreover, Weber underlines the importance of three further characteristics which are the foundations of a new morality, based on a sober life: the sense of duty, mystical religious practice and the concept of the Calling (*Beruf*). Nevertheless, Novak remarks, the attitudes that Weber calls 'Protestant' are shared by Calvinism and by other religious creeds. Modern Calvinists do not recognize themselves in Weber's theses. In fact, after Calvin's death and for some generations, in Geneva Calvinists did not establish credit banks, forbade loans at interest and investments of capital. In conclusion, the Weberian 'philosophy of avidity' – it is argued – is too extreme an argument to be a plausible example of the capitalistic ethic in practical life. Weber has rightly identified in capitalism a moral and cultural dimension, he has discovered a new cultural climate and spiritual attitude (*Geist*), social attitudes and practical discipline: self-sacrifice and the submitting of passions and pleasures to rigorous mental discipline. The heart of Capitalism is discovery, innovation and inventive power. Novak underlines the connection between capitalism and human creative ability, the crucial point – in his view – of Catholic ethics.

25 This is not the place to evaluate the differences between Sen's and Nussbaum's views, but it is useful to draw attention to Nussbaum's suggestion (which is not explicit in the works of Sen) of drawing up a list of basic capabilities.

26 It is important to stress that this does not mean that the economic approach to ethics does not rest on specific moral views. Although the dominant position falls within the utilitarian approach, Kantian ethics is at the basis of some economic theories on the 'social responsibility of firms', and many economic theories on non-profit organizations are based on Christian (or Catholic) ethics. I thank Prof. Stefano Zamagni for pointing this out.

27 Following this line of thought, Nicola Abbagnano (1971) suggests defining a norm as a rule or judgement criterion. The norm can derive from an actual case, a model or an example, but the actual case, the model or the example are norms if they can be considered as judgement criteria for other cases, or for things connected with the model or the example. The norm is different from the moral maxim because it is not solely a rule of conduct, but can be a rule or criterion for other operations or activities. And the norm is different from the moral law because it has no public sanction.

28 The social and economic dimension is not absent in moral philosophy, particularly in the contemporary debate, although it can produce two problems: first, if all moral norms – resulting from social dynamics in different cultures – are admissible, then this results in a relativist solution; second, when social facts are conceived as the basis for the formulation of moral principles, 'Hume's law' applies, that is, the logical impossibility of deriving 'ought' from 'is'. See Cremaschi (2005, pp. 55 ff. and 75 ff.).

29 Greer (2000, p. 53) maintains that 'the acceptance of an orthodox economic theory of *laissez-faire* implies an acceptance of an inherent 'goodness' of man, such that the economic decisions made by individuals are not made at the expense of other members of society'.

30 It is also necessary to assume that both individuals have a critical value of their intertemporal discount rate and that the probability of meeting again is quite high (see Costabile 1998, p. 19).

31 Following Costabile (2004), this theory falls within a conventionalist ethics, based on the idea that moral norms come to be established as *conventions*.

32 Bicchieri (1993, pp. 247 ff.) suggests that – within an evolutionary context – *learning* in strategic interaction may give rise, at the same time, to the acceptance of a code of behaviour in small groups and to its gradual spread to the whole population, if the

number of repetitions is sufficiently large. The key assumption underlying this theory is that (ibid., p. 231) 'a norm is there *because* everyone expects everyone else to conform, and each knows he is expected to conform, too', so that 'a norm is an equilibrium that is supported by a configuration of self-fulfilling expectations'. However, Bicchieri herself admits that this theory is unable to provide an explanation of the origin of individual expectations on rational bases and hence, in order to explain the origin of codes of behaviour in a *spontaneous order* approach, expectations must be assumed as given.

33 As a matter of fact, individual deviation from socially accepted moral norms produces different value judgements in relation to the (unforeseen) outcomes of individual behaviour. Consider, for instance, the case where individual A drives a car while drunk: if A kills someone, the 'weight' of social disapproval will be enormously higher than if driving a car while drunk produces no damages for A or for others.

34 For instance, if the reader wanted to memorize this text during his sleep to avoid the tedium of reading it, she/he might *wish* for a device that would enable her/him to memorize it, but she/he could not express a *demand*, since – at the time of writing – such a device simply does not exist (or if it exists, it is not on sale).

35 It is useful to recall the Keynesian definition of uncertainty: 'by uncertain [...] I do not mean merely to distinguish what is known for certain from what is only probable [but also what is unknown because] we simply do not know it' (Keynes 1973 [1936], p. 113). The issue will be discussed in Chapter 4.

36 Although this is not the place to explore Keynesian ethics, some considerations are worth noting. Undoubtedly, Keynes' economics is not a mere technicality but rests on deep philosophical, ethical and political grounds. However, while this thesis is widely accepted, there is no common interpretation at least on two basic issues: (i) the continuity of Keynes' convictions and (ii) his concept of morality. In what follows, the main arguments will be presented on these issues. In the influential book by O'Donnell (1989) it is argued that Keynes viewed history as intrinsically progressive and incessantly moving towards a higher goal. More precisely, O'Donnell maintains that, for Keynes, 'history has an evolutionary side, correcting its mistakes and proceeding towards greater understanding and higher degree of rationality' (p. 44). In this process, two obstacles are in operation: first, the purely economic problem; second, and more important, the moral problem. The first obstacle can be overcome *via* a strategy of managed capitalism, which would lead – in the very long run – to a dramatic increase in the average living standard. The second problem is related to the moral degradation of society, that is, the 'love of money' or the money-making passion. In this sense, following O'Donnell, capitalism is seen by Keynes as morally repugnant, although necessary for the time. His positive attitude towards the ability of human intelligence to correct mistakes and his belief in an enlightened bureaucracy (unlike Weber) leads him to think that the ultimate goal of a society is an *ethical–rational state*, where economic security is assured for each individual. O'Donnell (1989) also stresses the continuity in Keynes' thought, not only in the field of economics, but also in the matter of ethics. Furthermore, these two branches are strictly linked and the main signs of the continuity can be traced in (i) his theory of probability (elaborated from 1914 to 1921), which is the unifying centre of his whole work, and (ii) his methodology, that is, the view that economics is a means to achieve the ultimate ethical–political goal of ensuring the common good. J. E. King (2002, p. 182) recalls the Keynesian conviction that 'the study of economic behaviour was worthwhile only because it enabled informed and ethically defensible decisions to be made by politicians', and maintains that this conviction should be regarded as a key issue in the whole of Keynesian thought. By contrast, Davis (1991) argues that both in economic theory and in philosophical reflections, Keynes often changed his mind. This seems to be particularly applied to the shift from his early contrast with Moore's ethics – which lead him to theorize 'immoralism' – to his mature idea of the need to

pursue a common good. According to Holt (1998), in Keynes' view, what is good cannot be decided by individuals, but by the state. The argument is that – in a context where individuals have different bargaining powers – if public policies do not help define, say, labour relation laws, then firms' policies will define them for society.

37 Schematically, uncertainty can be regarded in the light of the following classifications: (i) *objective* uncertainty, that is, uncertainty, which is a realistic feature of future events and which cannot be removed because 'there is no scientific basis on which to form any calculable probability whatever; we simply do not know it' (Keynes 1973 [1937], pp. 113–114; see also Keynes 1971 [1926], p. 291; Keynes 1973 [1921]) and (ii) *perceived* uncertainty, where uncertainty is assumed as a 'fictitious' property of reality, in the sense that each event is not uncertain for itself but only for individuals. In this case uncertainty is only relative because of the lack of knowledge about the system that regulates the working of events whose perfect knowledge would lead to the achievement of certainty (see Knight 1971 [1921]). I thank Dr Andrea Pacella for drawing my attention to this issue. See also Chapter 4.

38 By contrast with the neoclassical picture, it is maintained here that scarcity of resources does not always and does not necessarily have an *objective* dimension (and, at the same time, it is not necessarily an *exogenous* scarcity, that is, deriving from natural constraints, see Chapter 4). Scarcity of resources is likely to depend (also) on power relationships and, particularly, on corporate price and wage policies in non-competitive markets.

39 This argument can be linked to Frank Knight's assumption (1960, p. 13) that education can make people 'more critical, less romantic' and, in this sense, it can facilitate 'intelligent' actions, that is, actions based on the knowledge of 'what is right, or best, not for the individual, but for society' (Greer 2000, p. 81).

40 Notice that, in this theoretical context, the increase in per-capita income can be considered a fact, in cases where, with no outside intervention, capitalism is seen as a self-propelling system capable of generating growth (and development) thanks solely to the operation of market mechanisms.

41 According to Maslow (1970), there are general types of needs (physiological, safety, love and esteem) that must be satisfied before a person can act *unselfishly*. He called these needs 'deficiency needs'. As long as we are motivated to satisfy these cravings, individuals are moving towards growth, towards self-actualization. In this perspective, actions devoted to causing damage to others (e.g. violence) are not the result of a natural propensity: they emerge in cases where individuals face constraints in satisfying their 'primary' needs.

42 An extensive discussion of Smith's approach to 'sympathy' is provided by Porta *et al.* (2001). See also the bibliography quoted there.

43 In *WN*, the conflict/cooperation dichotomy – which, in a sense, reflects the 'rapacity'/ 'prudence' dichotomy in *TMS* and in the debate with Jeremy Bentham (see Pesciarelli 1991) – is solved in the short/long-run dichotomy. In wage-bargaining – Smith argues – both parties know that, in the long term, they need to cooperate, while conflict prevails in the short term: 'In the long run the workman may be as necessary to his master as his master is to him' (Smith 1976a, p. 84).

44 The same conclusion is reached by Buchanan (1992), with specific reference to Smith's analysis of labour supply.

45 'No society can surely be flourishing and happy, of which the far greater part of the members are poor and miserable' (Smith 1976a, p. 96).

46 Here referring to the difference in the growth rates of labour demand and labour supply.

47 I thank Prof. Stefano Zamagni for drawing my attention to this issue. See S. Zamagni, *L'ancoraggio etico della responsabilità sociale d'impresa e la critica alla RSI*, mimeo 2005.

48 This theory derives from a rereading of Sidney and Beatrice Webb's *Industrial Democracy* (S. and B. Webb 1919b). Consistent with the earlier picture, they advocated union action and/or public intervention in view of the following arguments: (i) assuming that high wages increase labour productivity and demand, the prevalence of the unscrupulous entrepreneurs would lead to a volume of output lower than its potential value; (ii) state intervention – insofar as it is benefical to benevolent entrepreneurs – allows the spread of fair codes of behaviour. The Webbs' analysis will be further discussed in Appendix II.

49 An example might be the following. Take a worker 'abused' by his/her employer, who forces him/her for instance to do tasks unconnected to his/her position. The worker can experience an intolerance effect and react by, for instance, refusing to carry out the tasks. In this case he obviously risks retaliation (e.g. being fired). Therefore, the greater the psychological damage suffered and the more willing she/he is to take the risk of being fired, the more rapid and intense will his/her reaction be. Income distribution is likely to affect the timing and intensity of the reaction, owing to its effects on the degree of solidarity among weaker (i.e. 'poor') agents and hence on the individual propensity to risk.

50 Note that – following Sen (1987b) – the less chance people have of changing their lifestyle, the less they perceive their own poverty. The effects of the increase in advertising expenditure on income distribution will be discussed in Chapter 3.

51 It is also assumed that the choice to vote party x or y depends only on the monetary gains they are able to offer the individual citizen, both in the case of *past* improvement of living standards and in the case of its reasonable expectation, and that the number of workers is high enough to affect the outcome of elections.

52 This assumption can be relaxed, with no significant changes in the results of the schema proposed here, by accepting the idea that unemployed workers support deregulation. See Saint-Paul (2000).

53 In this context, one does not need a definite theory of union action; it is only assumed that union action, if successful, determines an increase in the average real wage, independently of the fact that – as stated in labour economics – unions maximize the expected utility of their members or maximize membership (see, among others, Pemberton 1988).

54 In his *A Theory of the Business Cycle* (1937), M. Kalecki found a similar result, arguing that taxation of capital – although profitable for economic growth – is normally opposed by capitalists, able to orient economic policy.

55 This is not the place to discuss the problem of free-riding which can occur in the individual decision of whether to join the union. It may be sufficient to recall the seminal work by Converse (1969), who argues that – in both the political and social arena – free-rider problems do not occur when there is strong 'partisan identification', which, in turn, depends on the learning process through participation in democratic institutions. Differences in partisan stability are explained in terms of different 'civic cultures'.

56 In anthropological terms, conflict may be seen as a 'struggle for recognition'. The issue is extensively explored by Axel Honneth (1996).

57 For the reasons that will be discussed in Chapter 4, job insecurity can be conceived as a form of 'unfairness'.

58 In this context, voting is not the result of a purely rational choice. The issue is discussed in Chapter 4.

59 The desired ('just') wage, giving rise to the most efficient macroeconomic outcome, should be such as to determine in – via consumption and effective demand – a full employment equilibrium.

60 In line with the discussion earlier, he also maintains (North 1990, p. 104) that 'Long-run economic change is the cumulative consequence of innumerable short-run decisions by political and economic entrepreneurs that both directly and indirectly (via external effects) shape performance'.

61 Jack Knight (1992, p. 16) convincingly points out that 'Social conflict implies the interaction among intentional actors who have competing interests in [social] outcomes.'

62 Altruism can be defined *prima facie* as an attitude to benefit other(s) without requiring payment. However, this definition cannot be used without referring to some theory of altruistic behaviour. In particular, three main problems arise. First, as Rand (1964) argues, altruists can be seen as 'irrational' *heroes*, who sacrifice themselves for no other reason than the well-being of others. Second, if – in contrast – altruistic behaviour is assumed to be based on reciprocity (Peter Singer 1982), it should be recognized that reciprocity is not necessarily always in operation, since 'reciprocators' may not *want* or may be *unable* to reciprocate. Third, as Yeager (2001, p. 159) notes, altruistic behaviour may be the outcome of 'the invitation to hypocrisy'; an example might be – in some circumstances – Christmas presents.

63 This terminology was proposed by Edgeworth.

64 For a clear and complete reconstruction of the debate, see Schneider (1974).

65 Preferences of *A* and *B* modify when they interact. In this context, 'I want to do x' means 'If I were alone (or non-altruist), I would do x'. Note also that the case described here concerns simultaneous consumption of a good/service. The paradox can also be extended to the case of exchanges of goods/services.

66 A similar result, obtained by assuming incomplete information, is reported by Bicchieri (1993, p. 214), with reference to what she names *the lover's paradox*. In a similar vein, Bernheim and Stark (1988) find a paradoxical result in the case where lovers (*A* the woman and *B* the man) are perfectly altruistic: if *A* suffers (owing to external causes), she will prefer him *not* to behave in an altruistic way, since – in this case – her level of utility will be greater than if he shares her suffering. For a criticism of this paradox, see Guy (in Sacco and Zamagni (2002), pp. 22 ff.).

67 On this theme, see Easterlin (2002).

68 A similar idea has been proposed by Brand Blanshard (1980, p. 295): 'To prize one's own happiness and be indifferent to another's is a clear case of irrationality'.

69 In more general terms, Paul A. Samuelson (*Journal of Political Economy*, 1958, quoted in Zamagni 1995 p. xv) wrote:

> Reverence for life, in Schweitzer's sense of respecting ants and flowers, might be a handicap in the Darwinian struggle for existence. But a culture where altruism abounds – because men do not think to behave like atomistic competitors or because men have by custom and law entered into binding social contracts – may have great survival and expansion powers.

70 See Steinberg (2004).

71 For this effect to be in operation, the propensity to consume on the part of the altruist must be lower than the propensity to consume on the part of the individuals who benefit; this is a recurrent assumption in post-Keynesian theories.

72 One the major representatives of this view, in the 1800s, is Samuel Smiles, especially in the work *Self-help* (London, 1859).

73 In his seminal book on *The Gift Relationship*, Titmuss (1973 [1970], p. 101) maintains that altruism can be conceived as a special case of interest: 'No donor type can, of course, be said to be characterized by complete, disinterested, spontaneous altruism [...] some expectation and assurance that a return gift may be needed and received at some future time.'

74 The name 'Fabian' or 'Fabianism' derives from the name of the Roman general Quintus Fabius, well known from the wars against Hannibal (see Minion 2000).

75 The dramatic conditions of workers of the period – with particular reference to 'sweating' – are described by Hobsbawm (1968, p. 93), who also refers to Booth's classical study on urban misery (p. 160). The role of the Webbs in the Edwardian tournament, which led to the Royal Commission on the Poor Laws of 1905–09, is explored by McBriar (1987).

76 For textual evidence, see Bland (1906); Besant (1886); Beveridge (1909); Cole (1918a, 1918b, 1920a, 1920b, 1920c, 1922, 1923a, 1923b, 1925, 1932, 1933, 1934); Olivier (1906); Shaw (1891, 1892, 1896, 1900, 1928, 1930); Wallas (1910).

77 The 'Preface' of *Industrial Democracy* is highly significant in this respect. The Webbs stress that (i) the 'primary task' of a scholar is 'to observe and dissect facts'; (ii) scientific discourse is composed of 'description of facts, generalizations, and moral judgements'.

78 In fact, before the publication of *Industrial Democracy* – considered their major work, aimed at giving a 'scientific analysis of Trade Unionism' (p. v), and the work this appendix will mainly examine – they published the *History of Trade Unionism* (1894) (S. and B. Webb 1919a), where, on the basis of the available data, they traced the origin and development of the trade union movement. A similar line of research is in S. and B. Webb (1936).

79 It should be recognized that more sophisticated versions of this theory were put forward by the classical authors, taking capitalists' consumption into consideration. See Forges Davanzati (2002).

80 So that there were no scientific grounds for supporting union action. As Hobsbawm (1968, p. 122) argues:

> Trade Unions were seen as either doomed to almost immediate failure, or as engines of economic catastrophe. Though they ceased to be illegal in 1824, every effort was made to destroy them where possible [...] [But] thanks to the efforts of the Philosophical Radicals, who argued that, if legal, their total uneffectiveness must soon become obvious, and the workers would therefore cease to be tempted by them.

81 With reference to Jevons's critique of the wages fund theory, see Forges Davanzati (1995).

82 A further argument can be traced in the neoclassical interpretation of the wages fund theory as being elementary on the analytical plane, in view of their more refined theory of labour demand.

83 As they clearly state, 'the theory [...] left no room for any elevation of the wage-earners even if the improvement justified itself by an increase in productive capacity' (S. and B. Webb 1919b, p. 607).

84 A reconstruction of the debate on the 'wage question' – with particular reference to the period between the end of the nineteenth century and the beginning of the twentieth century – has been provided by Forges Davanzati (1999).

85 As Mattew (2004, p. 410) remarks

> education became one of the key priorities for the 'National Efficiency' [in the Webbs' view. In particular] compulsory education was one of the elements in their project of a 'National Minimum': a set of standards below which no citizen should be allowed to fall.

86 BE's rationality, and his/her interest in long-run profits, is considered, by the Webbs, a minor feature. In approaching the question, they underline that the whole discussion on the nature and the aims of the benevolent entrepreneurs is 'Apart from these mere considerations of self-interest' (ibid., p. 662). On the other side, if BE were rational and had foresight there would be no space for competition, since she/he would pay high wages *independently of competitors' strategy*.

87 '[Human] actions [...]' – he writes (Olivier 1889, pp. 107–111) – 'are approved as moral [if they] tend to preserve the existence of society and the cohesion and convenience of its members'. He also argues (ibid., p. 112) that each individual acts to satisfy desires – which he splits into primary desires ('material needs') and secondary desires ('[the desires of] civilization [such as] art, culture, human intercourse, love') – and that the impossibility of satisfying these needs determines a lack of motivation on the part of workers.

88 For instance, the increase in prison costs following the increase in violence. In the *Fabian Essays*, G. B. Shaw describes a very peculiar form of conflict. In ordinary life, outside the workplace – he observes – entrepreneurs (i.e. the rich) try to avoid meeting workers (i.e. the poor), insofar as looking at suffering (or even at unrefined) people generates irritation. However, this process is costly, considering that the main means of reducing irritation is by giving alms (or even creating 'barriers to entry' in wealthy parts of the town). Note that – following this argument – capitalists have a double-sided behaviour: they are pure self-interested agents when they are capitalists and self-interested 'altruists' when they are citizens.

89 A further consequence is a reduction in the incentive to invest in innovation, since profits are now more easily made via wage cuts, and a fall in labour productivity. Accordingly, a rise in wages promotes high effort – on the part of the entrepreneurs – in order to avoid a reduction in their profits (ibid., p. 621 and also S. Webb 1912a, p. 982).

90 Promoting human capital accumulation (and hence an increase in labour productivity), in particular, is not profitable for the individual firm, insofar as it is a public good, which can be transferred – via labour mobility – from one firm to another. It is also worth noting that the claim for more education is a central theme in the Webbs' case. In this respect, one can recall that – also for other purposes (i.e. in order to promote the study of economic theory according to a 'heterodox approach') – they helped to found the London School of Economics (1895).

91 As the Webbs note, this may be true only in the very extreme case of a strike which makes it impossible for the firm to survive.

92 Two further arguments are presented to support this view. First, in the case of firing, the individual worker has to search for a new job in other cities or countries, in most cases, with consequent high psychological and financial costs. Second, he experiences a loss of reputation, insofar as firing is perceived socially as a signal of low productivity.

93 On the ways unions can raise funds to sustain workers – and on the possible conflicts in allocating them – see *Industrial Democracy*, ch. XII.

94 In this chapter, the Webbs deal with the question of competition among unions, noticing that each union tends to use different methods in order to enforce it and that, in this context, the outcome of wage bargaining depends on traditions and customs prevailing in local contexts.

95 It is worth noting that, in the Fabians' view, unions also promote *civil* growth, via education of the membership. As Olivier argues: unions are also responsible for 'moral education of individuals [who must] learn how to provide for the needs of bodily life in a manner that will not interfere with the freedom of the others to do the same'.

96 On the other hand, unemployment is an unavoidable evil of the capitalist system, where UE prevails, owing to its tendency to generate business cycles (ibid., p. 784), and, above all, owing to the employers' discipline device, that is, stipulating short-term contracts in order to create, when needed, a 'reserve army', necessary, in turn, to cut wages (ibid., p. 435). The existence of the *reserve army* – following the Webbs' analysis – is a further condition for a rational intervention by the state. In fact, the existence of unemployment allows firms to cut wages; this determines a reduction in aggregate demand and hence the necessity of public intervention to reach full employment. The Webbs report that the discontinuity of employment is convenient not only for firms, but also for (purely self-interested) unions. In fact, in the opposite case (i.e. long-term contracts), workers would increase their bargaining power and, for this very reason, would not need to enter the union.

97 As Sidney and Beatrice Webb write: 'A Trade Union [...] is a continuous association of wage earners for the purpose of improving the conditions of their employment' (Webb, S. and Webb, B. 1919a, p. 1).

98 In the minority report of the poor law commission that also describes the real labour conditions of workers in England between the 1800s and 1900s, and particularly in the section entitled 'Distress from Unemployment', the Webbs provide a classification of the types of unemployment: (i) *men from permanent situation* (unskilled workers), (ii) *men of discontinuous employment* (occasional workers), (iii) *the underemployed* (manual workers), (iv) the *unemployable* (invalids) (S. and B. Webb 1932, pp. 164–211).

99 They refer only to 'excessive claims' (ibid., p. 813 and *passim*).

100 Note that this interpretation is not in contrast with the Webbs' support for a gradual passage to socialism: while workers' conditions may improve via union action, the *prius* (i.e. the precondition for unions to emerge) is to be traced in increasing worker discontent.

101 This definition appears to be very close to Amartya Sen's concept of capability, conceived as the '[liberty] to lead freer and more worthwhile lives, [i.e.] freedom to live the kind of lives that people have reason to value'. This freedom is influenced by 'social development', that is, by 'all factors that causally influence the effective freedom that people actually enjoy, [such as] education, healthcare [and] medical attention' (Sen 1997, 1999, p. 1960).

102 The problems relating to the internal organization of the worker-managed firms (above all, the question of the right to vote attributable to workers themselves) are discussed, in particular, in S. and B. Webb (1921, pp. 39 ff.).

103 A similar view has been put forward – in the contemporary debate – by Bowles *et al.* (1993).

2 John Bates Clark: moral norms and the labour market in neoclassical economics

104 Tobin (1985) provides a detailed and very useful reconstruction on the spread of neoclassical economics in America.

105 After graduating from Amherst College in 1875, John Bates Clark (1847–1938) went to Germany, where he studied under Karl Knies in Heidelberg. On returning to the United States, Clark taught economics and history, in particular, at Carleton, Smith and Amherst colleges before coming into contact with graduate students at Johns Hopkins. In 1885 he helped found the American Economic Association, serving as its president (1893–95). In 1895, Clark finally achieved a post at Columbia University. According to Schumpeter, he was one of the discoverers of the neoclassical marginal approach and 'architect of one of its most significant theoretical structures'. As one of few American economists of the Marginalist School and a prominent apologist for the capitalist system, John Bates Clark was a great opponent of the Institutionalist School – and, therefore, became one of Thorstein Veblen's favourite targets. See Clark and Clark (1938).

106 Clark maintains that capital should be regarded as including only concrete, mechanical articles ('capital goods'), and rejects both the idea that capital is the fund devoted to paying workers and the idea that capital is money. In this respect, the critique by Veblen (1972 [1909], p. 181) is worth noting. He finds a contradiction between Clark's concept of capital and his treatment of capital mobility:

> it is plain that the 'transfer of capital' contemplated is a shift in investment and that it is, as indeed Mr. Clark indicates, not a matter of the mechanical shifting of physical bodies from one industry to the other. To speak of a transfer of 'capital' which does not involve a transfer of 'capital goods' is a contradiction of the main position that 'capital' is made up of 'capital goods'.

107 'Both production and distribution' – Clark (1883, p. 358) writes – 'ordinarily take place, not by a single operation, but by a succession of many. One producer begins

with crude nature, and so modifies it as but partially to prepare it for rendering its service to men; another and another continue the operation'.

108 '*The pay of labor in each industry tends to conform to the marginal product of social labor employed in connection with a fixed amount of social capital, as such*' (Clark 1965 [1899], ch. 9). In analytical terms, assume that firms maximize profits (P), that the unitary (real) wage (w) is given – in a context of perfect competition – and that production is a positive function of labour: $Q = f(L)$, with $f' > 0$ and $f'' < 0$. The profit function is: $P = f(L) - wL$ and its first derivative is $f'(L) - w$. Therefore, profits are at a maximum when $f'(L) = w$, and $f'(L)$ is labour marginal productivity.

109 This assumption has aroused extensive debate and this is not the place to discuss the whole controversy. In outline, one can approach the question in two distinct ways. First (the pure neoclassical view): the order of entry of workers into the production process is irrelevant. If workers A, B and C are homogeneous, and they are applied on a given quantity of land (or capital), when A is the 'first' she/he gives the maximum productivity. Otherwise, when B is the first, A gives a lower productivity. In other words, according to this approach, it is always *theoretically* possible to 'reshuffle' the order of entry, so that there is no definite way of identifying who is the 'first'. A second (non-neoclassical) approach assumes that A is *always* the first. Hence, owing to his/her higher productivity, the equilibrium condition implies paying him/her a wage higher than that of B, whose marginal productivity is lower. Therefore, wage differential emerges from the order of entry. On these issues, see, in particular, Robinson (1934) and Samuelson (1962). It should be noted that Clark is not always clear on this issue.

110 These assumptions may give rise to a theoretical problem regarding the *contemporary* neoclassical theory. If one considers that (i) production requires effort (e), and the willingness to work (i.e. effort itself) is the necessary condition for production not to be nil; (ii) Each worker knows the real wage she/he will receive *when she/he begins to work* and can choose the level of effort to be provided, and wages are paid *ex post* (see Graziani 1977, Glazer 2002, p. 5); (iii) Full employment exists, so that the threat of dismissal is not effective, then while workers *can* use the available capital, what ensures that they *do so*?

111 While the first statement (capital *is* a value) can be conceived as a theory of capital, the second statement (capital *has* a value) is a truism, since all goods – both inputs and outputs – have a value.

112 The wages fund theory is described and discussed in, Appendix II.

113 In his *Biography of Eugene Böhm-Bawerk* ('Ludwig von Mises Institute'), Roger W. Garrison observes:

> Formal or informal, the message is clear: An expansion of the capital structure is not to be viewed as a simultaneous and equiproportional increase in capital in each of the maturity classes; it is to be viewed as a reallocation of capital among the maturity classes. Overlooked by his predecessors and largely ignored by the modern mainstream, this is the market mechanism that keeps the economy's intertemporal production plans in line with the intertemporal preferences of consumers. The significance of this market mechanism was at issue in his debate with John B. Clark, who held that once capital is in place, the maintenance of capital is automatic and that production and consumption are, in effect, simultaneous. Although a modern reader may conclude that Böhm-Bawerk won the debate and that in later years Hayek was similarly victorious in his debate with Frank Knight, the development of mainstream macroeconomics reflects the implicit belief that it was Clark and Knight who won.

114 As Maurandi (2001, p. 100) points out, Clark's analysis lacks an assumption regarding labour supply. This leads Maurandi to argue that Clark's theory of the labour market does not allow us to determine the prices of inputs.

115 G. B. Shaw's critique of Clark's theory is also worth noting. He finds the main problem to be determining the contribution of the *individual* worker when the final output is the result of the joint effort of many workers and capital. In his own words: '[T]hat of giving to every person exactly what he or she has made by his or her labour, seems fair; but when we try to put it into practice we discover, first, that it is quite impossible to find out how much each person has produced' (Shaw, 1928, p. 21). Many economists have criticized Clark's view and the whole neoclassical theory on this point. See, in particular, Pullen (2001). John Bates Clark's son, John Maurice, although not explictly criticizing his father's thought, also raised some doubts (see Fiorito 2000).

116 Henry (1994, p. 110) is more sceptical in this respect, arguing that the origins of moral norms remain 'unspecified' in Clark's works.

117 Here defined as he who respects the code of 'equal exchange'.

118 A similar argument has been put forward, more recently, by many economists and philosophers (see, among others, Hansson and Stuart 1992). They show that agents who share genetically fixed 'altruistic' preferences have a competitive advantage simply because they behave cooperatively. See Appendix I.

119 On the basis of this argument, Prasch's (2002, p. 444) interpretation seems reasonable: 'While Clark was openly and unabashedly anti-socialist, it would be inaccurate to think of him as simply another apologist for business interests'.

120 This assumption may appear reasonable, although it does not explain how moral codes *initially* emerge.

121 According to Henry (1994) – and also on the basis of textual evidence – Clark believes in a providential design, which aims at converting conflictual into coopera-tive behaviour. Note that, as Henry himself (ibid., pp. 111 and 115) stresses, this hap-pens independently of the actions of religious officials, who are often 'allied with businessmen', and 'rather than promoting class harmony [are] now promoting "class antagonism" '.

122 It must be noted that Clark radically changes his opinion on the subject, maybe as a result of the transformation of American trusts at the end of the nineteenth century. In the article 'The Nature and Progress of True Socialism' (1879), he writes: 'When the corporation shall fairly pass the point in its development where it acquires a fully grown corporate soul, it will become a cooperative society, a beneficent form of true socialism.' In the article 'Disarming the Trust' (1900), he writes: 'Experience seems to show that a real monopolist power may form an alliance with its workmen [...] against the public.'

123 'Man may starve spiritually in consequence of material privation' (Clark 1880, p. 310).

124 As we know, Hayek maintains that rules of conduct, habits and customs derive from the limits of the human brain in interpreting the complex external world, and in calculating all the possible outcomes of one's actions. This remark is at the basis of the renewed interest in his thought within cognitive economics. See, among others, Rizzello (1999).

125 For a history of liberal thought, see Girvetz (1963).

126 The increase in money supply depends, in Hayek's view, on the acceptance of a sort of 'inflationary ideology', based on the Keynesian approach.

127 However, it could be argued that Pareto – in the *Cours d'économie politique* – refers to a non-standard (neoclassical) concept of competition, not considering the assump-tion of wage-taker firms. The 'intensity' of competition – one can argue – increases as the bargaining powers among agents tend to equalize.

128 See L. Bruni and G. Forges Davanzati, 'Pareto's theory of the labour market', paper presented at the VIII Eshet (European Society for the History of Economic Thought) Conference, February 2004, Treviso.

129 Hayek (p. 99) notes that the individual contribution to production is, in most cases, difficult to find, so that an 'objective' definition of merit appears nonsensical.

130 The interpretation of Hayek's ideas on cultural evolution is a controversial issue. See text and, among others, Caldwell (2000).
131 Note that Hayek includes Karl Marx in the list of the 'public figures of great prominence' (p. 128).
132 It is worth noting that Hayek's concept of 'spontaneous order' cannot be identified with the neoclassical equilibrium, since it does not presuppose the equality between demand and supply. See Donzelli (1986).

3 Thorstein Veblen: the institutionalist approach to income distribution and ethical codes

133 Thorstein Veblen was born in Valders Municipality of Cato (Wisconsin), on 30 July 1857 and lived with his family in the isolated Norwegian township of Wheeling, Rice County, Minnesota. In 1874 he entered Carleton College Academy and graduated in three years. He continued studying at Johns Hopkins University and at Yale. As an undergraduate, he worked under John Bates Clark. In 1884, he finished his final dissertation for his PhD in philosophy (*The Ethical Grounds of a Doctrine of Retribution*), studying Immanuel Kant with Noah Porter and economics with the Social Darwinist William Graham Sumner. In 1892, after futile attempts to find teaching positions, he moved to Chicago and worked as a teaching fellow at the University of Chicago, mainly thanks to the interest of Prof. J. Laurence Laughlin, head of economics. In 1906, he became assistant professor of political economy. Because of his inability to keep his courses well organized (or more generally, because of his non-academic attitude), he had a difficult academic career: in December 1906 the Chicago administration forced him out for flagrant marital infidelities. In 1918 he worked for the Food Administration in the US Government. He was one of the founders of the New School of Social Research in New York City and, from 1896, managing editor of the *Journal of Political Economy*. On 3 August 1929, he died from heart disease in the Menlo Park area (California). For further biographical information see Bates (1934).
134 Hodgson (1988, pp. 416 ff.) provides a detailed description – as well as an original interpretation – of the evolution of Veblen's thought, seen as discontinuous and involving a shift of interest (in the 1890s) from the Marxian and Spencerian theoretical framework to later contributions in biology and anthropology: Jacques Loeb, Georges Romanes and James Pierce, above all. A further complication in interpreting Veblen's thought is certainly his style of writing. Karl L. Anderson ([1933] in Tilman 2003, vol. II, p. 6) points out that 'his queer vocabulary makes interpretation very difficult, so that the accuracy of a compressed statement is somewhat uncertain'. A further complication arises because – as Joseph Dorfman ([1932] in Tilman 2003, vol. II. p. 474, italics added) notes – 'Thorstein Veblen's celebrated *Theory of the Leisure Class* has customarily been viewed as a *satire* upon the mannerisms' and not a real *scientific* work.
135 The widespread interpretation of Veblen's economic analysis is based on the idea that he simply proposed a naive variant of the Marxian critique of capitalism (see, among others, Harris 1958; Knight 1969; Sowell 1987).
136 See, for instance, *Cambridge Journal of Economics*, vol. 22, 4, July 1998, where Nicolai Fosse and Paul Twomey put forward a comparison between Veblen's reflections and contemporary evolutionary economics. Furthermore, Hodgson (1988, p. 397) finds in Veblen the idea of transaction costs, while Argyrous and Sethi (1996) attribute to him a theory of 'cumulative causation'. On this latter issue, see Cutrona (2003). In *The New Palgrave Dictionary of Economics* (1987), we read the following definition of the phenomenon of cumulative causation. The economy 'is conceived as a continuous process in which [...] forces interact upon one another in a cumulative way, thus making for changes in one direction to induce supporting changes which push the system further away from its initial position'.

137 The relationship between Veblen's and Marx's thought is the subject of a wide debate. Harris (in Tilman 2003, p. 150, italics added) argues that:

> As a social scientist Veblen sought to give a genetic account of capitalism, or enterprise system, as a unique mode of economic organization, and also to set forth the motivations and institutions peculiar to it. Like Marx, Veblen was a critic and historian of capitalism. Marx envisaged history as a succession of *class struggle* which, climaxed by the dictatorship of the proletariat, would end in a 'withering-away' of the state. But Veblen finds his moving principle of history and social change in *conflicting social habits* induced by the different types of occupations in which men are engaged in earning a living.

By contrast, Hunt ([1979] in Tilman 2003, pp. 123–150) maintains that the incompatibility between Veblen's and Marx's theoretical views is misleading: 'the two great thinkers' analyses of capitalism [are] not only compatible, but also significantly complement each other [...] Veblen's writings offer insights which remain critically important to contemporary Marxism' (p. 124). See also the section 'Income distribution'. The relation between Veblen and the Frankfurt School is explored by Tilman ([1999] in Tilman 2003, pp. 303–321).

138 One may conceive conspicuous consumption as a device for producing 'symbolic boundaries', that is, lines that include and define certain people, groups and things while excluding others (Epstein 1992, p. 232). As Lamont (2000) remarks – also with reference to Veblen – these distinctions can be expressed through normative interdictions (taboos), cultural attitudes and practices, and more generally through patterns of likes and dislikes. They play an important role in the creation of inequality and the exercise of power.

139 Veblen notes that the 'elegance' of a good is often connected to its 'visible imperfections' and that 'machine products' are generally regarded as vulgar (ibid., pp. 160–161).

140 The Veblen effect (i.e. the possible existence of a positive relation between price and quantity) has been incorporated in many contemporary textbooks, as an exceptional case (see Hardwick *et al.* 1990) deriving from 'snobbery' (Leibenstein 1976, p. 51). This approach usually reflects methological individualism and is based on the dominant microeconomics: Veblen goods are treated as a very peculiar case, where the 'law of demand' is not in operation and their consumption is the outcome of the *individual* rational choice. Campbell (1996, p. 80) has argued that Veblen is unclear in providing an answer to the question of whether the criteria underlying conspicuous consumption should 'be viewed as conscious, subconscious, or merely embodied in habitual practices'. However, as Tilman (in Tilman 2003, vol. I, p. xviii) clarifies,

> Veblen contended that individual utility preferences could not be understood except in relation to the utility preferences of others. Individuals were emulating others to strengthen their own sense of self-worth by commanding more social esteem. The assumption of atomistic individualism and consumer sovereignty, deemed valid by microeconomists, were thus shown to be specious on social-psychological grounds alone.

In other words, Veblen always refers to a process of *competitive emulatory consumption*. In a different theoretical perspective, neo-Marxists (see, for instance, Davis 1957) tried to approach the Veblen effect from a macroeconomic viewpoint. Although it is recognized that the 'struggle to excel', via ostentation, is a feature of contemporary capitalism, neo-Marxists criticize Veblen for not having seen that *the most important* feature of capitalism is the imperative to accumulate capital. In a similar way, Adorno (1967 [1941]) attributed to Veblen a 'puritanical' account of culture (see Tilman 1992). In contemporary microeconomic literature, it is also maintained that human capital accumulation may result in a positively shaped demand curve. Stigler and

Becker (1977) show that utility is also a function of investment in knowledge, insofar as knowledge allows consumers to appreciate a good more and thus get more utility from it (think, for instance, of the consumption of art). The demand curve can also be positively sloped when consumers attach positive moral judgements to the product. This is the case, for instance, of 'responsible consumption', where a (slightly) higher price – compared with other goods – is connected with higher consumption.

141 More recently, Colin Campbell ([1995] in Tilman 2003, vol. I, pp. 410–419), speaking of 'conspicuous confusion' criticized Veblen mainly in view of the lack of empirical support of his thesis.

142 Although ostentation can also involve comparison between individuals belonging to different groups. See following text.

143 This result is tenable mainly because the leisure class, by definition, does not contribute directly to the production process, and accumulates wealth via 'predatory behaviour' (see text). Moreover, as Hodgson ([1996] in Tilman 2003, vol. III, p. 126) remarks: Veblen 'saw production not primarily as a matter of "inputs" into some mechanical function, but as an outcome of an institutional ensemble of habits and routine'.

144 The use of the word 'instinct', in this context, may appear questionable. However, as O'Hara (1999, p. 162) remarks, 'Instincts, for Veblen, are not purely physiological, biological, and psychological, but are heavily conditioned by institutions.' Asso and Fiorito (2004, pp. 447–448) point out that 'Veblen conceives instincts as universal goals or propensity inborn in the human agent and transmitted as "hereditary traits".' Moreover, they also note, 'Although Veblen admitted that all instincts touch, blend, overlap, and interfere with each other, and therefore cannot be conceived as acting in isolation from others, he advanced his own taxonomy of instincts according to their "teleological content".' The authors provide a very interesting study on the evolution of the instinct-based theories of human behaviour within both the Institutionalist approach and the mainstream theoretical framework, in the history of economic thought.

145 The idea that 'scientific and technological effort is [...] as special kind of habitual behavior associated with the use of material and conceptual tools', involving 'causation', and that its development has 'to wait for the emancipation of human intelligence from animistic beliefs and practices' is also present in the works of the institutional economist Lawrence Kelso Frank, in the 1920s (Asso and Fiorito 2004, p. 564). But, as Asso and Fiorito (2004, p. 571) note, 'Frank was an admirer of Veblen [...]. However, it should be emphasized that Frank's analysis of institutional evolution is tainted by a sort of technological determinism that is lacking in Veblen.'

146 The spread of these codes is basically guaranteed by schooling: 'schools [...] are shaped by and rest upon a leisure-class culture', based on the humanities and erudition (Veblen 1975, p. 391).

147 These schemes of life becomes *habits*. Following Veblen, Lionel D. Edie (1922) conceives habits as *devices for saving mental energy*. However, as Asso and Fiorito (2004, p. 453) maintain: 'Unlike Veblen, however, Edie's instinct theory places more emphasis on human ability to interact with the circumstances of the economic environment.'

148 That is from the 'industrial revolution' to the middle of the nineteenth century.

149 Note that this idea is in contrast with the view that Veblen's analysis is based on the principle of 'institutional exploitation' (see text). The contradiction may be due to a lack of clarity in Veblen's works or to the evolution of his thought. However, it should be noticed that the interpretation based on 'institutional exploitation' refers only to the capitalism of Veblen's time.

150 J. A. Hobson ([1937] in Tilman 2003, vol. II, pp. 34–35) remarks that

> Living a generation after Marx and in a country where the sharp distinction of workers and owners, capital and labor, was less applicable than in early nineteenth-century England, [Veblen] saw a different array of economic forces and a different procedure of class conflict.

In particular, according to this interpretation, Veblen minimized 'the direct conflict between wage-earners and their employers as seen in the opposition of the latter to trade unions and collective bargaining'.

151 Within this line of research, some scholars conceive public expenditure as an effective device to increase research and development activities and to facilitate the accumulation of knowledge by workers.

152 Hodgson (1988) interprets Veblen's theory of the firm in view of the contemporary neo-institutionalist framework, namely the 'competence approach'. In a similar vein, although in a different theoretical framework, this interpretation can be linked to Alfred Marshall's (1920, p. 138) well-known argument that 'Knowledge is our most powerful engine of production [...] Organization aids knowledge.' The issue is debated by Loasby (2004), among others. See also the fundamental contribution by Nelson and Winter (1982).

153 A similar view is put forward by Banks ([1959] in Tilman 2003, vol. III, p. 244): 'It is difficult to read Veblen on pecuniary and industrial pursuits without being conscious of the underlying similarity between his point of view and that of the Durkheim of the *Division of Labour*.'

154 As Klein (1999, p. 95) points out: 'Thus today, for example, one can apply Veblenian distinctions to understand the conflict between the pecuniary pursuits of tobacco companies and the technological progress made in cancer research.'

155 In particular, the living standard of what Veblen (1975, p. 319) calls the 'indigent class'.

156 This rereading is based on the idea that his theories are helpful in understanding *contemporary* economic and social facts, in line with Klein (1999, p. 97): 'it seems [...] clear [...] that that [the Veblenian] perspective is enormously helpful in assessing current problems'.

157 In more general terms, Veblen – replying to Cummings' criticisms (Veblen, 1899) – states that

> In their discourse and in their thinking, men constantly and necessarily take an attitude of approval or disapproval toward the institutional facts of which they speak, for it is through such everyday approval or disapproval that any feature of the institutional structure is upheld or altered.

158 It is interesting to note that some contemporary economists re-propose this issue, approaching it as the 'market' for odium. See Glaeser (2002).

159 In this context, unproductive labour is labour in sectors producing goods acquired by those (the leisure class) who do not contribute to economic growth. O'Hara (2000, p. 86) gives these examples: growing corn is a productive activity, while advertising expenses and warfare are unproductive activities, generating waste. However, Veblen (1956 [1904], p. 252) also maintains that 'The wasteful expenditures enhance demand [...] increase profits and raise capitalization'; what O'Hara (2000, p. 86) calls the ' "Keynesian element" of effective demand (or absorption of the surplus)' in Veblen's thought.

160 One can argue that this argument appears close to that of Durkheim (1958 [1928], p. 200):

> What is needed if social order is to reign is that the mass of men be content with their lot. But what is needed for them to be content, is not that they have more or less, but that they are convinced that they have no right to more.

161 Phillip A. O'Hara (2000, p. 19) argues that 'there is sufficient continuity between Marx and Veblen to support, in a fundamental sense, a form of integration between Marxist and Veblenian political economy'. He believes (ibid., p. 49) that Veblen's analysis rests on materialistic grounds, although 'Veblen's materialism needs to be qualified by recognizing that it is a "softened materialism", broadly conceived to

include in the collective wealth the "immaterial" industrial arts and knowledge of the arts and sciences'. It should be pointed out that Veblen criticized Marx, attributing a theory of natural rights to him: 'The laborer's claim to the full product of labor, which is pretty constantly implied though not frequently avowed by Marx, he has in all probability taken from English writers of the early nineteenth century' (Veblen 1906, p. 412). A very similar view is shared by Husani (1980), while O'Hara (2000, pp. 50 ff.) supports a diametrically opposed point of view; that is, no textual evidence in favour of a Marxian 'natural rights' approach is – in his reconstruction – available.

162 Money plays a crucial role in the business cycle. In particular, the author emphasizes the failure to adapt on the part of the institution of the credit system which – owing to an accommodating policy – is always out of proportion compared with the real sector, generating false expectations of earnings. The constant creation of credit leads to an overvaluing of the monetary market value of capital compared with the value that, given real conditions – that is, given technology – guarantees real earnings. As credit grows, in fact, new investments are generated, and this leads to an increase in the monetary value of capital and in profit expectations. On the other hand, the actual value is lowered by the reduction in prices resulting from technological change. Since firms are not willing to accept a reduction in the real value of capital, fresh credit is generated, creating fresh investments. The consequent improvement in corporate expectations cannot be fulfilled – because of the excess of production – and this inevitably leads to a 'crisis'. This process is amplified by speculations in the capital market (see Leathers and Evans 1973).

163 Schooling is an important factor in forming workers' habits of thought. See text.

164 As seen earlier, the possible increase in wages may also be due to the increase in working hours for the aim of obtaining a set of goods which serves to improve the individual worker's reputation. This effect – although not explicit in Veblen – has been explored by Bowles and Park (2002). They also find empirical evidence supporting the idea that the greater the inequality in income distribution, the longer the working hours.

165 Recall that

> The subsistence minimum is of course not a rigidly determined allowance of goods, definite and invariable in kind and quantity [...] in a general way, the most ancient and ingrained of the habits which govern the individual's life – those habits that touch his existence as an organism – are the most persistent and imperative. Beyond these come the higher wants [...] *Some of the higher wants*, as for instance the use of certain stimulants, or the need of salvation (in the eschatological sense), or of good repute, *may in some cases take precedence of the lower or more elementary wants*.
>
> (Veblen 1975 [1889], p. 107)

This latter observation is worth noting since it casts doubts about the invariability of the 'scale of wants', as theorized by Maslow (see Chapter 1).

4 Ethical codes and income distribution in the neoclassical and institutionalist theoretical frameworks

166 Where external interventions involve union action, state intervention in fixing wages and prices and the activity of consumer associations. Moreover, in the neoclassical analysis (and in its further developments, i.e. monetarism and the 'new classical economics'), money is known to be neutral and exogenous. This latter point is strongly criticized by Keynesian economists and, particularly, by the supporters of the so-called monetary theory of production or monetary circuit approach, where it is assumed that money supply is endogenous, depending on firms' demand for money from the banking system. See Graziani (2003).

167 With specific regard to income distribution, as Saint-Paul (2000, p. 1) points out: 'Standard economic analysis holds that [...] institutions are harmful for job creation and typically increase unemployment.'

168 This issue, within a post-Keynesian framework, is treated by – among others – Forges Davanzati and Realfonzo (2000).

169 These questions are debated in G. Forges Davanzati and R. Realfonzo, *Towards a 'continuist' interpretation of Keynes: Labour market deregulation in a monetary economy*, mimeo.

170 Some authors adopt the assumption of bounded rationality within an institutionalist framework. See, for instance, Williamson (1985).

171 This is not the place to examine the critiques of the neoclassical criterion of rationality. It may be sufficient to recall the arguments of Herbert Simon (1983), who emphasizes the lack of realism of this criterion and suggests that individuals actually act in order to achieve *satisfying* (not optimal) ends, what is called 'bounded rationality'. In defence of the neoclassical criterion, from a 'conventionalist' point of view, Milton Friedman (1953) argues that the '*as if*' clause may be sufficient for its acceptance. The idea (the often quoted example is that of the billiard player) is that one can state that *if* an agent were rational, *then* she/he would behave in such a way as to obtain the maximum benefit.

172 Even if habits may have a *rational* foundation, when the decision is made, it is not purely rational if external circumstances have changed and the individual does not take these changes into account. However, as Brian J. Loasby (2004, p. 43), following Alfred Marshall, observes: 'if directed action fails to achieve its objective, the recognition of failure leads either to a modification of existing routines or to experimentation resulting in new routines'. Moreover, 'routines facilitate the creation of new knowledge'.

173 Moreover, if there is a friend of the immigrants, before the attack she/he could help by warning them, with the twofold possible outcome of becoming the next victim of the racists (in the case of warning) or of gaining benefits from helping friends.

174 Similarly, the instrumental criterion of rationality seems to be incompatible with *creative* behaviour, in the Schumpeterian meaning, as well as with the motive of *domination*. In the first case, this occurs because a 'pure' creative act presupposes an *instinctive* motive (and, hence, the absence of a complete calculation of means with respect to 'new' ends); in the second case, social relationships have to be admitted, violating the methodological individualism axiom.

175 Note that the hypothesis of self-interest does not necessarily imply the pursuit of certain short-term goals at the expense of future outcomes (provided that future outcomes may be foreseen, given the individual intertemporal discount rate), as happens in the Beckerian 'Rotten Kid Theorem'. A selfish child – it is argued – may find it profitable to obey his/her altruistic father, if this produces an increase in family income and, hence, in his/her future benefits.

176 For a detailed analysis of the concept of social capital see Coleman (1988) and Putnam (1993).

177 For a detailed reconstruction of the contemporary debate on the methodology of economics, see Backhouse (1994).

178 Douglass C. North (1990, p. 22) also emphasizes that institutions are social devices for reducing uncertainty. In particular, he observes that

> our lives are made up of routines in which the matter of choice appears to be regular, repetitive, and clearly evident, so that 90 percent of our actions in a day do not require much reflection [...]. We take them for granted, because the structure of exchange has been institutionalized in such a way as to reduce uncertainty.

179 Rereading Hume, Reisman (2002, p. 129) argues that scarcity is a function of intertemporal and interpersonal comparison, since 'The basepoint of another's felicity makes our own felicity appear more vivid or more muted through the contrast'.

180 Minsky (1996, p. 357) stresses 'the affinity between the economics of Keynes and the American institutionalists'.
181 This argument can also be related to the Keynesian view of choice under uncertainty. The relevance or irrelevance of situations can be interpreted in *objective* or in *subjective* terms. Knowing which type of relevance has more importance for an individual choice is not simple, and this difficulty is also clear in Keynes' thought. In his *Treatise on Probability*, in fact, Keynes places more emphasis on the objective relevance of a situation (the 'weight of argument'); that is, a situation is relevant if it reflects a series of known results in the past (Keynes 1973 [1921]; cf. Dequech 2003). On the other hand when he writes about 'animal spirits' he supposes that subjective relevance prevails in action, expressed as the 'spontaneous urge to action rather than inaction' (Keynes 1973 [1936]). I thank Dr Andrea Pacella for attracting my attention to this point.
182 The link between the marginal productivity of labour and the market wage can be seen in two different ways. First, worker productivity can be conceived as the *cause* of the existence of an average real wage higher than zero. This statement specifically applies to wage differentials, at least in the sense that – for a given labour supply and given the other inputs – the increase in workers' efficiency leads to an increase in the average real wage. Second, a worker's labour productivity can be seen simply as the *measure* of his/her contribution to the production process.
183 Although the authors emphasize the pointlessness of classifying their analysis as 'neoclassical' or 'Keynesian', their conviction – reflected in sophisticated models – that unemployment ultimately depends on labour market 'rigidities' leads to their contribution being interpreted as a re-proposal and a confirmation of the standard neoclassical view.
184 Since technical progress increases productivity and reduces costs – it is argued – the consequent reduction of prices determines an increase in the demand for goods and, therefore, in labour demand. As a result, unemployment – at least in the long term – cannot depend on technical progress.
185 Evidence on this point is ambiguous. See Bean (1994).
186 A reconstruction of the debate on the 'wages question' and the so-called shock theory – that is, the link between high wages and innovations – has been provided by Forges Davanzati (1999).
187 On condition that the individual worker's productivity can be measured by the employer.
188 The effect on labour productivity of unfair competition among co-workers appears to be ambiguous. If an individual worker *A* exercises mobbing activities on worker *B*, the consequent loss of productivity on the part of *B* may be compensated by the increase in *A*'s work intensity.

Bibliography

Abbagnano, N. 1971. *Dizionario di filosofia*, Turin: UTET.

Adorno, T. W. 1967 [1941]. *Prisms*, London: Neville Spearman.

Akerlof, G. A. 1970. 'The market for "lemons": quality uncertainty and the market mechanism', *Quarterly Journal of Economics*, vol. 84, pp. 488–500.

Akerlof, G. A. and Yellen, J. Y. 1986. *Efficiency wage models of the labor market*, Cambridge: Cambridge University Press.

Almender, R. 1984. 'The ethics of profits: Reflections on corporate responsibility', in T. R. Swartz and F. J. Bonello (eds) *Taking sides: clashing views on controversial economic issues*, Guilford, CT: Dushkin Publishing Group Inc.

Andreoni, J. 1990. 'Impure altruism and donations of public goods: a theory of warm-glowing giving', *Economic Journal*, vol. 100, 401, pp. 464–477.

Antiseri, D. 2000. 'Friedrick A. von Hayek e il problema della solidarietà', in G. Clerico and S. Rizzello (eds) *Il pensiero di Friedrich von Hayek. Società, istituzioni e stato*, Turin: UTET.

Argandoña, A. 2002. 'The social dimensions of labour market institutions', in A. Argandoña and J. Gual (eds) *The social dimension of employment. Institutional reforms in labour markets*, Cheltenham: Elgar.

Argyrous, G. and Sethi, R. 1996. 'The theory of evolution and the evolution of theory: Veblen's methodology in contemporary perspective', *Cambridge Journal of Economics*, pp. 475–495.

Asso, P. F. and Fiorito, L. 2004. 'Human nature and economic institutions: instinct psychology, behaviorism, and the development of American institutionalism', *Journal of the History of Economic Thought*, vol. 26, pp. 445–477.

Axelrod, R. 1984. *The evolution of cooperation*, New York: Basic Books.

Ayer, A. J. 1936. *Language, truth and logic*, reprinted New York: Dover, 1952.

Backhouse, R. 1994. *New directions in economic methodology*, London: Routledge.

Baglioni, G. 1969. *Sindacalismo e protesta operaia*, Milan: Angeli.

Baland, J. M. and Plateau, J. P. 1996. *Halting degradation of natural resources*, Rome: Food and Agriculture Organization of the United Nations.

Banner, M. 1999. *Christian ethics and contemporary moral problems*, Cambridge: Cambridge University Press.

Barry, B. 1995. *A treatise on social justice, II. Justice as impartiality*, Oxford: Oxford University Press.

Bates, E. S. 1934. 'Thorstein Veblen: a biography', *Scribner's Magazine*, December.

Bean, C. R. 1994. 'European unemployment: a survey', *Journal of Economic Literature*, vol. 32 (June), pp. 573–619.

Becker, G. S. 1976. 'Altruism, egoism, and genetic fitness: economics and sociobiology', *Journal of Economic Literature*, vol. 14, 3 (September), pp. 817–826.

Bentham, J. 1970 [1789]. *An introduction to the principles of morals and legislation*, London: Athlone Press.

Bergstrom, T. C. and Stark, O. 1993. 'How altruism can prevail in an evolutionary environment', *The American Economic Review*, vol. 83, 2 (May), pp. 149–155.

Bernheim, D. B. and Stark, O. 1988. 'Altruism within the family reconsidered: do nice guys finish last?', *The American Economic Review*, vol. 78 (December), pp. 1034–1045.

Besant, A. 1886. *Why I am a socialist*, London: printed by Annie Besant and Charles Bradlaugh.

Beveridge, W. 1909. *Unemployment: a problem of industry*, London: Longman, Green.

Bevir, M. 1989. 'Fabianism and the theory of rent', *History of Political Thought*, vol. 10, pp. 313–327.

Bevir, M. 2002. 'Sidney Webb: utilitarianism, positivism and social democracy', *Journal of Modern History*, vol. 74, 2 (June), pp. 217–252.

Bicchieri, C. 1993. *Rationality and coordination*, Cambridge: Cambridge University Press.

Bilodeau, M. and Gravel, N. 2004. 'Voluntary provision of a public good and individual morality', *Journal of Public Economics*, vol. 88, 3 (March), pp. 645–666.

Bland, H. 1906. 'Socialism and labor policy', *Fabian Society Tracts*, nos. 73–133. Tract no. 127.

Blank, R. M. and McGurn, W. 2004. *Is the market moral? A dialogue on religion, economics and justice*, Washington, DC: Brooking Institution.

Blanshard, B. 1980. 'Replies to my critics', in P. A. Schlipp (ed.) *The philosophy of Brand Blanshard*, Le Salle: Open Court.

Blaug, M. 1985. *Economic theory in retrospect*, Cambridge: Cambridge University Press.

Bordia, P., Hobman, E., Jones, E., Gallois, C. and Callan, V. J. 2004. 'Uncertainty during organizational change: types, consequences, and management strategies', *Journal of Business and Psychology*, vol. 18, pp. 507–532.

Bowles, S. and Gintis, H. 1976. *Schooling in capitalist America*, New York: Basic Books.

Bowles, S. and Gintis, H. 2002. *Prosocial emotions*, Santa Fe Institute, working paper no. 02-07-028 June.

Bowles, S. and Park, Y. 2002. *Emulation, inequality and work hours: was Thorstein Veblen right?* Santa Fe Institute, working paper, 12 November.

Bowles, S., Gintis, H. and Gustaffson B. 1993. *Markets and democracy. Participation, accountability and efficiency*, Cambridge: Cambridge University Press.

Brekkle, K. A., Kverndokk, S. and Nyborg, K. 2003, 'An economic model of moral motivation', *Journal of Public Economics*, vol. 87, 9 (September), pp. 1967–1983.

Bruni, L. 2002. *Vilfredo Pareto and the birth of the modern microeconomics*, Cheltenham: Elgar.

Buchanan, J. M. 1992. 'The supply of labour and the extent of the market', in M. Fry (ed.) *Adam Smith's legacy. His place in the development of modern economics*, London and New York: Routledge.

Buchanan, J. M. 1994. *Ethics and economic progress*, Norman and London: University of Oklahoma Press.

Bush, P. 1999. '*Veblen's* "Olympian Detachment" reconsidered', *History of Economic Ideas*, vol. 7, pp. 127–151.

Caldwell, B. 2000. 'The emergence of Hayek's ideas on cultural evolution', *Review of Austrian Economics*, vol. 13, pp. 5–22.

Camerer, C. 1997. 'Labor supply of New York City cabdrivers: one day at a time', *Quarterly Journal of Economics*, vol. 112, 2, pp. 407–441.

Campbell C. 1996. 'Veblen's theory of conspicuous consumption: a critical appraisal', *Yearbook of Sociology*, vol. 1, 1, pp. 61–82.

Checchi, D. and Lucifora, C. 2002. 'Unions and labour market institutions in Europe', *Economic Policy*, vol. 17, 35, pp. 361–408.

Clark, A. H. and Clark, J. M. 1938. *John Bates Clark: a memorial*, New York: Columbia University Press.

Clark, J. B. 1879. 'Business ethics, past and present', *New Englander and Yale Review*, vol. 38 (March), pp. 157–169.

Clark, J. B. 1880. 'Spiritual economics', *New Englander and Yale Review*, vol. 39, 156 (May), pp. 305–319.

Clark, J. B. 1882. 'Non competitive economics', *New Englander and Yale Review*, vol. 41 (November), pp. 837–848.

Clark, J. B. 1883. 'Recent theories of wages', *New Englander and Yale Review*, vol. 42 (May), pp. 354–364.

Clark, J. B. 1887. 'Christianity and modern economics', *New Englander and Yale Review*, vol. 47 (July), pp. 50–60.

Clark, J. B. 1890–91. 'Distribution as determined by a law of rent', *Quarterly Journal of Economics*, vol. 5 (April), pp. 289–318.

Clark, J. B. 1965 [1899]. *The distribution of wealth: a theory of wages, interest and profits*, New York: A. M. Kelley.

Cole, G. D. H. 1918a. *Labour in the Commonwealth: a book for the younger generation*, London: Headley Bros Ltd.

Cole, G. D. H. 1918b. *The payment of wages: a study in payment by results under the wage-system*, Westminster: Fabian Research Department; London: G. Allen and Unwin.

Cole, G. D. H. 1920a. *Chaos and order in industry*, London: Methuen.

Cole, G. D. H. 1920b. 'Guild socialism', *Fabian Society Tracts*, nos. 167–195. Tract. no. 192.

Cole, G. D. H. 1920c. *Social theory*, London: Methuen.

Cole, G. D. H. 1922. *The British labour movement: a historical introduction for classes and study circles*, London: Labour Research Department.

Cole, G. D. H. 1923a. *British trade unionism: problems and policy. A syllabus for classes and students*, London: Labour Research Department.

Cole, G. D. H. 1923b. *Trade unionism and munitions*, Oxford: Clarendon Press.

Cole, G. D. H. 1923c. *Unemployment: a study syllabus*, London: Labour Research Department.

Cole, G. D. H. 1925. *Industrial policy for socialists: a syllabus for classes and students*, London: ILP Information Committee.

Cole, G. D. H. 1932. 'How capitalism works', *Society for Socialist Inquiry and Propaganda [Publications]*, Study guides no. 5.

Cole, G. D. H. 1933. Socialist control of industry. A pamphlet prepared in the belief that to-day socialists want, not vague talk, but bold and concrete plans for the achievement of socialism in our time, *Society for Socialist Inquiry and Propaganda [Publications]*, Forum lecture series no. 6.

Cole, G. D. H. 1934. *Some relation between political and economic theory*, London: W. L. Kingsley.

Cole, M. 1972. 'Webb, Sidney and Beatrice', *International Encyclopedia of the Social Sciences*, vol. 15, New York: Macmillan, pp. 487–491.

Coleman, J. S. 1988. 'Social capital in the creation of human capital', *American Journal of Sociology*, vol. 94, Supplement 95–120.

Collard, D. 1975. 'Edgeworth's proposition on altruism', *Economic Journal*, vol. 85 (June), pp. 355–360.

Conte, R. and Castelfranchi, C. 1996. *La società delle menti*, Turin: UTET.

Converse, P. E. 1969. 'Of time and partisan stability', *Comparative Political Studies*, vol. 2, pp. 139–170.

Costabile, L. 1998. 'Ordine spontaneo o ordine negoziato? Conflitti e risoluzione dei conflitti nella nuova teoria economica delle istituzioni', in A. Amendola (ed.) *Istituzioni e mercato del lavoro*, Napoli: Edizioni scientifiche italiane.

Costabile, L. 2004. 'Labour commanded: credit, the employment relation and the property rights constraint', paper presented at the VIII National Conference of the Italian Association for the History of Economic Thought, Palermo.

Cremaschi, S. 2005. *L'etica del novecento. Dopo Nietzsche*, Rome: Carocci.

Crowley, B. 1987. *The self, the individual, and the community: liberalism in the political thought of F. A. Hayek and Sidney and Beatrice Webb*, Oxford: Clarendon Press.

Cummings, J. 1899. 'The theory of the leisure class', *Journal of Political Economy*, (September), pp. 425–455.

Cutrona, S. 2003. 'Cumulative causation in Veblen and Young', *Storia del pensiero economico*, vol. 45, pp. 55–89.

David, P. 1985. 'Clio and the economics of QWERTY', *American Economic Review – Papers and Proceedings*, vol. 75, pp. 332–337.

Davidson, P. 1994. *Post Keynesian macroeconomic theory*, Aldershot: Elgar.

Davis, A. K. 1957. 'Thorstein Veblen reconsidered', *Science and Society*, vol. 21, pp. 52–85.

Davis, J. B. 1991. 'Keynes's view of economics as a moral science', in B. W. Bateman and J. B. Davis (eds) *Keynes and philosophy*, pp. 89–103, Aldershot: Elgar.

Davis, J. B., Marciano, A. and Runde, J. (eds) 2004. *The Elgar companion to economics and philosophy*, Cheltenham: Elgar.

Dawkins, R. 1976. *The selfish gene*, New York: Oxford University Press.

Dequech, D. 2003. 'Uncertainty and economic sociology: a preliminary discussion', *American Journal of Economics and Sociology*, vol. 62, pp. 509–532.

Dickinson, T. 1905. *Unemployment. Its cause and cure*, London: ILP Publication Department.

Dobriansky, L. 1957. *Veblenism: a new critique*. Washington, DC: Public Affairs Press.

Domenighetti, G., D'Avanzo, B. and Bisig, B. 2000. 'Health effects of job insecurity among employees in the Swiss general population', *International Journal of Health Services*, vol. 30, 3, pp. 477–490.

Donzelli, F. 1986. *Il concetto di equilibrio nella teoria economica neoclassica*, Rome: Nuova Italia Scientifica.

Durkheim, E. 1958 [1928]. *Socialism and Saint Simon*, London: Routledge and Kegan.

Eagly, R. V. 1968. *Events, ideology, and economic theory: the determinants of progress in the development of economic analysis*, Detroit, MI: Wayne State University Press.

Easterlin, R. A. 1995. 'Will raising the incomes of all increase the happiness of all?', *Journal of Economic Behavior and Organization*, vol. 27, pp. 35–47.

Easterlin, R. A. (ed.) 2002. *Happiness in economics*, Cheltenham: Elgar.

Edgell, S. 1999. 'Veblen's theory of conspicuous consumption after 100 years', *History of Economic Ideas*, vol. 7, 3, pp. 99–125.

Edie, L. D. 1922. *Principles of the new economics*, New York: Thomas Y. Cromwell Co.

Edwards, P. 1965. *The logic of moral discourse*, New York: Free Press.

Epstein, C. F. 1992. 'Tinker-bells and pinups: the construction and reconstruction of gender boundaries at work', in M. Lamont and M. Fournier (eds) *Cultivating differences: symbolic boundaries and the making of inequality*, pp. 232–256, Chicago, IL: University of Chicago Press.

Eriksson, R. 1997. *Essays on the methodology and ethics of economics*, Abo: Abo Academy University Press.

Etzioni, A. 1986. 'The case for a multiple-utility concept', *Economics and Philosophy*, vol. 2, pp. 159–183.

Fiorito, L. 2000. 'John Maurice Clark on marginal productivity theory. A note on some unpublished correspondence', *Storia del pensiero economico*, vol. 40, pp. 181–201.

Fisscher, O., Nijhof, A. and Steensma, H. 2003. 'Dynamics in responsible behaviour in search of mechanisms for coping with responsibility', *Journal of Business Ethics*, 2–3 (May), vol. 44, 2, pp. 209–224.

Flanders, A. 1968. 'Per una teoria della contrattazione collettiva', *Economia e lavoro*, vol. 4, pp. 435–478.

Flux, A. W. 1894. 'Review: P. H. Wicksteed, "An essay on the coordination of the laws of distribution"', *Economic Journal*, vol. 4, pp. 305–313.

Fodor, G. 1983. *On the continuity of Keynes's thought*, Modena: Università di Modena.

Fontaine, P. 2004. 'Richard Titmuss on social cohesion: a comment', *European Journal of Political Economy*, vol. 20, 3 (September), pp. 795–797.

Forges Davanzati, G. 1995. 'W. S. Jevons: from the wage fund doctrine to the theory of individual supply of labour', *History of Economic Ideas*, vol. 3, 2, pp. 33–50.

Forges Davanzati, G. 1999. *Salario, produttività del lavoro e conflitto sociale. L'analisi delle determinanti dell'intensità dell'impegno lavorativo nella storia del pensiero economico*, Lecce: Milella.

Forges Davanzati, G. 2002. 'Wages fund, high wages and social conflict in a classical model of unemployment equilibrium', *Review of Radical Political Economics*, vol. 34, 4, pp. 1–24.

Forges Davanzati, G. and Realfonzo, R. 2000. 'Wages, labour productivity and unemployment in a model of the monetary theory of production', *Economie appliquée*, vol. 53, 4, pp. 117–138.

Forges Davanzati, G. and Realfonzo R. 2004. 'Labour market deregulation and unemployment in a monetary economy', in R. Arena and N. Salvadori (eds) *Money, credit and the role of the state. Essays in honour of Augusto Graziani*, Burlington, VT: Ashgate.

Fornero, G. 1993. 'La filosofia contemporanea', in N. Abbagnano (ed.) *Storia della filosofia*, vol. 4, Turin: UTET.

Frank, R. H. 1988. *Passions with reason: the strategic role of emotions*, New York: W.W. Norton.

Friedman, M. 1953. *Essays in positive economics*, Chicago, IL: University of Chicago Press.

Friedman, M. 1962. *Capitalism and freedom*, Chicago, IL: University of Chicago Press.

Friedrick, C. J. (ed.) 1949. *The philosophy of Kant*, New York: Modern Library.

Fudenberg, D. and Levine, D. 1989. 'Reputation and equilibrium selection in games with a patient player', *Econometrica*, vol. 57, pp. 759–778.

Garegnani, P. 1984. 'Value and distribution in the classical economists and Marx', *Oxford Economic Papers*, vol. 36, pp. 291–325.

Gasper, D. 1996. 'Needs and basic needs. A clarification of meanings, levels and different streams of work', Institute for Social Studies – The Hague, The Netherlands, working paper no. 210 (February).

Gick, E. 2003. 'Cognitive theory and moral behaviour: the contribution of F. A. Hayek to business ethics', *Journal of Business Ethics*, vol. 45, 1–2 (June), pp. 149–165.

Girvetz, H. K. 1963. *The evolution of liberalism*, New York: Collier Books.

Glaeser, E. 2002. 'The political economy of hatred', Harvard Discussion Paper no. 1970, May.

Glazer, A. 2002. 'Production with patriotic workers', University of California – Irvine, working paper, September.

Granovetter, M. 1985. 'Economic action and social structure: the problem of embeddedness', *American Journal of Sociology*, vol. 16, pp. 481–510.

Graziani, A. 1977. 'Scambi simultanei e successione ciclica nel processo economico', *Quaderni piacentini*.

Graziani, A. 1991. 'Nuove interpretazioni dell'analisi monetaria di Keynes', in J. Kregel (ed.) *Nuove interpretazioni dell'analisi monetaria di Keynes*, pp. 15–42, Bologna: Il Mulino.

Graziani, A. 1992. *Teoria economica. Macroeconomia*, Nuples: ESI.

Graziani, A. 2003. *The monetary theory of production*, Cambridge: Cambridge University Press.

Greer, W. B. 2000. *Ethics and uncertainty. The economics of John M. Keynes and Frank H. Knight*, Cheltenham: Elgar.

Griffin, R. and Karayiannis, A. D. 2002. 'T. Veblen's theory of entrepreneurship', *History of Economic Ideas*, vol. 10, 3, pp. 61–83.

Habermas, J. 1991. *Erläuterungen zur Diskursethik*, Frankfurt, a.m.: Suhrkamp Verlag.

Hansson, I. and Stuart, C. 1992. 'Socialization and altruism', *Journal of Evolutionary Economics*, vol. 4, 2, pp. 301–312.

Harcourt, G. 1972. *Some Cambridge controversies in the theory of capital*, Cambridge: Cambridge University Press.

Hardwick, P., Khan, B. and Langmead, J. 1990. *An introduction to modern economics*, 3rd edition, London: Longman.

Harris, A. 1958. *Economics and social reform*, New York: Harper and Brothers.

Harrison, R. J. 2000. *The life and the times of Sidney and Beatrice Webb, 1858–1905: the formative years*, Basingston: Macmillan.

Hausman, D. M. and McPherson, M. S. 1984. 'Economics, rationality and ethics', in D. M. Hausman (ed.) *The philosophy of economics*, Cambridge: Cambridge University Press.

Hayek, F. A. von, 1952. *The sensory order*, London: Routledge.

Hayek, F. A. von, 1960. *The constitution of liberty*, London: Routledge and Kegan.

Hayek, F. A. von, 1979. *Law, legislation and liberty: a new statement of the liberal principles of justice and political economy*, London: Routledge and Kegan.

Hazlitt, H. 1964. *The foundations of morality*, Princeton, NJ: Van Nostrand.

Henry, J. F. 1994. 'John Bates Clark's transformation', *Journal of the History of Economic Thought*, vol. 16, 1, pp. 106–125.

Hirsch, P. M. 1997. 'Review essay. Sociology without social structure: neoinstitutional theory meets brave new world', *American Journal of Sociology*, vol. 102, 6, pp. 1702–1723.

Hirschman, A. O. 1982. *Shifting involvements. Private interests and public action*, Princeton, NJ: Princeton University Press.

Hobsbawm, E. J. 1968. *Industry and empire*, vol. 3, The Penguin Economic History of Britain, London: Penguin Books.

Hochman, H. and Rodgers, J. 1969. 'Pareto optimal redistribution', *American Economic Review*, vol. 4, pp. 542–557.

Hodgson, G. M. 1988. *Economics and institutions. A manifesto for a modern institutional economics*, Oxford: Polity Press.

Hodgson, G. M. 1998. 'The approach of institutional economics', *Journal of Economic Literature*, vol. 36 (March), pp. 166–192.

Hogg, M. A. and Mullin, B. A. 1999. 'Join groups to reduce uncertainty: subjective uncertainty reduction and group identification', in D. Abrams and M. A. Hogg (eds) *Social identification and social cognition*, pp. 249–279, Oxford: Blackwell.

Holt, P. F. 1998. 'Keynes and the good life', paper presented at the History of Economics Society, Montreal, Canada, June.

Honneth, A. 1996. *The struggle for recognition. The moral grammar of social conflicts.* Cambridge, MA: MIT Press.

Huck, S. and Kübler, D. 2000. 'Social pressure, uncertainty, and cooperation', *Economics of Governance*, vol. 1, pp. 199–212.

Husani, Z. I. 1980. 'Marx on distributive justice', in M. Cohen, T. Nagel and T. Scanlon (eds) *Marx, justice and history*, Princeton, NJ: Princeton University Press.

Immergut, E. M. 1998. 'The theoretical core of the new institutionalism', *Politics and Society*, vol. 26, 1, pp. 5–34.

Jalledau, J. 1975. 'The methodological conversion of John Bates Clark', *History of Political Economy*, vol. 7, 2, pp. 209–226.

Jevons, W. S. 1879 [1871]. *The theory of political economy*, 2nd edition, London: Macmillan.

Jonas, H. 1979. *Das Prinzip Verantwortung. Versuch einer Ethics für die Technologische Zivilisation*, Frankfurt, a.m.: Insel Verlag.

Kahneman, D. and Tversky, A. 1979. 'Prospect theory: an analysis of decision under risk', *Econometrica*, vol. 47, 2, pp. 263–291.

Kahneman, D., Knetsch, J. and Thaler, R. 1986. 'Fairness as a constraint on profit seeking: entitlements in the market', *American Economic Review*, vol. 76, pp. 728–741.

Kamenka, E. 1972. *The ethical foundation of Marxism*, 2nd edition, London: Routledge and Kegan.

Kant, I. 1909 [1785]. 'Introduction to the methaphysics of morals', in Abbot (ed. and trans.) *Kant's theory of ethics*, Longmans.

Keynes, J. M. 1971 [1926]. 'The end of the laissez-faire', in *The collected writings of John Maynard Keynes*, vol. 9, London: Macmillan.

Keynes, J. M. 1973 [1921]. 'Treatise on probability', in *The collected writings of John Maynard Keynes*, vol. 8, London: Macmillan, St. Martin's Press; Cambridge: Cambridge University Press.

Keynes J. M. 1973 [1936]. *The general theory of employment, interest and money*, Cambridge: Cambridge University Press.

Keynes, J. M. 1973 [1936–1937]. 'The general theory and after: part II defence and development', in *The collected writings of John Maynard Keynes*, vol. 14, London: Macmillan, St. Martin's Press; and Cambridge: Cambridge University Press.

Khalil, E. L. 1990. 'Beyond self-interest and altruism: a reconstruction of Adam Smith's theory of human conduct', *Economic and Philosophy*, vol. 2, pp. 255–273.

Khalil, E. L. 2003. 'What is altruism?' *Journal of Economic Psychology*, vol. 1, pp. 97–123.

Kindlebergher, C. P. 1990. *Historical economics, art or science?* Berkeley, CA: University of California Press.

King J. E. 2002. *A history of post Keynesian economics since 1936*, Cheltenham and Northampton: Edward Elgar.

Klein, P. A. 1999. 'The theory of the leisure class, insipiration for the new millennium', *History of Economic Ideas*, vol. 7, 3, pp. 85–98.

Knight, F. H. 1929. 'Freedom as fact and criterion', *International Journal of Ethics*, vol. 39, 2, pp. 129–147.

Knight, F. H. 1935. 'Intellectual confusion on morals and economics', *International Journal of Ethics*, vol. 45 (January), pp. 200–220.

Knight, F. H. 1951. *The economic organization*, New York: Harper and Row.

Knight, F. H. 1960. *Intelligence and democratic action*, Cambridge, MA: Harvard University Press.

Knight, F. H. 1969. *Freedom and reform*, New York: Kennikatpress.

Knight, F. H. 1971 [1921]. *Risk, uncertainty and profits*, Boston, MA: Houghton Mifflin.

Knight, J. 1992. *Institutions and social conflict*, Cambridge: Cambridge University Press.

Kreps, D. and Wilson, R. 1982. 'Reputation and imperfect information', *Journal of Economic Theory*, vol. 27, pp. 257–279.

Lamont, M. 2000. *The dignity of working men: morality and the boundaries of race, class, and immigration*, New York and Cambridge, MA: Harvard University Press, Russell Sage Foundation.

Layard, R., Nickell, S. and Jackman R. 1994. *The unemployment crisis*, Oxford: Oxford University Press.

Leathers, C. G. and Evans, J. S. 1973. 'Thorstein Veblen and the new industrial state', *History of Political Economy*, vol. 5, 2, pp. 420–437.

Leibenstein, H. 1976 [1957]. *Beyond economic man*, Cambridge, MA: Harvard University Press.

Lim, C. 2003. 'Moral sentiments and equilibrium in moral codes', *International Journal of Social Economics*, vol. 30, 9 (13 August), pp. 985–999.

Lipsey, R. G. 1963. *An introduction to positive economics*, London: Weidenfeld and Nicolson.

Loasby, B. J. 2004. 'Cognitivism and innovation in economics', University of Milan 'Bicocca', working paper no. 77.

Lowenthal, E. 1911. *The Ricardian socialists*, New York: Columbia University Press.

Lucas, R. 1988. 'On the mechanics of economic development', *Journal of Monetary Economics*, vol. 22, pp. 3–42.

Lutz, M. A. and Lux, K. 1988. *Humanistic economics. The new challenge*, New York: Bootstrap Press.

McBriar, A. M. 1987. *An Edwardian mixed doubles: the Bosanquets versus the Webbs. A study in British social policy 1890–1929*, Oxford: Oxford University Press.

Machlup, F. 1980. *Knowledge: its creation, distribution, and economic significant. Knowledge and knowledge production*, vol. 1, Princeton, NJ: Princeton University Press.

Machlup, F. 1984. *Knowledge: its creation, distribution, and economic significant. The economics of information and human capital*, vol. 3, Princeton, NJ: Princeton University Press.

Mackie J. L. 1984. 'Rights, utility and universalization', in R. G. Frey (ed.) *Utility and rights*, Minneapolis, MN: University of Minnesota Press.

McNally, D. 1994. *Political economy and the rise of capitalism. A reinterpretation*, Berkeley, CA: University of California Press.

Marglin, S. A. 1974. 'What bosses do: the origins and the functions of hierarchy in capitalist production', *Review of Radical Political Economics*, vol. 6, 2, pp. 60–112.

Marshall, A. 1920. *Principles of economics*, London: Macmillan.

Marton, K. 2003. 'The fellowship of the new life: English ethical socialism reconsidered', *History of Political Thought*, vol. 24, 2, pp. 282–304.

Maslow, A. 1970. *Motivations and personality*, 2nd edition, vol. 24, New York: Harper and Row.

Mattew, T. 2004. 'No-one telling us what to do: anarchist schools in Britain, 1890–1916', *Historical Research*, vol. 77, 197, pp. 405–436.

Maurandi P. 2001. *John Bates Clark: un liberista critico del capitalismo*, Rome: Carocci.

Mauss, M. 1950. 'Essay sur le done', in *Sociologie et anthropologie*, Paris: PUF.

Mead, G. H. 1934 ' "Introduction" to George H. Meed' in C. W. Morris (ed.), *Mind, self and society*, Chicago, IL: University of Chicago Press.

Meijil, T. 2000. 'Modern morals in postmodernity: a critical reflection on professional codes of ethics', *Cultural Dynamics*, vol. 12, 1 (March), pp. 65–81.

Meltzer, A. 1988. *Keynes's monetary theory. An alternative interpretation*, Cambridge: Cambridge University Press.

Minion, M. 2000. 'The Fabian Society and Europe during the 1940s: the search for a socialist foreign policy', *European History Quarterly*, 2, pp. 237–270.

Minsky, H. P. 1996. 'Uncertainty and the institutional structure of capitalist economies', *Journal of Economic Issues*, vol. 30, 2, pp. 357–368.

Moore, G. E. 1903. *Principia ethica*, Cambridge: Cambridge University Press.

Mueller, D. C. 1989. *Public choice II. A revised edition of public choice*, Cambridge: Cambridge University Press.

Napoleoni, C. 1982. *Valore*, Milan: Mondadori.

Nayaradou, M. 2004. 'The influence of firm strategy on business cycles in Veblen's economic theory', *Oeconomicus*, vol. 7, pp. 37–56.

Negishi, T. 1989. *History of economic theory*, Amsterdam: Elsevier Science Publishers.

Nelson, R. R. and Winter, S. G. 1982. *An evolutionary theory of economic change*, Cambridge, MA: Harvard University Press.

North, D. C. 1990. *Institutions, institutional change and economic performance*, Cambridge: Cambridge University Press.

Novak, M. 1993. *The Catholic ethic and the spirit of capitalism*, London: Macmillan.

Nozick, R. 1974. *State, anarchy and utopia*, New York: Basic Books.

Nussbaum, M. 1992. 'Human functioning and social justice: in defence of Aristotelian essentialism', *Political Theory*, vol. 20, 2, pp. 202–246.

O'Donnell, R. M. 1989. *Keynes: philosophy, economics, politics*, London: Macmillan.

O'Hara, P. A. 1999. 'Thorstein Veblen's theory of collective social wealth, instincts and property relations', *History of Economic Ideas*, vol. 7, 3, pp. 153–179.

O' Hara, P. A. 2000. *Marx, Veblen, and contemporary institutional political economy*, Cheltenham: Elgar.

Olivier, S. 1891 [1889]. 'The moral basis of Socialism', in G. B. Shaw and H. G. Wilshire (eds) *Fabian essays in Socialism*, New York: Humbert Publishing Co.

Olivier, S. 1906. *White capital and coloured labour*, London: printed for the Standing Joint Committee of the Independent Labour Party and the Fabian Society.

Pacella, A. 2005. 'Uncertainty, social norms and the labour market: a monetary circuit approach' paper presented at the 9th Eshet Conference, Stirling, June.

Pareto, V. 1964 [1896–1897]. *Cours d'économie politique*, Geneva: Droz.

Pasinetti, L. 1974. *Growth and income distribution. Essays in economic theory*, Cambridge: Cambridge University Press.

Patinkin, D. 1956. *Money, interest and prices*, New York: Harper and Row.

Patinkin, D. 1987. *Keynes, John Maynard*, vol. 3, The New Palgrave, London: Macmillan, pp. 19–41.

Pease, E. R. 1963. *The history of the Fabian Society*, New York: Barnes and Noble.

Pemberton, J. 1988. 'A "managerial" model of the trade union', *Economic Journal*, vol. 98, pp. 755–771.

Pesciarelli, E. 1991. 'Smith, Bentham and the development of contrasting ideas on entrepreneurship', in M. Blaug (ed.) *Adam Smith (1723–1790)*, vol. I, Aldershot: Elgar; also in *History of Political Economy*, vol. 21, 3, pp. 521–536, 1989.

Picchio, A. 1993. 'Longe, Marshall, Webb. A game of chess or a struggle for survival?', *Studi e ricerche* – Dipartimento di Economia Politica, Università degli studi di Modena.

Piderit, J. J. 1993. *The ethical foundations of economics*, Washington, DC: Georgetown University Press.

Porta, P. L., Scazzieri, R. and Skinner, A. 2001 (eds) *Knowledge, social institutions and the division of labour*, Cheltenham: Elgar.

Powell, W. W. and Di Maggio, P. J. 1991. 'Introduction', in W. W. Powell and P. J. Di Maggio (eds) *The new institutionalism in organizational analysis*, Chicago, IL: University of Chicago Press.

Prasch, R. E. 2002. 'An introduction to "Anarchism, socialism and social reform" by John Bates Clark', *Journal of the History of Economic Thought*, vol. 24, 4, pp. 443–449.

Prideaux, S. 2001. 'New labour, old functionalism: the underlying contradictions of welfare reform in the US and in the UK', *Social Policy and Administration*, vol. 35, 1, pp. 85–115.

Pullen, J. 2001. 'A linguistic analysis of the marginal productivity theory of distribution; or, the use and abuse of the proprietorial "of" ', University of New England – School of Economics, working paper no. 4 – February.

Putnam, R. D. 1993. *Making democracy work: civic tradition in modern Italy*, Princeton, NJ: Princeton University Press.

Rand, A. 1964. *The virtue of selfishness*, New York: New American Library.

Rawls, J. 1971. *A theory of justice*, Cambridge, MA: Harvard University Press.

Rawski, G., Carte, S. B., Cohen, J. S., Cullimberg, S., Lindert, P. H., McCloskey, D. N., Rockoff, H. and Sutch, R. 1996. *Economics and the historian*, Berkeley, CA: University of California Press.

Rees, A. 1973. *The economics of work and pay*, New York: Harper and Row.

Reisman, D. 2002. *Institutional economy. Demand and supply*, Cheltenham: Elgar.

Rizzello, S. 1999, *The economics of mind*, Cheltenham: Elgar.

Robbins, L. 1932. *An essay on the nature and significance of economic science*, London: Macmillan.

Robinson, J. V. 1934. 'Euler's theorem and the problem of distribution', *Economic Journal*, vol. 44, pp. 398–414.

Romani, R. 2003. 'La teoria del salario in Italia (1890–1900)', paper presented at the 7th Eshet Conference, Paris, January.

Romer, P. 1989. 'Capital accumulation in the theory of long run growth', in R. Barro (ed.) *Modern business cycle theory*, Cambridge, MA: Harvard University Press.

Roncaglia, A. 1993. 'Toward a post-Sraffian theory of income distribution', *Journal of Income Distribution*, pp. 3–27.

Ruse, M. 1990. 'Evolutionary ethics and the search for predecessors: Kant, Hume and all the way back to Aristotle?', *Social Philosophy and Policy*, vol. 8, (Autumn), pp. 58–85.

Sacco, P. L. and Zamagni, S. 2002. *Complessità relazionale e comportamento economico*, Bologna: Il Mulino.

Sacconi, L. 1997. *Economia, etica, organizzazione*, Bari-Roma: Laterza.

Sahlins, M. 1965. 'On the sociology of primitive exchange', in M. Banton (ed.) *The relevance of models for social anthropology*, London: Tavistock.

Saint-Paul, G. 2000. *The political economy of labour market institutions*, Oxford: Oxford University Press.

Salop, J. and Salop, S. 1976. 'Self-selection and turnover in the labour market', *Quarterly Journal of Economics*, vol. 90, pp. 619–628.

Samuelson, P. A. 1962. 'Parable and realism in capital theory: the surrogate production function', *Review of Economic Studies*, vol. 29, 3, pp. 193–206.

Sartre, J. P. 1936. *L'Immagination*, Paris: Alcan.

Schlict, E. 2002. *Social evolution, corporate culture and exploitation*, University of Munich, discussion paper no. 651, November.

Schmid, A. A. 2004. *Conflict and cooperation. Institutional and behavioral economics*, Oxford: Blackwell.

Schneider, H. K. 1974. *Economic man. The anthropology of economics*, New York: Free Press.

Schotter, A. 1986. 'The evolution of social institutions', in R. Langlois (ed.) *Economics as a process*, Cambridge: Cambridge University Press.

Schultz, T. 1961. 'Investment in human capital', *American Economic Review*, vol. 51, pp. 1–17.

Schumpeter, J. A. 1934 [1912]. *The theory of economic development*, Cambridge, MA: Harvard University Press.

Schumpeter, J. A. 1950. *Capitalism, socialism and democracy*, 3rd edition, New York: Harper and Row.

Schumpeter J. A. 1954. *History of economic analysis*, London: Allen and Unwin [1986].

Scott, W. R. 1995. *Institutions and organizations*, Thousand Oaks, CA: Sage Publications.

Selten, R. 2001. 'John C. Harsany, system builder and conceptual innovator', *Games and Economic Behaviour*, vol. 36, pp. 31–46.

Sen, A. K. 1977. 'Rational fools: a critique of the behavioural foundations of economic theory', *Philosophy and Public Affairs*, vol. 6, pp. 317–344.

Sen, A. K. 1979. 'Utilitarianism and welfarism', *Journal of Philosophy*, vol. 76, pp. 463–480.

Sen, A. K. 1984. *Resources, values and development*, Cambridge, MA: Harvard University Press.

Sen, A. K. 1987a. *On ethics and economics*, Oxford: Blackwell.

Sen, A. K. 1987b. 'The standard of living', in G. Hawthorn (ed.) *The standard of living*, Cambridge: Cambridge University Press.

Sen, A. K. 1997. 'Human capital and human capability', *World development*, Elsevier science, vol. 25, 12 December, pp. 1959–1961.

Sen, A. K. 1999. *Commodities and capabilities*, Oxford: Oxford University Press.

Serrano F. and Cesaratto S. 2002. 'The laws of return in the neoclassical theories of growth: a Sraffian critique'; available from http://networkideas.org

Shapiro, C. and Stiglitz, J. E. 1984. 'Equilibrium unemployment as worker discipline device', *American Economic Review*, vol. 74, pp. 433–444.

Shavell, S. 1987. 'The optimal use of nonmonetary sanctions as a deterrent', *American Economic Review – Papers and Proceedings*, vol. 77, pp. 107–110.

Shaw, B. 1891. '*What socialism is*', *Fabian Society Tracts*, nos. 1–72. Tract no. 13.

Shaw, B. 1892. 'The Fabian society: what it has done and how it has done it', paper presented at the Conference of the London and Provincial Fabian Societies at Essex Hall on the 6 February 1892, pp. 125–160.

Shaw, B. 1896. 'The Fabian Society: its early history'. *Fabian Society Tracts*, nos. 1–72. Tract no. 41.

Shaw, B. 1900. *Fabian and the empire: a manifesto*, London: Grant Richards.

Shaw, B. 1928. *The intelligent woman's guide to socialism and capitalism*, London: Constable and Company Ltd.

Shaw, B. 1930. 'Socialism: principle and outlook and Fabianism', *Fabian Society Tracts*, Tract. no. 233.

Sidgwick, H. 1907 [1874]. *The method of ethics*, London: Macmillan.

Silver, M. A. 1974. 'Political revolution and repression: an economic approach', *Public Choice*, vol. 17, 1, Spring, pp. 63–71.

Simon, H. A. 1983. *Reason in human affairs*, Stanford, CA: Stanford University Press.

Singer, P. 1982. *The expanding circle: ethics and sociobiology*, New York: New American Library.

Skorupski, J. 1999. *Ethical exploration*, Oxford: Oxford University Press.

Smith, A. 1976a [1776]. *An inquiry into the nature and the causes of the wealth of nations*, London: Oxford University Press.

Smith, A. 1976b [1759]. *The theory of moral sentiments*, in D. D. Raphael and A. L. Macfie (eds), vol. 1 of *The Glasgow edition of the works and correspondence of Adam Smith*, in D. D. Raphael and Andrew Skinner (eds), Oxford: Clarendon Press.

Snooks, G. D. 1993. *Historical analysis in economics*, London: Routledge.

Sober, E. 1991. 'Organisms, individuals, and units of selection', in A. I. Tauber (ed.) *Organism and the origins of self*, pp. 275–296, Dordrecht, Netherlands: Kluwer.

Solow, R. M. 1956. 'A contribution to the theory of economic growth', *Quarterly Journal of Economics*, vol. 70, pp. 65–94.

Solow, R. M. 1990. *The labour market as a social institution*, Oxford: Basil Blackwell.

Soskice, D. 1990. 'Wage determination. The changing role of institutions in advanced industrialized countries', *Oxford Review of Economic Policy*, vol. 6, 4, pp. 36–61.

Sowell, T. 1987. *A conflict of visions*, New York: William Morrow.

Sraffa, P. 1926. 'The laws of return under competitive conditions', *Economic Journal*, vol. 40 (December), pp. 538–550.

Stabile, D. 1997. 'The intellectual antecedents of Thorstein Veblen: a case for John Bates Clark', *Journal of Economic Issues*, vol. 31, pp. 817–825.

Standing, G. 1999. *Global labour flexibility. Seeking distributive justice*, London: Macmillan.

Steinberg, R. 2004 (ed.). *The economics of nonprofit enterprises*, Cheltenham: Elgar.

Stigler, G. J. 1946 [1941]. *Production and distribution theories*, New York: Macmillan.

Stigler, G. J. and Becker, G. S. 1977. 'De gustibus non est disputandum', *American Economic Review*, vol. 67, 2, pp. 76–90.

Sudgen, R. 1986. *The economics of rights, cooperation and welfare*, Oxford: Basil Blackwell.

Sumner, L. W. 1984. 'Rights deneutralized', in R. G. Frey (ed.) *Utility and rights*, Minneapolis, MN: University of Minnesota Press.

Taylor, M. 1987. *The possibility of cooperation*, Cambridge: Cambridge University Press.

Thurow, L. 1975. *Generating inequalities*, New York: Basic Books.

Tilman, R. 1992. *Thorstein Veblen and his critics, 1891–1963*, Princeton, NJ: Princeton University Press.

Tilman, R. 2003. *The legacy of Thorstein Veblen*, 3 vols, Cheltenham: Elgar.

Titmuss, R. M. 1973 [1970]. *The gift relationship*, Harmondsworth: Penguin Books.

Tobin, J. 1985. 'Neoclassical theory in America: J. B. Clark and Fisher', *Cowles Foundation Discussion Paper* no. 776, September.

Trentmann, F. 1997. 'Wealth versus welfare: the British left between free trade and national political economy before the First World War', *Historical Research*, vol. 70, 171, pp. 70–98.

Tullock, G. 1971. 'The paradox of revolution', *Public Choice*, vol. 11 (Fall), pp. 89–100.

Vanberg, V. 1987. *Morality and economics: De moribus est disputandum*, New Brunswick, NJ: Transaction Books.

Vanberg, V. 1993. 'Rational choice, rule-following and institutions: an evolutionary perspective', in U. Maki, B. Gustafsson and C. Knudsen (eds), *Rationality, institutions and economic methodology*, London: Routledge.

Van Dun, F. 1994. 'Hayek and natural law: the Human connection', in J. Birner and R. van Zijp (eds) *Hayek, co-ordination and evolution*, London and New York: Routledge.

Van Staveren, I. 2001. *The values of economics. An Aristotelian perspective*, London: Routledge.

Varian, H. 1974. 'Equity, envy and efficiency', *Journal of Economic Theory*, vol. 9, pp. 63–91.

Varian, H. 1992. *Microeconomic analysis*, 3rd edition, New York: Norton.

Varian, H. 1996. *Intermediate microeconomics. A modern approach*, New York: Norton.

Veblen, T. B. 1899. 'Mr. Cummings's strictures on the "Theory of the leisure class"' (in Notes), *Journal of Political Economy*, vol. 8, 1 (December), pp. 106–117. Review of John Cummings, 'The theory of the leisure class', *Journal of Political Economy*, vol. 7, 4 (September), pp. 425–455.

Veblen, T. B. 1904. *The theory of business enterprise*, New York: Scribner's.

Veblen, T. B. 1906. 'The socialist economics of Karl Marx and his followers: 1. The theories of Karl Marx', *Quarterly Journal of Economics*, vol. 20, pp. 575–595.

Veblen, T. B. 1908. 'On the nature of capital. I: the productivity of capital goods', *Quartely Journal of Economics*, vol. 22, 3 (August), reprinted in *The place of science in modern civilization*, New York: Russell and Russell, 1961, pp. 324–351.

Veblen, T. B. 1956 [1904]. *The theory of business enterprise*, New York: A. M. Kelley.

Veblen, T. B. 1964 [1914]. *The instinct of workmanship and the state of industrial arts*, New York: A. M. Kelley.

Veblen, T. B. 1964 [1923]. *Absentee ownership and business entreprise in recent times: the case of America*, New York: A. M. Kelley.

Veblen, T. B. 1972 [1909]. 'Professor Clark's economics', in E. K. Hunt and J. B. Schwartz (eds) *A critique of economic theory*, Baltimore, MD: Penguin Books.

Veblen, T. B. 1975 [1899]. *The theory of the leisure class*, New York: A. M. Kelley.

Veblen, T. B. 1994 [1923]. 'Absentee ownership and business entreprise in recent times: the case of America', in *The collected works of Thorstein Veblen*, London: Routledge.

Viano, C. A. 1990. *Teorie etiche contemporanee*, Turin: Boringhieri.

Walker, D. 1977. 'Thorstein Veblen's economic system', *Economic Inquiry*, vol. 15, pp. 217–222.

Walker, F. A. 1968 [1876]. *The wages question*, New York: A. M. Kelley.

Wallas, G. 1910. *Human nature in politics*, London: Constable and Company Ltd.

Wallas, G. 1914. *The great society: a psychological analysis*, New York: The Macmillan Company.

Warr, P. 1999. 'Well-being in the workplace', in D. Kahneman (ed.) *Well-being: the foundations of hedonic psychology*, New York: Russell Sage.

Webb, S. 1891. *The case for the eight hours bill*, London: published for the Fabian Society by John Heywood.

Webb, S. 1899. 'A labor policy for public authorities', *Fabian Society Tracts*, nos. 1–72.

Webb, S. 1905. *Labour in the longest reign (1837–1897)*, London: Fabian Society.

Webb, S. 1906. *The economics of direct employment: with an account of the fair wages policy*, London: Fabian Society.

Webb, S. 1912a. 'The economic theory of legal minimum wage', *Journal of Political Economy*, vol. 20.

Webb, S. 1912b. '*How the government can prevent unemployment*', *War against poverty* [cover title], London: Printed for the Joint Standing Committee of the Independent Labour Party and the Fabian society.

Webb, S. 1912c. 'The legal minimum wage', *War against poverty* [cover title] London: printed for the Standing Joint Committee of the Independent Labour Party and the Fabian society.

Webb, S. 1914a. 'The war and workers: handbook of some immediate measures to prevent unemployment and relieve distress', *Fabian Society Tracts*, nos. 167–195. Tract. no. 176.

Webb, S. 1914b. *The difficulties of individualism*, Westminster: Fabian Society.

Webb, S. 1923. 'The Labour Party on the threshold', *Fabian Society Tracts*, nos. 196–229. Tract no. 207.

Webb, S. 1927. W*ork for the workless: how the labour government has handled unemployment*, London: Labour Publication Department.

Webb, S. and Cox, H. 1891. *The eight hours day*, London: Walter Scott.

Webb, S. and Webb, B. 1898. *Problems of modern industry*, London: Longmans, Green and Co.

Webb, S. and Webb, B. 1909. 'The public organization of the labour market, in *The minority report of the poor law commission*, reprinted New York: A. M. Kelley Publishers, 1974.

Webb, S. and Webb, B. 1919a. *The history of trade unionism 1666–1920*, London: printed by the authors for the students of the workers educational association.

Webb, S. and Webb, B. 1919b. *Industrial democracy*, London: Longman, Green and Co.

Webb, S. and Webb, B. 1921. *The consumers' cooperative movement*, London: printed by the authors for cooperative members and trade unionists.

Webb, S. and Webb, B. 1932. *Methods of social study*, London: Longman, Green and Co.; reprinted New York: A. M. Kelley Publishers, 1974.

Webb, S. and Webb, B. 1936. 'Le leghe operaie dal 1890 al 1920', in C. Arena (ed.) *Lavoro*, vol. 11, Turin: Torinese.

Wicksteed P. H. 1910. *The common sense of political economy*, London: Routledge and Kegan [1967].

Wilkinson, F. 1998. 'Co-operation, the organization of work and competitiveness', University of Cambridge (UK), – working paper no. 85, March.

Williamson, O. 1985. *The economic institutions of capitalism: firms, markets, relational contracting*, New York: Free Press.

Wilson, D. S. 1983. 'The group selection controversy: history and current status', *Annual review of ecology and systematics*, vol. 14, pp. 159–188.

Wright, T. 1987. *Socialism old and new*, London: Routledge.

Yaari, M. E. 1996. 'Remarks on rationality and morality', in F. Farina, F. Hahn and S. Vannucci (eds) *Ethics, rationality and economic behaviour*, Oxford: Clarendon Press.

Yeager, L. B. 2001. *Ethics as a social science. The moral philosophy of social cooperation*, Cheltenham: Elgar.

Zagari, E. 1991. *Storia dell'economia politica*, vol. 1, Turin: Giappichelli.

Zamagni, S. (ed.) 1995. *Economics of altruism*, Aldershot: Elgar.

Index